Istio: Up and Running
Using a Service Mesh to Connect, Secure, Control, and Observe

Lee Calcote and Zack Butcher

Beijing · Boston · Farnham · Sebastopol · Tokyo

Istio: Up and Running

by Lee Calcote and Zack Butcher

Published by O'Reilly Media, Inc., 1005 Gravenstein Highway North, Sebastopol, CA 95472.

O'Reilly books may be purchased for educational, business, or sales promotional use. Online editions are also available for most titles (*http://oreilly.com*). For more information, contact our corporate/institutional sales department: 800-998-9938 or *corporate@oreilly.com*.

Acquisitions Editor: Nikki McDonald	**Proofreader:** Christina Edwards
Development Editor: Corbin Collins	**Indexer:** Ellen Troutman
Production Editor: Deborah Baker	**Cover Designer:** Karen Montgomery
Interior Designer: David Futato	**Illustrator:** Rebecca Demarest
Copyeditor: Octal Publishing, LLC	

October 2019:   First Edition

Revision History for the First Edition
2019-09-26:   First Release
2019-11-27:   Second Release

See *http://oreilly.com/catalog/errata.csp?isbn=9781492043782* for release details.

978-1-492-04378-2

[LSI]

Table of Contents

Preface

Who Should Read This Book

Whether as a side project, or for your core work, a service mesh is a necessary tool in your cloud native infrastructure. This book is for anyone looking to get started with Istio. It is expected that readers are comfortable with Docker and Kubernetes before starting this book, but having basic knowledge of networking and Linux should be sufficient to learn Istio through this text. Knowledge of Go or another programming language is not needed or expected.

We touch on many cloud native tools and topics such as Prometheus, Jaeger, Grafana, Meshery, Envoy, and OpenTracing. Familiarity with these is ideal, but only preliminary knowledge is sufficient to digest the contents of this book.

Why We Wrote This Book

The era of service meshes ushers in a new layer of intelligent network services that are changing the architecture of modern applications and the confidence with which they are delivered. Istio, as one of many service meshes, but one with a vast set of features and capabilities, needs an end-to-end guide.

The aim of this book is to provide that step-by-step guide to getting started with Istio. It wraps the reader's arms all the way around it, so that their fingertips touch on the other side. Each concept is provided in a logical, organized fashion, that builds on the previously covered one. With so many moving parts and an active community, this book can't cover all advanced use cases, but instead focuses on the core building blocks and more timeless aspects of the project. We point readers to additional resources as appropriate.

When you have worked your way through to the end of *Istio: Up and Running*, you should be familiar with all of Istio's major capabilities and be able to deploy Istio in your own environments with confidence.

Conventions Used in This Book

The following typographical conventions are used in this book:

Italic
> Indicates new terms, URLs, email addresses, filenames, and file extensions.

`Constant width`
> Used for program listings, as well as within paragraphs to refer to program elements such as variable or function names, databases, data types, environment variables, statements, and keywords.

`Constant width bold`
> Shows commands or other text that should be typed literally by the user.

`Constant width italic`
> Shows text that should be replaced with user-supplied values or by values determined by context.

 This element signifies a tip or suggestion.

 This element signifies a general note.

 This element indicates a warning or caution.

Using Code Examples

Supplemental material (code examples, exercises, etc.) is available for download at *https://oreil.ly/istio-up-and-running*.

This book is here to help you get your job done. In general, if example code is offered with this book, you may use it in your programs and documentation. You do not need to contact us for permission unless you're reproducing a significant portion of the code. For example, writing a program that uses several chunks of code from this book does not require permission. Selling or distributing a CD-ROM of examples from O'Reilly books does require permission. Answering a question by citing this book and quoting example code does not require permission. Incorporating a significant amount of example code from this book into your product's documentation does require permission.

We appreciate, but do not require, attribution. An attribution usually includes the title, author, publisher, and ISBN. For example: "*Istio: Up and Running* by Lee Calcote and Zack Butcher (O'Reilly). Copyright 2020 Lee Calcote and Zack Butcher, 978-1-492-04378-2."

If you feel your use of code examples falls outside fair use or the permission given above, feel free to contact us at *permissions@oreilly.com*.

O'Reilly Online Learning

 For almost 40 years, *O'Reilly Media* has provided technology and business training, knowledge, and insight to help companies succeed.

Our unique network of experts and innovators share their knowledge and expertise through books, articles, conferences, and our online learning platform. O'Reilly's online learning platform gives you on-demand access to live training courses, in-depth learning paths, interactive coding environments, and a vast collection of text and video from O'Reilly and 200+ other publishers. For more information, please visit *http://oreilly.com*.

How to Contact Us

Please address comments and questions concerning this book to the publisher:

O'Reilly Media, Inc.
1005 Gravenstein Highway North
Sebastopol, CA 95472
800-998-9938 (in the United States or Canada)
707-829-0515 (international or local)
707-829-0104 (fax)

We have a web page for this book, where we list errata, examples, and any additional information. You can access this page at *http://www.oreilly.com/catalog/9781492043782*.

To comment or ask technical questions about this book, send email to *bookquestions@oreilly.com*.

For more information about our books, courses, conferences, and news, see our website at *http://www.oreilly.com*.

Find us on Facebook: *http://facebook.com/oreilly*

Follow us on Twitter: *http://twitter.com/oreillymedia*

Watch us on YouTube: *http://www.youtube.com/oreillymedia*

Acknowledgments

Thanks to Nikki McDonald, John Devins, Virginia Wilson, Corbin Collins, Deborah Baker, and the rest of the team at O'Reilly.

And special thanks to everyone who reviewed our manuscript as this book came together, especially our technical reviewers Myles Steinhauser, Girish Ranganathan, and Jess Males.

Lee would like to personally acknowledge: Jill, your fortitude and love is the foundation upon which I stand. Our double ewes are most precious because of you. Dr. G, the journey has only begun, my friend. Thank you for accompanying me on it. Keith, I covet our time together and find refuge in the true friendship you give me.

## CHAPTER 1

Introducing the Service Mesh

What Is a Service Mesh?

Service meshes provide policy-based, network services for network-connected workloads by enforcing desired behavior of the network in the face of constantly changing conditions and topology. Conditions that change can be load, configuration, resources (including those affecting infrastructure and application topology of intracluster and intercluster resources coming and going), and workloads being deployed.

Fundamentals

Service meshes are an addressable infrastructure layer that allow you to manage both modernizing existing monolithic (or other) workloads as well as wrangling the sprawl of microservices. Service meshes are an addressable infrastructure layer brought to bear in full force. They're beneficial in monolithic environments, but we'll blame the microservices and containers movement—the cloud native approach to designing scalable, independently delivered services—for their brisk emergence. Microservices have exploded what were internal application communications into a mesh of service-to-service remote procedure calls (RPCs) transported over networks. Among their many benefits, microservices provide democratization of language and technology choice across independent service teams—teams that create new features quickly as they iteratively and continuously deliver software (typically as a service).

The field of networking being so vast, it's no surprise that there are many subtle, near-imperceptible differences between similar concepts. At their core, service meshes provide a developer-driven, services-first network: one primarily concerned with obviating the need for application developers to build network concerns (e.g., resiliency) into their code; and one that empowers operators with the ability to declaratively define network behavior, node identity, and traffic flow through policy.

This might seem like software-defined networking (SDN) reincarnate, but service meshes differ here most notably by their emphasis on a developer-centric approach, not a network administrator–centric one. For the most part, today's service meshes are entirely software based (although hardware-based implementations might be coming). Though the term *intent-based networking* is used mostly in physical networking, given the declarative policy-based control service meshes provide, it's fair to liken a service mesh to a cloud native SDN. Figure 1-1 shows an overview of the service mesh architecture. (We outline what it means to be cloud native in Chapter 2.)

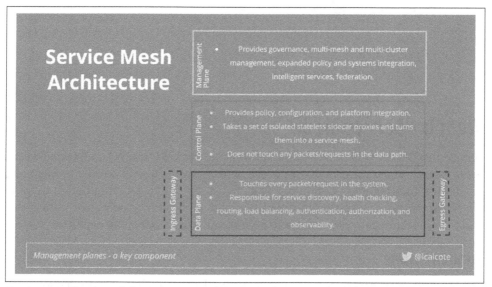

Figure 1-1. If it doesn't have a control plane, it ain't a service mesh.

Service meshes are built using service proxies. Service proxies of the data plane carry traffic. Traffic is transparently intercepted using iptable rules in the pod namespace.

This uniform layer of infrastructure combined with service deployments is commonly referred to as a *service mesh*. Istio turns disparate microservices into an integrated service mesh by systemically injecting a proxy among all network paths, making each proxy cognizant of one another, and bringing these under centralized control; thus forming a service mesh.

Sailing into a Service Mesh

Whether the challenge you face is managing a fleet of microservices or modernizing your existing noncontainerized services, you can find yourself sailing into a service mesh. The more microservices that are deployed, the greater these challenges become.

Client Libraries: The First Service Meshes?

To deal with the complicated task of managing microservices, some organizations have started using *client libraries* as frameworks to standardize implementations. These libraries are considered by some to be the first service meshes. Figure 1-2 illustrates how the use of a library requires that your architecture has application code either extending or using primitives of the chosen library(ies). Additionally, your architecture needs to accommodate the potential use of multiple language-specific frameworks and/or application servers to run them.

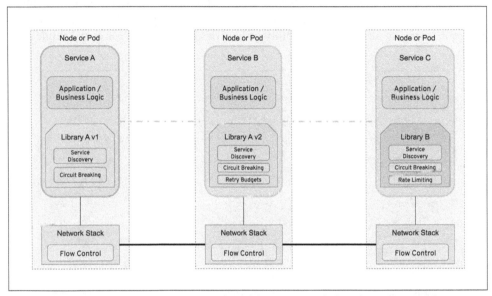

Figure 1-2. Services architecture using client libraries coupled with application logic

The two benefits of creating client libraries are that resources consumed are locally accounted for each and every service, and that developers are empowered to self-service their choice of an existing library or building a new language-specific library. Over time, however, the disadvantages of using client libraries brought service meshes into existence. Their most significant drawback is the tight coupling of infrastructure concerns with application code. Client libraries' nonuniform, language-specific design makes their functionality and behavior inconsistent, which leads to poor observability characteristics, bespoke practices to augment services that are more or less controllable by one another, and possibly compromised security. These language-specific resilience libraries can be costly for organizations to adopt wholesale, and they can be either difficult to wedge into brownfield applications or entirely impractical to incorporate into existing architectures.

Networking is hard. Creating a client library that eliminates client contention by introducing jitter and an exponential back-off algorithm in the calculation of timing the next retry attempt isn't necessarily easy, and neither is attempting to ensure the same behavior across different client libraries (with the varying languages and versions of those libraries). Coordinating upgrades of client libraries is difficult in large environments as upgrades require code changes, rolling a new release of the application and, potentially, application downtime.

Figure 1-3 shows how with a service proxy next to each application instance, applications no longer need to have language-specific resilience libraries for circuit breaking, timeouts, retries, service discovery, load balancing, and so on. Service meshes seem to deliver on the promise that organizations implementing microservices could finally realize the dream of using the best frameworks and language for their individual jobs without worrying about the availability of libraries and patterns for every single platform.

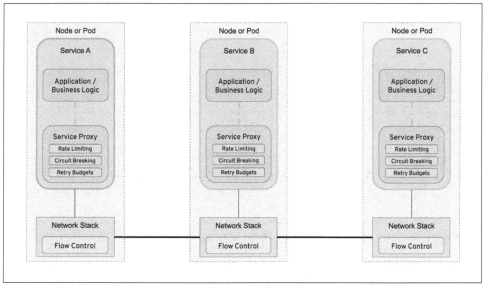

Figure 1-3. Services architecture using service proxies decoupled from application logic

Why Do You Need One?

At this point, you might be thinking, "I have a container orchestrator. Why do I need another infrastructure layer?" With microservices and containers mainstreaming, container orchestrators provide much of what the cluster (nodes and containers) needs. They focus largely on scheduling, discovery, and health, primarily at an infrastructure level (necessarily so), leaving microservices with unmet, service-level needs. A service mesh is a dedicated infrastructure layer for making service-to-service communication safe, fast, and reliable, at times relying on a container orchestrator or integration with another service discovery system. Service meshes might deploy as a separate layer atop container orchestrators, but don't require them, as control and data-plane components might be deployed independent of containerized infrastructure. In Chapter 3, we look at how a node agent (including a service proxy) as the data-plane component is often deployed in noncontainer environments.

The Istio service mesh is commonly adopted à la carte. Organization staff we've spoken to are adopting service meshes primarily for the observability that they bring through instrumentation of network traffic. Many financial institutions in particular are adopting service meshes primarily as a system for managing the encryption of service-to-service traffic.

Whatever the catalyst, organizations are adopting posthaste. And service meshes are not only valuable in cloud native environments, to help with the considerable task of runing microservices. Many organizations that run monolithic services (those running on metal or virtual machines, on- or off-premises) keenly anticipate using service meshes because of the modernizing boost their existing architectures will receive from this deployment.

Figure 1-4 describes the capabilities of container orchestrators (asterisks denotes an essential capability). Service meshes generally rely on these underlying layers. The lower-layer focus is provided by container orchestrators.

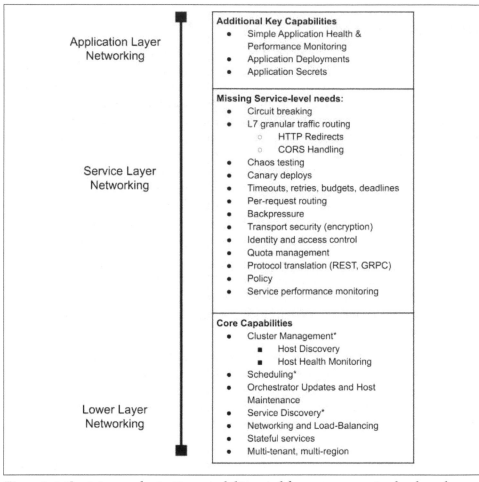

Figure 1-4. Container orchestration capabilities and focus versus service-level needs

Don't We Already Have This in Our Container Platforms?

Containers simplify and provide generic, non-language-specific, application packaging and essential life cycle management. As a generic, non-language-specific platform, *container orchestrators* take responsibility for forming clusters, efficiently scheduling their resources, and managing higher-level application constructs (deployments, services, service-affinity, anti-affinity, health checking, scaling, etc.). Table 1-1 shows how container orchestrators generally have service discovery mechanisms—load balancing with virtual IP addresses built in. The supported load-balancing algorithms are typically simplistic in nature (round robin, random) and act as a single virtual IP to communicate with backend pods.

Kubernetes handles the registration/eviction of instances in the group based on their health status and whether they match a grouping predicate (labels and selectors). Then, services can use DNS for service discovery and load balancing regardless of their implementation. There's no need for special language-specific libraries or registration clients. Container orchestrators have allowed us to move simple networking concerns out of applications and into the infrastructure, freeing the collective infrastructure technology ecosystem to advance our focus to higher layers.

Now you understand how service meshes complement underlying layers: what about other layers?

Landscape and Ecosystem

The service mesh landscape (*https://oreil.ly/57P0j*) is a burgeoning ecosystem of tooling that's not relegated to cloud native applications; indeed, it also provides much value to noncontainerized, nonmicroservice workloads. As you come to understand the role a service mesh plays in deployments and the value it provides, you can begin selecting a service mesh and integrating it with your incumbent tooling.

Landscape

How should you select a service mesh? Of the many service meshes currently available, their significant differences don't make it easy for people to discern what actually is a service mesh and what isn't. Over time, more of their capabilities are converging, making it easier to characterize and compare them.

Interestingly, but not surprisingly, many service meshes have been based on some of the same proxies, such as Envoy and NGINX.

Ecosystem

As far as how a service mesh fits in with other ecosystem technologies, we've already looked at client libraries and container orchestrators. API gateways address some similar needs and are commonly deployed on a container orchestrator as an edge proxy. Edge proxies provide services with Layer 4 (L4) to Layer 7 (L7) management while using the container orchestrator for reliability, availability, and scalability of container infrastructure.

API gateways interact with service meshes in a way that puzzles many, given that API gateways (and the proxies they're built upon) range from traditional to cloud-hosted to microservices API gateways. The latter can be represented by a collection of microservices-oriented, open source API gateways, which use the approach of wrapping existing L7 proxies that incorporate container orchestrator native integration and developer self-service features (e.g., HAProxy, Traefik, NGINX, or Envoy).

With respect to service meshes, API gateways are designed to accept traffic from outside your organization or network and distribute it internally. API gateways expose your services as managed APIs, focused on transiting north-south traffic (in and out of the service mesh). They aren't as well suited for traffic management within the service mesh (east-west) necessarily, because they require traffic to travel through a central proxy, and add a network hop. Service meshes are designed primarily to manage east-west traffic internal to the service mesh.

Given their complementary nature, you'll often find API gateways and service meshes deployed in combination. API gateways wotk with other API management functions to handle analytics, business data, adjunct provider services, and implementation of versioning control. Today, there is overlap as well as gaps between service mesh capabilities, API gateways, and API management systems. As service meshes gain new capabilities, use cases overlap more.

The Critical, Fallible Network

As noted, in microservices deployments, the network is directly and critically involved in every transaction, every invocation of business logic, and every request made to the application. Network reliability and latency are among the chief concerns for modern, cloud native applications. One cloud native application might comprise hundreds of microservices, each with many instances that might be constantly rescheduled by a container orchestrator.

Understanding the network's centrality, you want your network to be as intelligent and resilient as possible. It should:

- Route traffic away from failures to increase the aggregate reliability of a cluster.
- Avoid unwanted overhead like high-latency routes or servers with cold caches.
- Ensure that the traffic flowing between services is secure against trivial attack.
- Provide insight by highlighting unexpected dependencies and root causes of service communication failure.
- Allow you to impose policies at the granularity of service behaviors, not just at the connection level.

Also, you don't want to write all of this logic into your application.

You want Layer 5 management, a services-first network; you want a service mesh.

The Value of a Service Mesh

Currently, service meshes provide a uniform way to connect, secure, manage, and monitor microservices.

Observability

Service meshes give you visibility, resiliency, and traffic control, as well as security control over distributed application services. Much value is promised here. Service meshes are transparently deployed and give visibility into and control over traffic without requiring any changes to application code (for more details, see Chapter 2).

In this, their first generation, service meshes have great potential to provide value; Istio, in particular. We'll have to wait and see what second-generation capabilities spawn when service meshes are as ubiquitously adopted as containers and container orchestrators have been.

Traffic control

Service meshes provide granular, declarative control over network traffic to determine, for example, where a request is routed to perform a canary release. Resiliency features typically include circuit-breaking, latency-aware load balancing, eventually consistent service discovery, retries, timeouts, and deadlines (for more details, see Chapter 8).

Security

When organizations use a service mesh, they gain a powerful tool for enforcing security, policy, and compliance requirements across their enterprise. Most service meshes provide a certificate authority (CA) to manage keys and certificates for securing service-to-service communication. Assignment of verifiable identity to each service in the mesh is key in determining which clients are allowed to make requests of different services as well as in encrypting that request traffic. Certificates are generated per service and provide a unique identity for that service. Commonly, service proxies (see Chapter 5) are used to take on the identity of the service and perform life cycle management of certificates (generation, distribution, refresh, and revocation) on behalf of the service (for more on this, see Chapter 6).

Modernizing your existing infrastructure (retrofitting a deployment)

Many people consider that if they're not running many services, they don't need to add a service mesh to their deployment architecture. This isn't true. Service meshes offer much value irrespective of how many services you're running. The value they provide then only increases with the number of services you run and with the number of locations from which your services deploy.

While some greenfield projects have the luxury of incorporating a service mesh from the start, most organizations will have existing services (monoliths or otherwise) that they'll need to onboard to the mesh. Rather than a container, these services could be running in VMs or bare-metal hosts. Service meshes help with modernization, allowing organizations to upgrade their services inventory without rewriting applications, adopting microservices or new languages, or moving to the cloud.

You can use *facade services* to break down monoliths. You could also adopt a *strangler pattern* of building services around the legacy monolith to expose a more developer-friendly set of APIs.

Organizations can get observability support (e.g., metrics, logs, and traces) as well as dependency or service graphs for each of their services (microservice or not), as they adopt a service mesh. In regard to tracing, the only change required within the service is to forward certain HTTP headers. Service meshes are useful for retrofitting uniform and ubiquitous observability tracing into existing infrastructures with the least amount of code change.

Decoupling at Layer 5

An important consideration when digesting the value of a service mesh is the phenomenon of decoupling service teams and the delivery speed this enables, as demonstrated in Figure 1-5.

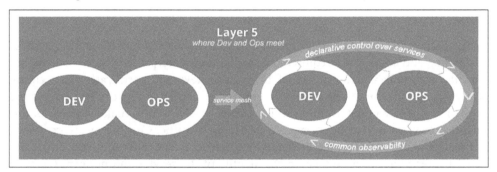

Figure 1-5. Layer 5 (L5), where Dev and Ops meet

Just as microservices help decouple feature teams, creating a service mesh helps decouple operators from application feature development and release processes, in turn giving operators declarative control over how their service layer is running. Creating a service mesh doesn't just decouple teams, it eliminates the diffusion of responsibility among them and enables uniformity of practice standards across organizations within our industry. Consider this list of tasks:

- Identify when to break a circuit and facilitate it.
- Establish end-to-end service deadlines.
- Ensure distributed traces are generated and propagated to backend monitoring systems.

- Deny users of "Acme" account access to beta versions of your services.

Whose responsibility is this—the developer or the operator? Answers likely would differ from organization to organization; as an industry, we don't have commonly accepted practices. Service meshes help keep these responsibilities from falling through the cracks or from one team blaming the other for lack of accountability.

The Istio Service Mesh

Let's now embark on our journey into the Istio service mesh.

> ## Project Etymology
>
> With Kubernetes being such a significant presence in the cloud native ecosystem, its Greek etymological heritage has given rise to a proliferation of associated projects with names that start with "K," as well as others named for associated Greek words. *Kubernetes* (κυβερνήτης (https://oreil.ly/azC7B) in the Greek alphabet) is Greek for "helmsman" or "pilot." It is also the root word for "cybernetics" and "gubernatorial," terms with important meaning in control theory, and control being at the center of Kubernetes's focus.
>
> *Istio* (in the Greek alphabet, ιστίο (https://oreil.ly/8lwcR)) is Greek for "sail," and is pronounced "iss-teeh-oh." And, of course, Istio's accompanying command-line interface (CLI), istioctl, is pronounced "iss-teeh-oh-c-t-l," because you use it to control Istio, not cuddle with it.

The Origin of Istio

Istio is an open source implementation of a service mesh first created by Google, IBM, and Lyft. What began as a collaborative effort among these organizations has rapidly expanded to incorporating contributions from many other organizations and individuals. Istio is a vast project; in the cloud native ecosystem, it's second in scope of objectives to Kubernetes. It ingests a number of Cloud Native Computing Foundation (CNCF)–governed projects like Prometheus, OpenTelemetry, Fluentd, Envoy, Jaeger, Kiali, and many contributor-written adapters.

Akin to other service meshes, Istio helps you add resiliency and observability to your services architecture in a transparent way. Service meshes don't require applications to be cognizant of running on the mesh, and Istio's design doesn't depart from other service meshes in this regard. Between ingress, interservice, and egress traffic, Istio transparently intercepts and handles network traffic on behalf of the application.

Using Envoy as the data-plane component, Istio helps you to configure your applications to have an instance of the service proxy deployed alongside it. Istio's control plane is composed of a few components that provide configuration management of the data-plane proxies, APIs for operators, security settings, policy checks, and more. We cover these control-plane components in later chapters of this book.

Although it was originally built to run on Kubernetes, Istio's design is deployment-platform agnostic. So, an Istio-based service mesh can also be deployed across platforms like OpenShift, Mesos, and Cloud Foundry, as well as traditional deployment environments like VMs and bare-metal servers. Consul's interoperability with Istio can be helpful in VM and bare-metal deployments. Whether running monoliths or microservices, Istio is applicable—*the more services you run, the greater the benefit.*

The Current State of Istio

As an evolving project, Istio has a healthy release cadence, this being one way in which open source project velocity and health are measured. Figure 6-1 presents the community statistics from May 2017, when Istio was publicly announced as a project, to February 2019. During this period, there were roughly 2,400 *forks* (GitHub users who have made a copy of the project—either in the process of contributing to the project or using its code as a base for their own projects) and around 15,000 *stars* (users who have favorited the project and see project updates in their activity feed).

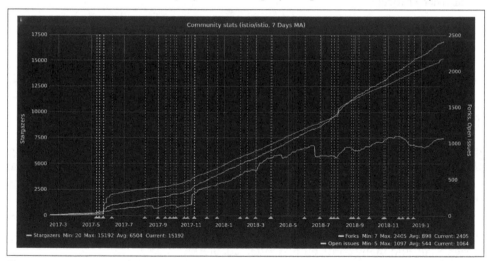

Figure 1-6. Istio contribution statistics

A simple number of stars, forks, and commits is moderately indicative of project health in terms of velocity, interest, and support. Each of these raw metrics can be improved upon. Reporting the rates of commits, reviews, and merges over time perhaps better indicates project velocity, which is most accurately measured relative to itself, and relative to its own timeline. When determining a project's health, you should look at whether the rates of these activities are increasing or decreasing, whether the the release cadence is consistent; and how frequently and how many patches are released to improve a low-quality major or minor feature release?

Cadence

Like many software projects, Istio's versioning semantics are laid out in a familiar (to Semantic Versioning (*https://semver.org*)) style (e.g., version 1.1.1), and, like other projects, Istio defines its own nuances to release frequency, setting expectations of longevity of support (see Table 1-1). Though daily and weekly releases are available, these aren't supported and might not be reliable. However, as Table 1-1 shows, the monthly snapshots are relatively safe and are usually packed with new features. But, if you are looking to use Istio in production, look for releases tagged as "LTS" (Long-Term Support). As of this writing, 1.2.x is the latest LTS release.

Table 1-1. Istio's build and release cadence (see this Istio doc page (https://oreil.ly/szQfK))

Type	Support level	Quality and recommended use
Daily build	No support	Dangerous; might not be fully reliable. Useful for experimentation.
Snapshot release	Support is provided for only the latest snapshot release.	Expected to be stable, but use in production should be limited to an as-needed basis. Usually only adopted by bleeding-edge users or users seeking specific features.
LTS release	Support is provided until three months after the next LTS.	Safe to deploy in production. Users are encouraged to upgrade to these releases as soon as possible.
Patches	Same as the corresponding Snapshot/LTS release.	Users are encouraged to adopt patch releases as soon as they are available for a given release.

As a frame of reference, Kubernetes minor releases occur approximately every three months, so each minor release branch is maintained for approximately nine months.

By comparison, because it is an operating system, Ubuntu quite necessarily needs to prioritize stability over speed of feature release, and thus publishes its LTS releases every two years in April. It's worth noting that the LTS releases are much more heavily used (something like 95% of all Ubuntu installations are LTS releases).

Docker uses a time-based release schedule, with time frames generally as follows:

- Docker CE Edge releases happen monthly.
- Docker CE Stable releases happen quarterly, with patch releases as needed.
- Docker EE releases happen twice per year, with patch releases as needed.

Updates and patches release as follows:

- Docker EE releases receive patches and updates for at least one year after they are released.

- Docker CE Stable releases receive patches and updates for one month after the next Docker CE Stable release.

- Docker CE Edge releases do not receive any patches or updates after a subsequent Docker CE Edge or Stable release.

Releases

The original plan was that Istio would have one point release every quarter, followed by *n* patch releases. Snapshots were intended as monthly releases that would mostly meet the same quality bar as a point release, except that it's not a supported release and can have breaking changes. A history of all releases is available on Istio's Releases page (*https://oreil.ly/2fZ4x*) on GitHub. Table 1-2 presents Istio's release cadence over a 10-month period.

Table 1-2. Cadence of Istio releases from June 2018 to April 2019

Release date	Release number	Days from last release
4/16/19	1.1.3	11
4/5/19	1.1.2	0
4/5/19	1.0.7	11
3/25/19	1.1.1	6
3/19/19	1.1.0	3
3/16/19	1.1.0-rc.6	2
3/14/19	1.1.0-rc.5	2
3/12/19	1.1.0-rc.4	4
3/8/19	1.1.0-rc.3	4
3/4/19	1.1.0-rc.2	5
2/27/19	1.1.0-rc.1	6
2/21/19	1.1.0-rc.0	8
2/13/19	1.1.0-snapshot.6	0
2/13/19	1.0.6	19
1/25/19	1.1.0-snapshot.5	0
1/25/19	1.1.0-snapshot.4	48
12/8/18	1.0.5	11
11/27/18	1.1.0-snapshot.3	6
11/21/18	1.0.4	26
10/26/18	1.0.3	3
10/23/18	1.1.0-snapshot.2	26
9/27/18	1.1.0-snapshot.1	21
9/6/18	1.0.2	8

Release date	Release number	Days from last release
8/29/18	1.1.0-snapshot.0	5
8/24/18	1.0.1	24
7/31/18	1.0.0	8
7/23/18	1.0.0-snapshot.2	3
7/20/18	1.0.0-snapshot.1	22
6/28/18	1.0.0-snapshot.0	27
6/1/18	0.8.0	

Feature Status

In true Agile style, Istio features individually go through their own life cycle (dev/alpha/beta/stable). Some features are stabilizing while others are being added or improved upon, as demonstrated in Table 1-3.

Table 1-3. Istio's feature status categories (see: https://oreil.ly/qV8b0)

	Alpha	Beta	Stable
Purpose	Demo-able; works end-to-end but has limitations	Usable in production, not a toy anymore	Dependable, production hardened.
API	No guarantees on backward compatibility	APIs are versioned	Dependable, production-worthy. APIs are versioned, with automated version conversion for backward compatibility.
Performance	Not quantified or guaranteed	Not quantified or guaranteed	Performance (latency/scale) is quantified, documented, with guarantees against regression.
Deprecation policy	None	Weak: three months	Dependable, firm. One-year notice will be provided before changes.

Future

Working groups are iterating on designs toward a v2 architecture, incorporating learnings from running Istio at scale and usability feedback from users. With more and more people learning about service meshes in the future, ease of adoption will be key to helping the masses successfully reach the third phase of their cloud native journey → containers → orchestrators → meshes.

What Istio Isn't

Istio doesn't account for specific capabilities that you might find in other service meshes, or offered by management plane software. This is because it's subject to change or to be commonly augmented with third-party software.

With the prominent exception of facilitating distributed tracing, Istio is not a white-box application performance monitoring (APM) solution. The generation of additional telemetry surrounding and introspecting network traffic and service requests that is available with Istio does provide additional black-box visibility. Of the metrics and logs available with Istio, these provide insight into network traffic flows, including source, destination, latency, and errors; top-level service metrics, not custom application metrics exposed by individual workloads or cluster-level logging.

Istio plug-ins integrate service-level logs with the same backend monitoring system you might be using for cluster-level logging (e.g., Fluentd, Elasticsearch, Kibana). Also, Istio uses the same metrics collection and alarming, which might well be the same utility (e.g., Prometheus) that you're using already.

It's Not Just About Microservices

Kubernetes doesn't do it all. Will the infrastructure of the future be entirely Kubernetes-based? Not likely. Not all applications, notably those designed to run outside of containers, are a good fit for Kubernetes (currently, anyway). The tail of information technology is quite long considering that mainframes from decades ago are still in use today.

No technology is a panacea. Monoliths are easier to comprehend, because much of the application is in one place. You can trace the interactions of its different parts within one system (or a limited more or less stagnant set of systems). However, monoliths don't scale, in terms of development teams and lines of code.

Nondistributed monoliths will be around for a long time. Service meshes help in their modernization and can provide facades to facilitate evolutionary architecture. Deployment of a service mesh gateway as an intelligent facade in front of the monolith will be an approach many take to strangle their monolith by siphoning path-based (or otherwise) requests away. This approach is gradual, leading to migrating parts of the monolith into modern microservices, or simply acting as a stopgap measure pending a fully cloud native redesign.

Terminology

Here are some important Istio-related terms to know and keep in mind:

Cloud
    A specific cloud service provider.

Cluster
    A set of Kubernetes nodes with common API masters.

Config store
    A system that stores configuration outside of the control plane itself for example, etcd in a Kubernetes deployment of Istio or even a simple filesystem.

Container management

Loosely defined as OS virtualization provided by software stacks like Kubernetes, OpenShift, Cloud Foundry, Apache Mesos, and so on.

Environment

The computing environment presented by various vendors of infrastructure as a service (IaaS), like Azure Cloud Services (*https://oreil.ly/mDkY5*), AWS (*https://aws.amazon.com/*), Google Cloud Platform (*https://oreil.ly/39fXT*), IBM Cloud (*https://oreil.ly/N-1xd*), Red Hat Cloud computing (*https://oreil.ly/ZCMj_*), or a group of VMs or physical machines running on-premises or in hosted datacenters.

Mesh

A set of workloads with common administrative control; under the same governing entity (e.g., a control plane).

Multienvironment (aka hybrid)

Describes heterogeneous environments where each might differ in the implementation and deployment of the following infrastructure components:

Network boundaries

Example: one component uses on-premises ingress, and the other uses ingress operating in the cloud.

Identity systems

Example: one component has LDAP, the other has service accounts.

Naming systems like DNS

Example: local DNS, Consul-based DNS.

VM/container/process orchestration frameworks

Example: one component has on-premises locally managed VMs, and the other has Kubernetes-managed containers running services.

Multitenancy

Logically isolated, but physically integrated services running under the same Istio service mesh control plane.

Network

A set of directly interconnected endpoints (can include a virtual private network [VPN]).

Secure naming

Provides mapping between a service name and the workload principals authorized to run the workloads implementing a service.

Service

A delineated group of related behaviors within a service mesh. Services are named using a service name, and Istio policies such as load balancing and routing are applied to service names. A service is typically materialized by one or more service endpoints.

Service endpoint

The network-reachable manifestation of a service. Endpoints are exposed by workloads. Not all services have service endpoints.

Service mesh

A shared set of names and identities that allows for common policy enforcement and telemetry collection. Service names and workload principals are unique within a mesh.

Service name

A unique name for a service that identifies it within the service mesh. A service may not be renamed and maintain its identity: each service name is unique. A service can have multiple versions, but a service name is version-independent. Service names are accessible in Istio configuration as the `source.service` and `destination.service` attributes.

Service proxy

The data-plane component that handles traffic management on behalf of application services.

Sidecar

A methodology of coscheduling utility containers with application containers grouped in the same logical unit of scheduling. In Kubernetes's case, a pod.

Workload

Process/binary deployed by operators in Istio, typically represented by entities such as containers, pods, or VMs. A workload can expose zero or more service endpoints; a workload can consume zero or more services. Each workload has a single canonical service name associated with it, but can also represent additional service names.

Workload name

Unique name for a workload, identifying it within the service mesh. Unlike service name and workload principal, workload name is not a strongly verified property and should not be used when enforcing access control lists (ACLs). Workload names are accessible in Istio configuration as the `source.name` and the `destination.name` attributes.

Workload principal

Identifies the verifiable authority under which a *workload* runs. Istio service-to-service authentication is used to produce the workload principal. By default, workload principals are compliant with the SPIFFE ID (*http://spiffe.io*) format. Multiple workloads may share a workload principal, but each workload has a single canonical workload principal. These are accessible in Istio configuration as the `source.user` and the `destination.user` attributes.

Zone (Istio control plane)

Running set of components required by Istio. This includes Galley, Mixer, Pilot, and Citadel.

- A single zone is represented by a single logical Galley store.
- All Mixers and Pilots connected to the same Galley are considered part of the same zone, regardless of where they run.
- A single zone can operate independently, even if all other zones are offline or unreachable.
- A single zone may contain only a single *environment.*
- Zones are not used to identify *services* or *workloads* in the *service mesh*. Each *service name* and *workload principal* belongs to the service mesh as a whole, not an individual zone.
- Each zone belongs to a single service mesh. A service mesh spans one or more zones.
- In relation to clusters (e.g., Kubernetes clusters) and support for multienvironments, a zone can have multiple instances of these. But Istio users should prefer simpler configurations. It should be relatively trivial to run control-plane components in each cluster or environment and limit the configuration to one cluster per zone.

Operators need independent control and a flexible toolkit to ensure they're running secure, compliant, observable, and resilient microservices. Developers require freedom from infrastructure concerns and the ability to experiment with different production features, and deploy canary releases without affecting the entire system. Istio adds traffic management to microservices and creates a basis for value-add capabilities like security, monitoring, routing, connectivity management, and policy.

## CHAPTER 2

Cloud Native Approach to Uniform Observability

In this chapter, we walk through a cloud native approach to uniform observability through the lens of service meshes. Split into three sections, this chapter breaks down the concepts of *cloud native*, *observability*, and *uniform observability*. In the first section, we examine the amorphous concept of cloud native by characterizing its various facets. Then we'll consider the difference between the act of monitoring a service and the property of a service being observable. In the last section, we reflect on the power of having autogenerated telemetry that provides ubiquitous and consistent insight into your running services. As service meshes are a product of cloud native, so let's start our discussion by defining what cloud native really means.

What Does It Mean to Be Cloud Native?

"Cloud native" as an umbrella term is a combination of both *technology* and *process*. Driven by the need for both machine and human efficiency, cloud native technology spans application architecture, packaging, and infrastructure. Cloud native process embodies the full software life cycle. Often, but not always, cloud native process reduces historically separate organizational functions and life cycle steps (e.g., architecture, QA, security, documentation, development, operations, sustaining, and so on) to two functions: *development* and *operations*. Development and operations are the two primary functions of individuals who deliver software as a service, commonly employing DevOps practices and culture. Cloud native software is commonly, but not always, continuously delivered as a service.

The more services you deploy, the greater the return on investment you'll see from using a service mesh. Cloud native architectures lend themselves to higher numbers of services, hence our need to understand what it means to be cloud native. Service meshes provide value to noncontainerized workloads as well as monolithic services. Examples of this added value are highlighted throughout this book.

Cloud native applications typically run in a public or private cloud. Minimally, they run on top of programmatically addressable infrastructure. That said, *lifting and shifting* an application into a cloud doesn't quite make it cloud native.

The following are characteristics of cloud native applications:

- They run on programmatically addressable infrastructure, and are dynamic and decoupled from physical resources by one or more layers of abstraction across compute, network, and storage resources.
- They are distributed and decentralized with the focus often being on how the application behaves, not on where it's running. They account for software life cycle events to allow for (rolling) updates, smoothly upgrading services without service disruption.
- They are resilient and scalable, designed to run redundantly without single points of failure and to survive continually.
- They are observable through their own instrumentation and/or that provided by underlying layers. Given their dynamic nature, distributed systems are relatively more difficult to inspect and debug, and so their observability must be accounted for.

The Path to Cloud Native

For most organizations, the path to cloud native is an evolutionary act of applying cloud native principles to existing services, whether through retrofit or rewrite. Others are fortunate enough to have started projects after cloud native principles and tools were generally available and accepted. Whether your journey calls for dealing with an existing service or writing a new collection of them, service meshes offer considerable value—*value that increases as you increase the number of services that you own and run*. Service meshes are the next logical step after a container orchestration deployment. Figure 2-1 outlines various cloud native paths.

As some service meshes are easier to deploy than others and some meshes offer more value than others, depending on which mesh you deploy, you might need a certain number of microservices to make the deployment useful. In time, service meshes (and extensions to them) will alleviate developers of common application-level considerations (e.g., cost accounting and price planning) in that the service mesh simply provides these ubiquitous concerns.

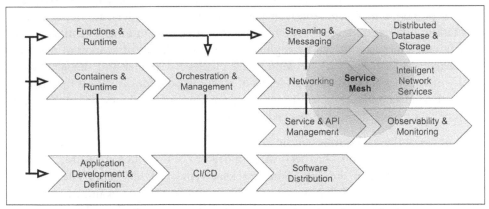

Figure 2-1. The paths taken to cloud native are varied and replete with choice.

Depending upon your teams' experience levels and your specific projects, your path to cloud native will use different combinations of software development process, operational practices, application architecture, packaging and runtimes, and application infrastructure. Applications and teams exhibiting cloud native characteristics use one, a combination of, or all of the approaches highlighted in Figure 2-2.

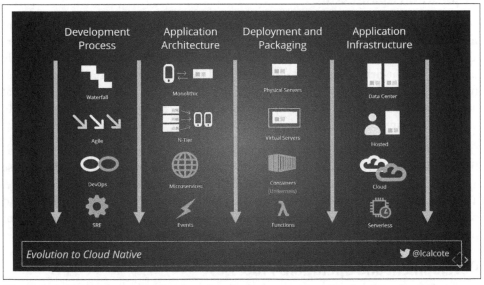

Figure 2-2. The evolution to cloud native through process and technology (architecture, packaging, and infrastructure)

Packaging and Deployment

Cloud native technology often takes the form of microservices (engaged through service endpoints), built-in containers (engaged through a scheduler), and function augmentation (engaged through event notifications). Evolutionary shifts in the packaging patterns are driven by engineers' need for efficient utilization of machines and delivery speed. The path to cloud native pushes for smaller and smaller units of deployment, enabled through high levels of resource isolation. Isolation through virtualization and containerization provide higher levels of efficiency as smaller packages make for more tightly bin-packed servers.

Each phase of the packaging evolution, from bare-metal servers to VMs to containers to unikernels to functions, has seen varying degrees of use when measured by number of deployments in the wild. Some package types provide better guarantees of portability, interoperability, isolation, efficiency, and so on. For example, containers deliver higher degrees of portability and interoperability than VMs. Though they're lightweight, isolated, and infinitely scalable, functions suffer in regard to portability, exhibiting possibly the highest degree of lock-in among the various types of packaging. Irrespective of your chosen packaging—whether you deploy services directly on the host OS, in a VM, in a container, as a unikernel, or a function—service meshes can provide connection, control, observability, and security.

Application Architecture

More important than the form they take are the characteristics exhibited by cloud native application architecture. Central to cloud native are qualities such as ephemerality, actively scheduled workloads, loose coupling with dependencies explicitly described, event-driven, horizontally scaled, and cleanly separated stateless and stateful services. Cloud native applications often exemplify an architectural approach that is commonly declarative and incorporating resiliency, availability, and observability as upfront design concerns.

Cloud native technologies empower organizations to build and run scalable applications in dynamic environments such as public, private, and hybrid clouds. Here, these applications are centered around declarative APIs to interface with the infrastructure. These techniques enable loosely coupled systems that are resilient, manageable, and observable. Istio and other open source service meshes deliver the next generation of networking designed for cloud native applications.

Development and Operations Processes

Developer and operator experience is also central to the philosophy of cloud native design and process, which fosters code and component reuse and a high degree of automation. When married with infrastructure as code (IaC), operators aggressively

---

automate the methods by which cloud native applications and their infrastructure are deployed, monitored, and scaled. When combined with robust automation, microservices enable engineers to make high-impact changes frequently and predictably with minimal toil, typically using multiple continuous integration (CI) and continuous delivery (CD) pipelines to build and deploy microservices.

High levels of granular observability is a key focus of systems and services that site reliability engineers monitor and manage. Istio generates metrics, logs, and traces pertaining to requests sent across the mesh, facilitating instrumentation of services so that metrics creation and log and trace generation is done without code changes (save for context propagation in traces). Istio, and service meshes in general, insert a dedicated infrastructure layer between Dev and Ops, separating common concerns of service communication by providing independent control over services. Without a service mesh, operators would still be tied to developers for many concerns as they'd need new application builds to control network traffic, shaping, affecting access control, and which services talk to downstream services. The decoupling of Dev and Ops is key to providing autonomous independent iteration.

Cloud Native Infrastructure

Public, hybrid, and private cloud are clearly core to the definition of what it means to be cloud native. In a nutshell, the cloud is software-defined infrastructure. The use of APIs as the primary interface to infrastructure is a principal cloud concept. Natively integrated workloads use these APIs (or abstractions of these APIs) instead of nonnative workloads ignorant of their infrastructure. As the definition of "cloud native" advances, so do cloud services themselves. Broadly, cloud services have evolved from IaaS to managed services to serverless offerings. Given that most FaaS compute systems execute inside a container, these FaaS platforms can run on a service mesh and benefit from *uniform observability*.

Cloud native technology and process radically improves machine efficiency and resource utilization while reducing costs associated with maintenance and operations and significantly increasing the overall agility and maintainability of applications. Though employing a container orchestrator addresses a layer of infrastructure needs, it doesn't meet all application or service-level requirements. Service meshes provide a layer of tooling for the unmet service-level needs of cloud native applications.

What Is Observability?

Proper definition of any new terms we use is important not only to facilitate common nomenclature (and understanding) and avoid debate. The notion of a system being *observable* versus being *monitored* has been discussed at length within the industry. To clarify, let's define *monitoring* (a verb) as a function performed, an activity; whereas *observability* (an adjunct noun) is an attribute of a system.

When speaking of a system's observability, you describe how well and in what way the system provides you with signals to monitor. Observable software is typically instrumented to capture and expose information (telemetry/measurements), allowing you to reason over complex software.

In contrast, monitoring is the action of observing and checking the behavior and outputs of a system and its components over time, evaluating system state. Your ability to monitor a system is improved by its number of observable attributes (its observability). Monitoring asserts whether a state is true or not true (e.g., a system is degraded or not).

Consider monitorability (a noun) as the condition of being monitorable; the ability to be monitored. Monitoring is being on the lookout for failures, typically through polling observable endpoints. Simplistically, early monitoring systems target uptime as a key metric to measure resilience. Modern monitoring tooling is oriented toward top-level services metrics like latency, errors (rate of requests that fail), traffic volume (by requests per second for web service or transactions retrievals per second for a key/value store), and saturation (a measurement of how utilized a resource is). Modern monitoring systems are often infused with analytics for identifying anomalous behavior, predicting capacity breaches, and so on. Service meshes bridge observability and monitoring by providing some of both by way of generating, aggregating, and reasoning over telemetry. Various service meshes incorporate monitoring tooling as a capability or easy add-on.

 Debate would subside if we were to use "monitoring" and "monitorability." This verb and its noun adjunct can be left alone in synonymous company with its sister "observing" and "observability." That said, we'll need to offer a new term for vendors to claim, coin, wield, and posture around. Lacking a term and definition to debate would be like a quinceañera without a piñata to beat up.

Is observability for developers, and monitoring for operators? Maybe, but that's beside the point. Until service meshes arrived, it was unclear whose responsibility it was to make a system observable and to perform monitoring of it. Most teams give different answers to the question of whose responsibility it is to define and deliver a service-level objective for a given service. Responsibilities such as these are often diffused. Service meshes decouple development and delivery teams by introducing a management layer—Layer 5 (L5)—between the lower-layer infrastructure and higher-layer application services.

Pillars of Telemetry

Observability can include logs in the form of events and errors; traces in the form of spans and annotations; and metrics in the form of histograms, gauges, summaries, and counters, as depicted in Figure 2-3.

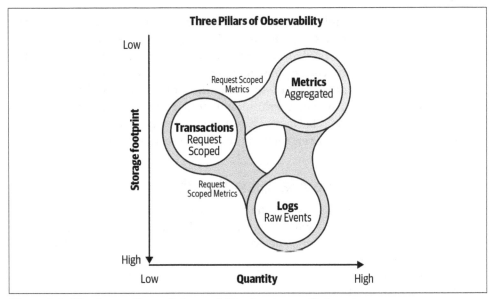

Figure 2-3. The three pillars of observability: key types of telemetry

Logs

Logs provide additional context for data such as metrics, They're well suited for debugging, making it difficult to strike the correct balance in tuning which logs to centrally save versus which to allow to eventually rotate out. However, logs are also costly in terms of performance because they tend to be of the highest volume and require the most storage. Though structured logging doesn't have the downsides inherent in pure string-based log manipulation, it still takes up far more storage and is slower to query and process (as is evident from log-based monitoring vendors' pricing models. Some best practices for logging include enforcing quotas and dynamic rate of adjustment of log generation.

Metrics

Metrics, unlike logs, have a constant overhead and are good for alerts. Taken together, logs and metrics give insight into individual systems, but they make it difficult to see into the lifetime of a request that has traversed multiple systems. This is pretty common in distributed systems. Metrics can be powerful and, when aggregated, quite insightful—good for identifying known-unknowns. The high compression rate on metrics only pushes them to have a smaller footprint, considering that they're optimized for storage (a good Gorilla implementation can get a sample down to 2.37 bytes) and enable historical trends through long-term retention.

Traces

Tracing allows you to granularly track request segments (spans) as the request is processed across various services. It's difficult to introduce later, as (among other reasons) third-party libraries used by the application also need to be instrumented. Distributed tracing can be costly; thus, most service mesh tracing systems employ various forms of sampling to capture only a portion of the observed traces. When traces are sampled, performance overhead and storage costs are reduced, but so is visibility. The sampling rate is balanced against the frequency by which traces are captured (typically expressed as a percentage in relation to service request volume).

Trace Sampling Algorithms

Each sampling algorithm comes with trade-offs. These algorithms tend to fall into two categories: *head-based* and *tail-based*. Head-based consistent sampling (or upfront sampling) makes the sampling decision once per trace at the trace's start. Tail-based sampling makes the sampling decision at the end of the request execution so that additional criteria can be considered in whether a trace should be saved. Here are some different sampling algorithms:

Probabilistic sampling
    This decision is based on a coin toss with a certain probability.

Rate limiting sampling
    This decision employs a rate limiter to ensure that only a fixed number of traces are sampled per time interval.

Adaptive sampling
    This decision dynamically adjusts sampling parameters to align the actual amount of traces generated to a preset desired rate of generation.

Context-sensitive sampling
    This one is used for ad hoc or debug sampling (e.g., using a special header to signal the tracing instrumentation that a given request should be sampled).

Whereas most current tracing systems implement head-based sampling, some newer systems employ tail-based sampling. With either approach's application and infrastructure overhead being imposed, it's important to weigh the ROI of your telemetry (i.e., are year-over-year comparisons necessary for this signal?). Various sampling algorithms can be used to tune the sampling behavior and negate the impact on tracing backends in the management plane.

Combining Telemetry Pillars

A maximally observable system exploits each internal signal, including synthetic checks, end-user experience monitoring (real user monitoring), and tooling for distributed debugging. Black-box testing and synthetic checks are still needed because they are end-to-end validation of everything you might not have observed.

Figure 2-4 presents a spectrum demonstrating how collecting telemetry in production is a compromise between cost, in terms of storage and performance (CPU, memory, and request latency) overhead, and the value of information collection, typically in terms of how expressive it is or useful in fixing slow or errored responses.

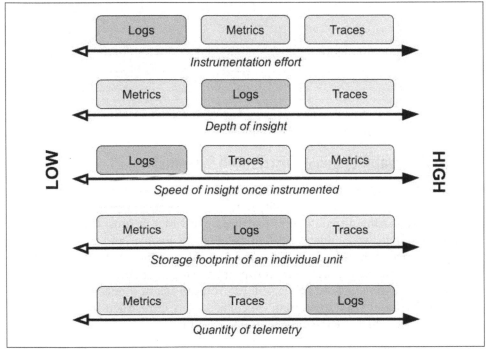

Figure 2-4. A comparative spectrum showing value provided by each pillar versus cost

Arguably, metrics provide the best ROI. Given that some service meshes facilitate distributed tracing, you could argue that distributed tracing provides the greatest value from the least investment (relative to level of insight provided). Ideally, your instrumentation allows you to dial back the verbosity levels and sampling rate to give control over your overhead costs versus desired observability.

Many organizations are now used to having individual monitoring solutions for distributed tracing, logging, security, access control, and so on. Service meshes centralize and assist in solving these observability challenges. Istio generates and sends multiple telemetric signals based on requests sent into the mesh, as shown in Figure 2-5.

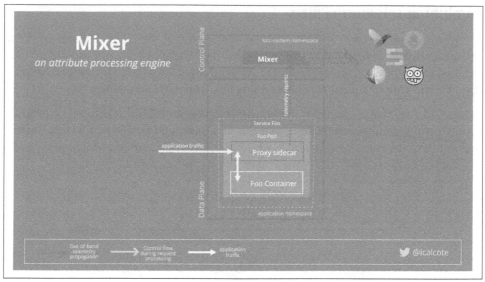

Figure 2-5. Istio's Mixer can collect and send telemetric signals to backend monitoring, authentication, and quota systems via adapters.

Why Is Observability Key in Distributed Systems?

The ability to aggregate and correlate logs, metrics, and traces together when running distributed systems is key to your ability to reason over what's happening within your application across the disparate infrastructure upon which it runs. When running a distributed system, you understand that failures *will* happen and can account for some percentage of these known-unknowns. You will not know beforehand all of the ways in which failure will occur (unknown-unknowns); therefore, your system must be granularly observable (and debuggable) so you can ask new questions and reason over the behavior of your application (in context of its infrastructure). Of the many signals available, which are the most critical to monitor?

As a service owner, you need to explore these complex and interconnected systems and explain anomalies based on telemetry delivered from your instrumentation. It's through a combination of internal observables and external monitoring that service meshes illuminate service operation, where you might otherwise be blind.

Which KPIs Are Most Significant?

Popular methodologies have different descriptions as to what key performance indicators (KPIs) should be measured, and how:

- USE stands for "utilization, saturation, and errors." These are resource scoped (e.g., CPU, memory, etc.).
- RED stand for "rate, errors, and duration." These are request scoped. Duration is explicitly taken to mean distributions, not averages.
- The four golden signals are: latency, requests, saturation, and errors.

Reviewing the popular methodologies of USE, RED, and the four golden signals, you'll find that they have *requests*, *latency*, and *errors* in common.

Requests
  This measures how much demand is being placed on your system and is measured in requests per second.

Latency
  This is the time it takes to service a request typically separating the latency of successful requests from that of the latency of failed requests.

Errors
  This is the rate by which requests fail.

Monitoring is an activity you perform, by simply observing the state of a system over a period of time. Observability (the condition of being observable) is a measure of how well the internal states of a system can be inferred from knowledge of its external outputs; a measure of the extent to which something is observable.

Rather than attempting to overcome distributed systems concerns by writing infrastructure logic into application code, you can manage these challenges with a service mesh. A service mesh helps ensure that the responsibility of service management is centralized, avoiding redundant instrumentation, and making observability ubiquitous and uniform across services.

Uniform Observability with a Service Mesh

Insight (observability) is the number one reason why people deploy a service mesh. Not only do service meshes provide a level of immediate insight, but they also do so *uniformly* and *ubiquitously*. You might be accustomed to having individual monitoring solutions for distributed tracing, logging, security, access control, metering, and so on. Service meshes centralize and assist in consolidating these separate panes of glass by generating metrics, logs, and traces of requests transiting the mesh. Taking advantage of automatically generated span identifiers from the data plane, Istio provides a baseline of distributed tracing in order to visualize dependencies, request volumes, and failure rates. Istio's default attribute template (more on attributes in Chapter 9) emits metrics for global request volume, global success rate, and individual service responses by version, source, and time. When metrics are ubiquitous across your cluster, they unlock new insights, and also free developers from having to instrument code to emit these metrics.

The importance of ubiquity and uniformity of insight (and control over request behavior) is well illustrated by the challenges that arise from using client libraries.

Client Libraries

Client libraries (sometimes referred to as microservices frameworks) are yesterday's go-to tooling for developers looking to infuse resilience into their microservices. There are a number (*https://layer5.io/landscape/*) of popular language-specific client libraries that offer resiliency features like timing out a request or backing off and retrying when a service isn't responding in a timely fashion.

Client libraries became popular as microservices gained a foothold in cloud native application design, as a means of avoiding having to rewrite the same infrastructure and operational logic in every service. One problem with microservices frameworks is that they couple those same infrastructure and operational concerns with your code. This leads to code duplication across your services and inconsistency in what different libraries provide and how they behave. As shown in Figure 2-6, when running multiple versions of the same library or different libraries, getting service teams to update their libraries can be an arduous process. When these distributed systems concerns are embedded into your service code, you need to chase your engineers to update and correct their libraries (of which there might be a few, used to varying degrees). Getting a consistent and recent version deployed can take some time. Achieving and enforcing consistency is challenging.

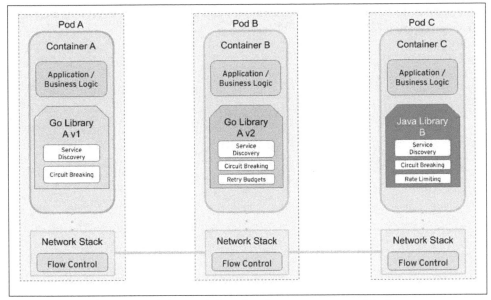

Figure 2-6. Applications tightly coupled with infrastructure control logic

Interfacing with Monitoring Systems

From the application's vantage point, service meshes largely provide black-box monitoring (observing a system from the outside) of service-to-service communication, leaving white-box monitoring (observing a system from within—reporting measurements from inside out) of an application as the responsibility of the microservice. Proxies that comprise the data plane are well positioned (transparently, in-band) to generate metrics, logs, and traces providing uniform and thorough observability throughout the mesh as a whole. Istio provides adapters to translate this telemetry and transmit to your monitoring system(s) of choice.

Driven by the need for speed of delivery, potential global scale, and judicious resource utilization, cloud native applications run as immutable, isolated, ephemeral packages on what is typically shared infrastructure.

Client libraries and microservices frameworks come with challenges. Service meshes move these concerns into the service proxy and decouple from the application code.

Is your application easy to monitor in production? Many applications are, but sadly, some are designed with observability as an afterthought. Ideally you should consider observability in advance, as this is one important factor of running apps at scale, just like backups, security, auditability, and the like. In this way, you can make the trade-offs consciously. Whether observability was considered upfront in your environments or not, a service mesh offers much value.

There's a cost to telemetry. Various techniques and algorithms are used to gather only what signals are most insightful.

## CHAPTER 3

Istio at a Glance

As organizations mature in their operations of container deployments, many will come to utilize a service mesh within their environment. This topic causes significant buzz within the cloud native ecosystem. Currently, many administrators, operators, architects, and developers are seeking an understanding and guidance with respect to how, when, and why to adopt a service mesh, so let's look at Istio.

As you learned in Chapter 2, Istio, like other service meshes, introduces a new layer into modern infrastructure, creating the potential to implement robust and scalable applications with granular control over them. If you're running microservices, these challenges are exacerbated as you deploy ever more microservices. You might not be running microservices, however. Even though the value of a service mesh shines most brightly in microservices deployments, Istio also readily accounts for services running directly on the OS running in your VM and bare-metal server.

Service Mesh Architecture

At a high level, service mesh architectures including Istio commonly comprise two planes: a *control* plane and *data* plane, while a third (management) plane might reside in incumbent/infrastructure systems. Istio's architecture adheres to this paradigm. Figure 3-1 presents the divisions of concern by planes.

For a more thorough explanation of service mesh deployment models and approaches to evolutionary architectures, see *The Enterprise Path to Service Mesh Architectures* (*https://oreil.ly/TTO4p*).

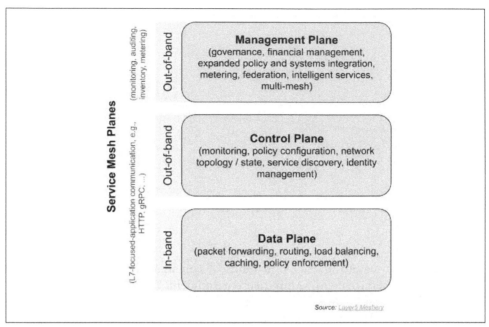

Figure 3-1. Istio and other service meshes are composed of two planes. A third plane is commonly deployed to enable additional network intelligence and ease of management in heterogenous environments.

Planes

Istio's data plane intercepts every packet in the request and is responsible for health checking, routing, load balancing, authentication, authorization, and generation of observable signals. Operating in band, service proxies are transparently inserted, and as applications make service-to-service calls, applications are unaware of the data plane's existence. Data planes are responsible for intracluster communication as well as inbound (*ingress*) and outbound (*egress*) cluster network traffic. Whether traffic is entering or leaving the mesh, application service traffic is directed first to the service proxy for handling. With Istio, traffic is transparently intercepted using iptables rules and redirected to the service proxy. The Istio data plane touches every packet/request in the system and is responsible for service discovery, health checking, routing, load balancing, authentication, authorization, and observability.

The control plane in Istio provides a single point of administration for service proxies, which need programmatic configuration to be efficiently managed and have their configuration updated in real-time as services are rescheduled across your environment (i.e., container cluster). Control planes provide policy and configuration for services in the mesh, taking a set of isolated, stateless proxies and turning them into a service mesh. They do not directly touch any network packets in the mesh; control planes operate out of band. They typically have a CLI and user interface (UI) with which to interact, each of which provide access to a centralized API for holistically controlling proxy behavior. You can automate changes to control-plane configuration through its APIs (e.g., by a CI/CD pipeline), where, in practice, configuration is most often version controlled and updated.

The Istio control plane does the following:

- Provides policy and configuration for services in the mesh via APIs for operators to specify desired routing/resilience behavior
- Combines a set of isolated stateless sidecar proxies into a service mesh:
  - APIs for the data plane to consume localized configuration
  - Service discovery abstraction for the data plane
- Uses APIs for specifying usage policies via quota and usage restrictions
- Provides security via certificate issuance and rotation
- Assigns workload identity
- Handles routing configuration:
  - Doesn't touch any packets/requests in the system
  - Specifies network boundaries and how to access them
  - Unifies telemetry collection

Istio Control-Plane Components

In this section, we introduce the functionality of each control-plane component at a high level. In later chapters, we'll do a deep dive into each component's behavior, configuration, and troubleshooting capability.

Pilot

Pilot is the head of the ship in an Istio mesh, so to speak. It stays synchronized with the underlying platform (e.g., Kubernetes) by tracking and representing the state and location of running services to the data plane. Pilot interfaces with your environment's service discovery system, and produces configuration for the data-plane service proxies (we'll examine istio-proxy as a data-plane component later).

As Istio evolves, more of Pilot's focus will be the scalable serving of proxy configuration and less on interfacing with underlying platforms. Pilot serves Envoy-compatible configurations by coalescing configuration and endpoint information from various sources and translating this into xDS objects. Another component, Galley, will eventually take responsibility for interfacing directly with underlying platforms.

Galley

Galley is Istio's configuration aggregation and distribution component. As its role evolves, it will insulate the other Istio components from underlying platform and user-supplied configurations by ingesting and validating configurations. Galley uses the Mesh Configuration Protocol (MCP) as a mechanism to serve and distribute configuration.

Mixer

Capable of standing on its own, Mixer is a control-plane component designed to abstract infrastructure backends from the rest of Istio, where infrastructure backends are things like Stackdriver or New Relic. Mixer bears responsibility for precondition checking, quota management, and telemetry reporting. It does the following:

- Enables platform and environment mobility
- Provides granular control over operational policies and telemetry by taking responsibility for policy evaluation and telemetry reporting
- Has a rich configuration model
- Abstracts away most infrastructure concerns with intent-based configuration

Service proxies and gateways invoke Mixer to do precondition checks to determine whether a request should be allowed to proceed (check), whether communication between the caller and the service is allowed or has exceeded quota, and to report telemetry after a request has completed (report). Mixer interfaces to infrastructure backends through a set of native and third-party adapters. Adapter configuration determines which telemetry is sent to which backend and when. Service mesh operators can use Mixer's adapters as the point of integration and intermediation with their infrastructure backends as it operates as an attribute processing and routing engine.

 The Mixer v2 design that is currently underway proposes a significantly different architecture. However, its scope and focus are planned to remain much the same as in Mixer v1.

Citadel

Citadel empowers Istio to provide strong service-to-service and end-user authentication using mutual Transport Layer Security (mTLS), with built-in identity and credential management. Citadel's CA component approves and signs certificate-signing requests (CSRs) sent by Citadel agents, and it performs key and certificate generation, deployment, rotation, and revocation. Citadel has an optional ability to interact with an identity directory during the CA process.

Citadel has a pluggable architecture in which different CAs can be used so that it's not using its self-generated, self-signed signing key and certificate to sign workload certificates. The CA pluggability of Istio enables and facilitates the following:

- Integrates with your organization's public key infrastructure (PKI) system.
- Secures communication between Istio and non-Istio legacy services (by sharing the same root of trust).
- Secures the CA signing key by storing it in a well-protected environment (e.g., HashiCorp Vault, hardware security module, or HSM)

Service Proxy

You can use service mesh proxies to gate ingress network traffic, traffic between services, and traffic egressing services. Istio uses proxies between services and clients. Service proxies are usually deployed as sidecars in pods. (Examples of other deployment models can be found in the book, *The Enterprise Path to Service Mesh Architectures* (*https://oreil.ly/Up2H7*).) The proxy-to-proxy communication is what truly forms the mesh. Inherently, it follows that for an application to be onboarded to the mesh, a proxy must be placed between the application and the network, as illustrated in Figure 3-2.

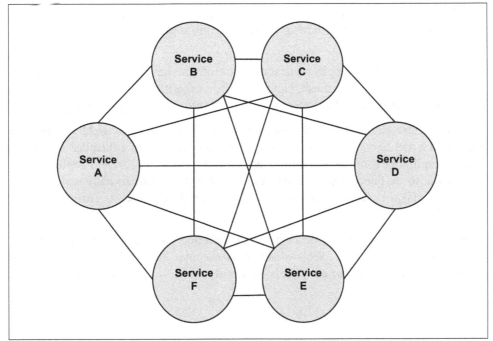

Figure 3-2. Fully interconnected service proxies form the mesh.

A sidecar adds behavior to a container without changing it. In that sense, the sidecar and the service behave as a single, enhanced unit. The pods host the sidecar and service as a single unit.

Istio Data-Plane Components

Istio uses an extended version of the Envoy proxy, a high-performance proxy developed in C++, to mediate all inbound and outbound traffic for all services in the service mesh. Istio uses Envoy's features such as dynamic service discovery, load balancing, TLS termination, HTTP/2 and gRPC Remote Procedure Call (gRPC) proxying, circuit breakers, health checks, staged rollouts with percent-based traffic split, fault injection, and rich metrics.

Envoy is deployed as a sidecar to the relevant service in the same Kubernetes pod. This allows Istio to extract a wealth of signals about traffic behavior as attributes, which in turn it can use in Mixer to enforce policy decisions and send to monitoring systems to provide information about the behavior of the entire mesh.

Injection

The sidecar proxy model also allows you to add Istio capabilities to an existing deployment with no need to redesign or rewrite code. This is a significant attraction to using Istio. The promises of an immediate view of top-level service metrics, of detailed control over traffic, and of automated authentication and encryption between all services without having to change your application code *or* change your deployment manifests.

Using Istio's canonical sample application Bookinfo, makes clear how service proxies come into play and form a mesh. Figure 3-3 shows the Bookinfo application without the service proxies. (We take a closer look at Bookinfo and deploy it in Chapter 4.)

In Kubernetes, automatic proxy injection is implemented as a webhook using a Kubernetes API Server with the mutating webhook admission controller. It is stateless, depending only on the injection template and mesh configuration configmaps as well as the to-be-injected pod object. As such, it is easily horizontally scaled, either manually via the Deployment object, or automatically via a Horizontal Pod Autoscaler (HPA).

Injection of the sidecar proxy into a newly created pod takes an average of 1.5 µs (per microbenchmark) for the Webhook itself to execute. Total injection time will be higher when accounting for network latency and API Server processing time.

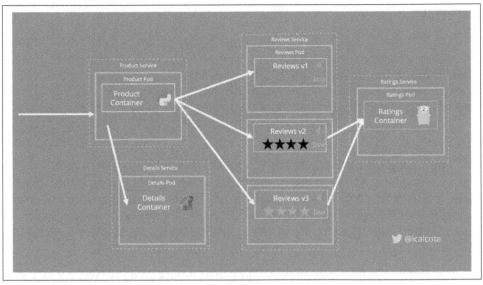

Figure 3-3. Istio's sample application, Bookinfo, shown without service proxies

Istio addresses the well-known distributed systems challenge of not having homogeneous, reliable, unchanging networks. It does so through deployment of lightweight proxies deployed between your application containers and the network. Figure 3-4 demonstrates how the full architecture of Istio includes the control and data planes with each of their internal components. A full-mesh deployment also includes ingress and egress service gateways.

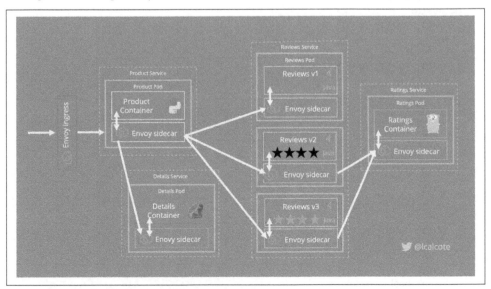

Figure 3-4. Bookinfo shown with service proxies

Gateways

Istio 0.8 introduced the concept of ingress and egress gateways. Symmetrically similar, ingress and egress gateways act as reverse and forward proxies, respectively, for traffic entering and exiting the mesh. Like other Istio components, the behavior of an Istio Gateway is defined and controlled through configuration, giving you control over which traffic to allow in and out of the service mesh, at what rate, and so on.

Ingress

Configuring ingress gateways enables you to define traffic entryways into the service mesh for incoming traffic to flow through. Consider that ingressing traffic into the mesh is a reverse proxy situation—akin to traditional web server load balancing. Configuration for egressing traffic out of the mesh is a forward proxy situation in which you identify which traffic to allow out of the mesh and where it should be routed.

As an example, the following gateway configuration sets up a proxy to act as a load balancer exposing port 80 and 9080 (HTTP), 443 (HTTPS), and port 2379 (TCP) for ingress. The gateway will be applied to the proxy running on a pod with labels `app: my-gateway-controller`. Even though Istio will configure the proxy to listen on these ports, it is the responsibility of the user to ensure that external traffic to these ports is allowed into the mesh (for more details, see Istio's gateway documentation (*https://oreil.ly/e5pIQ*)):

```
apiVersion: networking.istio.io/v1alpha3
kind: Gateway
metadata:
  name: my-gateway
spec:
  selector:
    app: my-gateway-controller
  servers:
  - port:
      number: 80
      name: http
      protocol: HTTP
    hosts:
    - uk.bookinfo.com
    - eu.bookinfo.com
    tls:
      httpsRedirect: true # sends 301 redirect for http requests
  - port:
      number: 443
      name: https
      protocol: HTTPS
    hosts:
    - uk.bookinfo.com
    - eu.bookinfo.com
```

```
  tls:
    mode: SIMPLE #enables HTTPS on this port
    serverCertificate: /etc/certs/servercert.pem
    privateKey: /etc/certs/privatekey.pem
- port:
    number: 9080
    name: http-wildcard
    protocol: HTTP
  hosts:
  - "*"
- port:
    number: 2379 # to expose internal service via external port 2379
    name: mongo
    protocol: MONGO
  hosts:
  - "*"
```

Egress

Traffic can exit an Istio service mesh in two ways: directly from the sidecar or funneled through an egress gateway, where you can apply traffic policy.

> By default, Istio-enabled applications are unable to access URLs external to the cluster.

Direct from a service proxy

If you want traffic destined to an external source to bypass the egress gateway, you can provide configuration to the ConfigMap of the `istio-sidecar-injector`. Set the following configuration in the sidecar injector, which will identify cluster-local networks and keep traffic destined locally within the mesh while forwarding traffic for all other destinations externally:

```
--set global.proxy.includeIPRanges="10.0.0.1/24"
```

After you've applied this and Istio proxies are updated with this configuration, external requests bypass the sidecar and route directly to the intended destination. The Istio sidecar will intercept and manage only internal requests within the cluster.

Route through an egress gateway

You may need to use an egress gateway in order to provide connectivity from your cluster's private IP address space, monitoring, or cross-cluster connectivity.

An egress gateway allows Istio monitoring and route rules to be applied to traffic exiting the mesh. It also facilitates communication between applications running in a cluster where the nodes do not have public IP addresses, preventing applications in the mesh from accessing the internet. Defining an egress gateway, directing all the egress traffic through it, and allocating public IPs to the egress gateway nodes allows the nodes (and applications running on them) to access external services in a controlled way, as depicted in Figure 3-5.

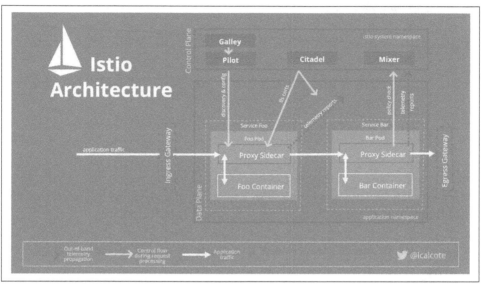

Figure 3-5. Istio's architecture and components

Why Use Istio Gateways and Not Kubernetes Ingresses?

In general, the Istio v1alpha3 APIs use gateways for richer functionality given that Kubernetes Ingress has proven insufficient for Istio applications. Compared to Kubernetes Ingress, Istio gateways can operate as a pure Layer 4 (L4) TCP proxy and support all protocols that Envoy supports.

Another consideration is the separation of trust domains between organizational teams. The Kubernetes Ingress API merges specification for L4 to Layer 7 (L7), making it difficult for different teams in organizations with separate trust domains (like SecOps, NetOps, ClusterOps, and Developers) to own ingress traffic management.

Extensibility

Although not an explicit goal for some service meshes, Istio is designed to be customized. As an extensible platform, its integrations come in two primary forms: swappable sidecar proxies and telemetry/authorization adapters.

Customizable Sidecars

Within Istio, though Envoy is the default service proxy sidecar, it is possible to use another service proxy for your sidecar. Although there are multiple service proxies in the ecosystem, beyond Envoy, only two have currently demonstrated integration with Istio: Linkerd and NGINX. Linkerd2 is not currently designed as a general-purpose proxy; rather, it focuses on being lightweight, having extensibility as a secondary concern in offering extension via the gRPC plug-in.

Though it's more likely that you'd choose to run a different service mesh altogether, you might want to use Istio with one of the following alternative service proxies:

Linkerd
> You might want to use this if you're already running Linkerd and want to begin adopting Istio control APIs like `CheckRequest`, which is used to get a thumbs-up/thumbs-down before performing an action.

NGINX
> Based on your operational expertise and need for battle-tested proxies, you might select NGINX. You might be looking for caching, web application firewall, or other functionality available in NGINX Plus as well.

Consul Connect
> You might choose to deploy Consul Connect based on ease of deployment and simplicity of needs.

The arrival of choice in service proxies for Istio has generated a lot of excitement. Linkerd's integration was created early in Istio's 0.1.6 release. Similarly, the ability to use NGINX as a service proxy through the nginMesh (*https://oreil.ly/axVOR*) project was provided early in Istio's release cycle.

> Although nginMesh is no longer in active development, you might find this article, "How to Customize an Istio Service Mesh" (*https://oreil.ly/p72P8*), and its related webcast (*https://oreil.ly/KHPOG*) helpful in better understanding Istio's extensibility with respect to swappable service proxies.

Without configuration, proxies lack instructions to perform their tasks. Pilot is the head of the ship in an Istio mesh, so to speak, keeping synchronization with the underlying platform by tracking and representing its services to `istio-proxy`. As the default proxy, `istio-proxy` contains an extended version of Envoy. Typically, the same `istio-proxy` Docker image is used by Istio sidecar and Istio ingress and egress gateways. `istio-proxy` contains not only the service proxy, but also the Istio Pilot agent, which pulls configuration down from Pilot to the service proxy at frequent intervals so that each proxy knows where to route traffic. In this case, nginMesh's translator agent performs the task of configuring NGINX as the `istio-proxy`. Pilot is responsible for the life cycle of `istio-proxy`.

Extensible Adapters

Istio's Mixer control-plane component is responsible for enforcing access control and usage policies across the service mesh and collecting telemetry data from the sidecar proxy. As Istio's main point of extensibility, Mixer categorizes adapters based on the type of data they consume, as illustrated in Figure 3-6.

The In-Process Adapter authoring model for Mixer adapters is now a deprecated concept in Istio. Like other open source projects before it, Istio began with conveniently incorporating adapters in-tree. As Istio has evolved and matured, this model has been converted to that of keeping adapters separate from the main project so as to remove the burden on the core project teams and encourage ownership by what are typically separate development teams that have created an integration to other backend systems.

Future extensibility might come in the form of secure key stores for HSMs and better support for swapping out distributed tracing infrastructure backends. Additionally, we expect management planes to play a more prominent role as Istio and other service meshes are adopted.

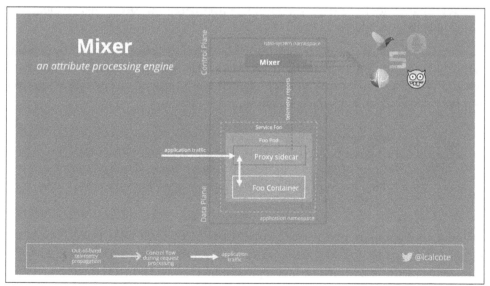

Figure 3-6. Mixer acts as an attribute processing engine, collecting, transforming, and transmitting telemetry.

Scale and Performance

Like many, you might be saying to yourself, "These features are great, but what's the overhead of running a service mesh?" It's true that these features come at a cost. Running a proxy per service and intercepting each packet takes a certain amount of continual overhead. Costs can be analyzed by data and control planes. And answers to performance questions always begin with "it depends." Here, depending on how many of Istio's features you use, the resources needed vary (*https://oreil.ly/9puvE*). Some cost/resources are as follows:

- 1 virtual CPU (vCPU) per peak thousand requests per second for the sidecar(s) with access logging (which is off by default in v1.1) and 0.5 without. Fluentd on the node is a big contributor to that cost because it captures and uploads logs.
- Assuming a typical cache hit ratio (>80%) for Mixer checks: 0.5 vCPU per peak thousand requests per second for the mixer pods.
- Latency of approximately 8 ms is added to the 90th percentile latency.
- Mutual TLS (mTLS) costs are negligible on AES-NI capable hardware in terms of both CPU and latency.

Overhead for both the data plane and control plane is a common concern in the minds of those adopting a service mesh. As far as the data plane is concerned, maintainers of Envoy understand that this service proxy is in the critical path and have worked to tune its performance. Envoy has first-class support for HTTP/2 and TLS in either direction and minimizes overhead by multiplexing requests and responses across single, long-lived TCP connections. In this way, its support of HTTP/2 achieves lower latency than HTTP/1.1 otherwise would.

Although Envoy project maintainers do not currently publish any official performance benchmarks, they encourage users to benchmark it in their own environments with a configuration similar to what you plan on using in production. To fill this void, tools like Meshery (*https://oreil.ly/MNUQC*) have cropped up within the open source community. Meshery is an open source, multiservice mesh-management plane that provisions different service meshes and sample applications and benchmarks the performance of service mesh deployments. It facilitates benchmarking various configuration scenarios of Istio, as well as comparison of performance of services (applications) on and off the mesh and across meshes. It vets mesh and service configuration against deployment best practices. Some service mesh projects use Meshery as their release benchmark tool. It is complemented by other load-generation tools (*https://oreil.ly/pZxU9*) commonly used for service mesh performance testing.

In larger deployments, as the service proxy (Envoy) fleet grows, the central role the control plane plays can become a bottleneck or source of latency. For example, depending on the verbosity of the instrumentation and rate of sampling, trace data can exceed the volume of the actual business traffic sustained by an application. Collection of this telemetry, and sending it to the tracing backend (directly or via the control plane), can have a real effect on the application's latency and throughput.

Deployment Models

Istio supports different deployment models, some of which deploy only select components of its architecture. Figure 3-7 shows a full Istio deployment in all its glory.

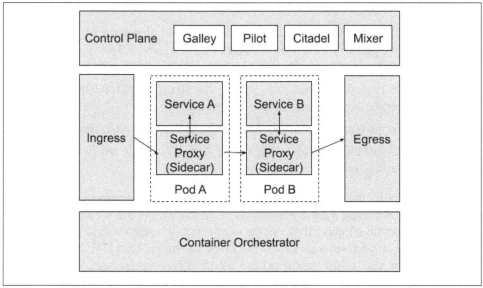

Figure 3-7. Istio deployment on Kubernetes

Service meshes come in various shapes and sizes. To explore other mesh deployment models, see *The Enterprise Path to Service Mesh Architectures* (*https://oreil.ly/70pu7*). You're learning more about Istio, a service mesh, because you're ready to layer up—ready for enhanced service management. Istio aims to directly address service management challenges by providing a new layer of visibility, security, and control.

In this chapter, we've covered how the Istio control plane provides a single point of visibility and control, while the data plane facilitates traffic routing. Also, Istio is an example of a service mesh designed with customizability in mind. Finally, we covered how decoupling of control and unification of responsibility over microservices as a new layer of infrastructure, L5, avoids finger-pointing between Dev and Ops teams.

## CHAPTER 4

Deploying Istio

To gain familiarity with the complete set of Istio's capabilities, we need to get Istio up and running. Let's begin by understanding its supported platforms and preparing our environment for deployment. Istio is a large project, providing a number of capabilities and quite a few deployment options. In this chapter, we perform a basic installation on your local machine and deploy a few services onto the mesh. Later chapters dive deeper into various aspects of Istio functionality.

Preparing Your Environment for Istio

In addition to Istio, we'll deploy its sample application, Bookinfo. Our Istio and Bookinfo deployments will lay down a number of containers. We will use Kubernetes as the platform to manage these containers. Kubernetes (*https://kubernetes.io*) is a robust container orchestration system capable of forming clusters (a collection of nodes) and scheduling containers across nodes within the fleet of host machines (nodes) that form the cluster. Nodes are Linux or Windows servers capable of running containers that have a Kubernetes agent, kubelet, installed. As one of a number of to-be-supported underlying platforms, Kubernetes is the first and best-supported platform. So, we use Kubernetes throughout our examples. To be clear, Istio is not dependent on Kubernetes. Designed to be platform agnostic, Istio supports multiple deployment platforms, including those without a container orchestrator.

Docker Desktop as the Installation Environment

There are many options for deploying Kubernetes. In this book, we use Docker Desktop as a convenient option. Docker Desktop is an easy-to-install application for your Mac or Windows environment that enables you to start running Kubernetes and Istio from your local machine.

To install Docker Desktop and verify that you have a functional Docker environment, on the command line, run ++$ docker run hello-world++. A "Hello from Docker!" message confirms that Docker was able to pull images, create new instances, and is running as expected.

 We chose Docker Desktop (*https://oreil.ly/HRKvu*) as a convenient Kubernetes platform that requires manual deployment of Istio (so you can see Istio's innards without needing to fuss with Kubernetes cluster deployment). You can also use the management plane, Meshery (*https://oreil.ly/0Oa9X*), which quickly deploys Istio and the sample application, Bookinfo. No matter which tool you use to deploy Istio, the examples used here should work within any Istio environment running on Kubernetes. For a list of supported platforms, see the Istio documentation (*https://oreil.ly/LeGw5*).

As of July 2018, Docker Desktop for Mac and Windows includes support for running a standalone Kubernetes server and client as well as Docker CLI integration. We use Docker Desktop to run Kubernetes and Kubernetes as the platform to deploy Istio. The Docker Desktop–managed Kubernetes server runs locally within your Docker instance, is not configurable, and is a single-node Kubernetes cluster.

The Docker Desktop for Mac Kubernetes integration provides the Kubernetes CLI executable at */usr/local/bin/kubectl*. The Docker Desktop for Windows Kubernetes integration provides the Kubernetes CLI executable at *C:\>Program Files\Docker \Docker\Resources\bin\kubectl.exe*. This location might not be in your shell's PATH variable; if so, type the full path of the command or add it to the PATH. For more information about kubectl, see the official documentation (*https://oreil.ly/BaEUI*).

Configuring Docker Desktop

To ensure that your Docker Desktop VM has enough memory to run Kubernetes, Istio, and Istio's sample application, Bookinfo, you will need to configure your Docker VM with at least 4 GB of memory. This amount of memory allocation is required for all Istio and Bookinfo services to run. Pilot, specifically, might have trouble running as it requests 2 GB of memory in an Istio deployment with default settings (for a quick review of Pilot's purpose, see Chapter 3). Docker Desktop's default limit also happens to be 2 GB, so Pilot might refuse to start due to insufficient resources, if this isn't increased in your Docker installation.

Instead of increasing the amount of memory allocated to your Docker Desktop installation, as shown in Figure 4-1, you might, alternatively, reduce the amount of memory that Pilot requests of your Kubernetes cluster. There are a couple of ways you can do this, depending upon whether you're using a package manager like Helm or simply Kubernetes spec files directly.

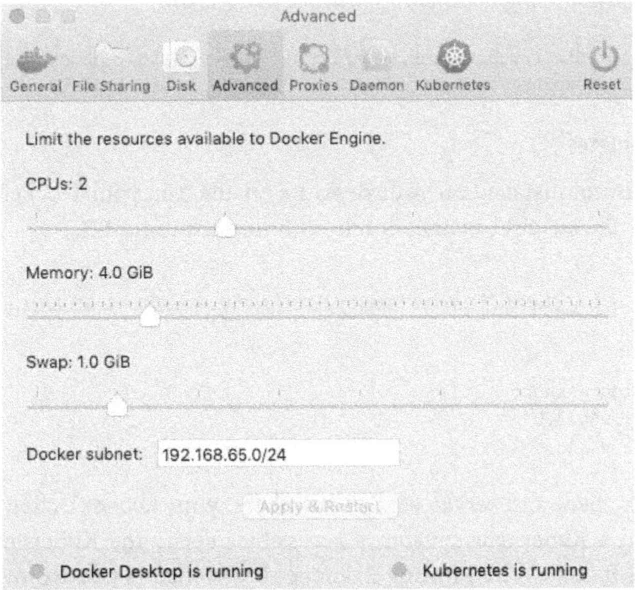

Figure 4-1. Increasing Docker's memory limit in the Advanced pane

Using *install/kubernetes/istio-demo.yaml* as an example manifest, Example 4-1 high-lights which section of the Pilot specification to edit in order to reduce the 2 GB of memory requested by Pilot to something smaller, like 512 MB.

Example 4-1. istio-demo.yaml showing memory resource requested for Pilot container

```
apiVersion: extensions/v1beta1
kind: Deployment
metadata:
  name: istio-pilot
  namespace: istio-system
...
        resources:
          requests:
            cpu: 500m
            memory: 2048Mi
...
```

Or you can provide a custom configuration when using Helm (a package manager for Kubernetes) to deploy Istio. To customize Istio install using Helm, use the `--set <key>=<value>` option in the Helm command to override one or more values, as demonstrated in Example 4-2.

Example 4-2. Customizing Istio's configuration using Helm

```
$ helm template install/kubernetes/helm/istio --name istio --namespace istio-system
    --set pilot.resources.requests.memory="512Mi" | kubectl apply -f -
```

Deploying Kubernetes

If Kubernetes is not installed on your desktop, enable it in your Docker Desktop preferences. Verify the kubectl installation by running Example 4-3.

Example 4-3. Listing client (kubectl binary) and server (Kubernetes cluster) version numbers

```
$ kubectl version --short
Client Version: v1.13.0
Server Version: v1.13.0
```

If you see both client and server version numbers, your kubectl client is installed in your PATH, and a Kubernetes cluster is accessible. Verify the Kubernetes installation and your current context by running $ kubectl get nodes (see Example 4-4), which will confirm that your *kubeconfig* (typically located at *~/.kube/config*) is correctly configured to the docker-desktop context and your single-node cluster is up.

Example 4-4. List of Kubernetes nodes as retrieved by kubectl

```
$ kubectl get nodes
NAME             STATUS   ROLES    AGE   VERSION
docker-desktop   Ready    master   32m   v1.13.0
```

 This installation creates sample users, secrets, applications, and other objects within your cluster. Objects created in this tutorial are for illustrative and educational purposes only. Do not run this configuration in a production environment.

Installing Kubernetes Dashboard

Kubernetes Dashboard is a web-based UI for managing your cluster and its resources. You can use it to deploy and troubleshoot containerized applications. Kubernetes Dashboard also provides information on the state of Kubernetes resources in your cluster and on any errors that might have occurred. Dashboard is useful for reinforcing your understanding of how Istio is running. The easiest and most common way to access the cluster is through kubectl proxy, which creates a local web server that securely proxies data to Dashboard through the Kubernetes API Server. Deploy the Kubernetes Dashboard by running the following command:

```
$ kubectl create -f https://raw.githubusercontent.com/kubernetes/dashboard/
    master/aio/deploy/recommended/kubernetes-dashboard.yaml
```

Then access Dashboard by using the `kubectl` command-line tool by running the following command:

```
$ kubectl proxy
```

This command creates a local web server that securely proxies data to Dashboard through the Kubernetes API Server. Understand that you can access Dashboard only from the machine where the command is executed. See `kubectl proxy --help` for more options and Kubernetes Dashboard documentation (*https://oreil.ly/El-cx*) for more information. `kubectl` makes Dashboard available, as illustrated in Figure 4-2.

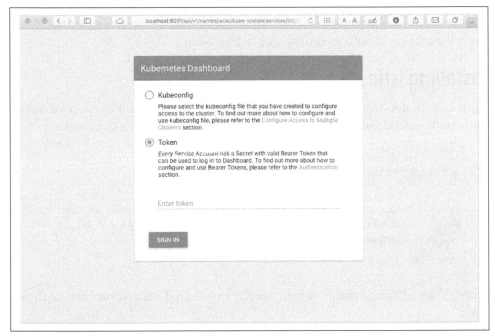

Figure 4-2. Authenticating to the Kubernetes Dashboard

To protect your cluster data, Dashboard deploys with a minimal role-based access control (RBAC) configuration by default. Currently, Dashboard only supports logging in with a bearer token. You can either create a sample user (*https://oreil.ly/qwiNm*) and use its token or use an existing token provided by your Docker Desktop deployment, as shown here:

```
$ kubectl -n kube-system describe secret $(kubectl -n kube-system get secret |
    awk '/default-token/ {print $1}')
```

This prints something like Example 4-5.

Example 4-5. Output of describing a Kubernetes secret

```
Name:          default-token-tktcn
Namespace:     kube-system
Labels:        <none>
Annotations:   kubernetes.io/service-account.name: default
               kubernetes.io/service-account.uid: 3a0a68b1-4abd-11e9-8561-025...

Type:  kubernetes.io/service-account-token

Data
====
ca.crt:        1025 bytes
namespace:     11 bytes
token:         eyJhbGciOiJSUzI1NiIsImtpZCI6IiJ9.eyJpc3MiOiJrdWJlcm5ldGVzL3NlcnZp...
```

Copy the token and use it to authenticate in Dashboard.

Installing Istio

With Kubernetes deployed and Dashboard up, it's time to install our service mesh. You can download the latest Istio release by running the following command:

```
$ curl -L https://git.io/getLatestIstio | sh -
```

This script fetches the latest Istio release candidate and untars it.

 Mac and Linux users should find `curl` readily available on their system. Windows users may need to download curl for Windows (*https://oreil.ly/2QiWB*).

To fetch a particular version of Istio, specify the desired version number, as shown here:

```
$ curl -L https://git.io/getLatestIstio | ISTIO_VERSION=1.1.0 sh -
```

Even though Istio as a project provides backward compatibility from minor version to minor version (unless noted in release changelogs), you might want to specify `ISTIO_VERSION=1.1.0` to ensure that the examples in this book function as described.

You can also download Istio from the Istio release page (*https://oreil.ly/6GzRG*). You can choose from Windows, macOS, and Linux releases. Irrespective of which OS you use, after you've downloaded the distribution for your OS, extract the compressed file to a directory and familiarize yourself with the contents of the distribution.

Each release includes `istioctl` (this binary will be specific to your OS), configuration samples, a sample application, and platform-specific installation resources. Also installable via your favorite package manager, `istioctl` is an important CLI for service operators to debug and diagnose their Istio service mesh.

 After downloading, be sure to move the release distribution to a folder where it will not be deleted.

To explore release contents on macOS or Linux, for example, change directory to *istio-x.x.x*, as shown here (as of this writing, the latest version of Istio is 1.1.7):

```
$ cd istio-1.1.0
```

This directory (see Example 4-6) contains the files necessary for installing Istio, sample files, and also `istioctl`.

Example 4-6. Contents of the top-level folder containing an Istio release

```
$ ls -l
total 48
-rw-r--r--   1 lee   staff   11343 Mar 18 16:08 LICENSE
-rw-r--r--   1 lee   staff    5921 Mar 18 16:08 README.md
drwxr-xr-x   3 lee   staff      96 Mar 18 16:08 bin
drwxr-xr-x   7 lee   staff     224 Mar 18 16:08 install
-rw-r--r--   1 lee   staff     602 Mar 18 16:08 istio.VERSION
drwxr-xr-x  16 lee   staff     512 Mar 18 16:08 samples
drwxr-xr-x  21 lee   staff     672 Mar 18 16:08 tools
```

The installation directory contains Istio installation YAML files for Kubernetes in *install/*, sample applications in *samples/*, and the `istioctl` client binary in the *bin/* directory. The *istio.VERSION* configuration file contains a list of Istio components and their version numbers for the release's distribution.

You can use the `istioctl` CLI for creating routing rules and policies. You also can use it when you're manually injecting Envoy as a service proxy. Other uses include creating, listing, modifying, and deleting configuration resources in the Istio system. Let's add it to your PATH environment variable:

```
$ export PATH=$PWD/bin:$PATH
```

You can verify your `istioctl` installation by running:

```
$ istioctl version
```

This should validate the path and `istioctl` command options (see Example 4-7). If not, see the "Istio Installation, Upgrade, and Uninstall" on page 194.

Example 4-7. Confirmation that istioctl runs on your machine

```
version.BuildInfo{
Version:"1.1.0", GitRevision:"82797c0c0649a3f73029b33957ae105260458c6e",
User:"root",
Host:"996cd064-49c1-11e9-813c-0a580a2c0506", GolangVersion:"go1.10.4",
DockerHub:"docker.io/istio",
BuildStatus:"Clean",
GitTag:"1.1.0-rc.6"
}
```

Now that we have downloaded an Istio distribution and verified that the `istioctl` CLI is functional on our local machine, let's perform a basic installation.

Istio Installation Options

There are many different installation methods and deployment architectures. Commonly, installations generally fall across the categories in the following subsections.

Choice of security configuration

Install with strict mTLS authentication
> Recommended for a fresh Kubernetes cluster. This method enforces authentication between sidecars by default.

Install with permissive mTLS authentication between sidecars
- This is recommended if you have existing clusters and services.
- Use this if you have applications where services with an Istio sidecar need to communicate with other non-Istio Kubernetes services.

Custom deployments that include or exclude certain default Istio components
- This is recommended if a function of one of Istio's components isn't necessary or desired in your environment (e.g., removal of Citadel if mTLS is not to be used).

Choice of deployment utility

Consider the following when choosing a deployment utility:

- Does it render Kubernetes manifests directly with kubectl?
- Is it recommended for understanding Istio's underpinnings more explicitly?
- Will it render Kubernetes manifests with a package/configuration management system like Helm or Ansible?
- Is it recommended for production deployments with templated configuration?

This list isn't exhaustive; however, no matter which approach you take to installing Istio, each will include installation of Kubernetes custom resource definitions (CRDs) for Istio. CRDs allow definition and registration of nondefault Kubernetes resources. When Istio CRDs are deployed, Istio's objects are registered as Kubernetes objects, providing a highly integrated experience with Kubernetes as a deployment platform.

What Are CRDs?

Introduced in Kubernetes 1.7, CRDs are extensions of the Kubernetes API. CRDs are a powerful feature you can use to add custom objects to your Kubernetes cluster. A *resource* is an endpoint in the Kubernetes API that stores a collection of API objects of a certain kind. For example, the built-in pods resource contains a collection of Pod objects.

The standard Kubernetes distribution ships with many built-in API resources (objects). A *custom resource* is an extension of the Kubernetes API that is not necessarily available in a default Kubernetes installation. It represents a customization of a particular Kubernetes installation. However, many core Kubernetes functions are now built using custom resources, making Kubernetes more modular.

Custom resources come into the picture when you want to introduce your objects into your Kubernetes cluster. After you apply a CRD to your Kubernetes cluster, they are stored in the etcd cluster, providing durability through replication and life cycle management. The Kubernetes API (kube-api) represents these new resources as endpoints that you can use as you would any other native Kubernetes object (e.g., a Pod object). As such, you are able to take advantage of all of the features of Kubernetes, such as its CLI, security, API services, RBAC, and more when interfacing with and managing your custom resources, saving you the overhead of implementing them on your own.

For more information, see the Kubernetes Custom Resources (*https://oreil.ly/rKU4N*) documentation.

Registering Istio's Custom Resources

Now, with an understanding of the power and convenience of custom resources under your belt, let's register Istio's CustomResourceDefinitions with your Kubernetes cluster. Use the following command to apply Istio's CustomResourceDefinition objects to your cluster:

```
$ for i in install/kubernetes/helm/istio-init/files/crd*yaml;
    do kubectl apply -f $i; done
```

This installation does not use Helm. The generally preferred method for any installation of Istio that might find its way into production is to use Helm or Ansible; both are included in the distribution you just downloaded. With Helm or Ansible, you gain flexibility regarding which components you install, and you can customize things in detail.

Example 4-8. Istio's CRDs, loaded as resources into kube-api and available for interaction

```
$ kubectl  api-resources | grep istio
meshpolicies        authentication.istio.io    false   MeshPolicy
policies            authentication.istio.io    true    Policy
adapters            config.istio.io            true    adapter
apikeys             config.istio.io            true    apikey
attributemanifests  config.istio.io            true    attributemanifest
authorizations      config.istio.io            true    authorization
bypasses            config.istio.io            true    bypass
checknothings       config.istio.io            true    checknothing
circonuses          config.istio.io            true    circonus
cloudwatches        config.istio.io            true    cloudwatch
...
```

Istio registers new CRDs (see Example 4-8), which you can manipulate (create/ update/delete) just like any other Kubernetes object:

```
$ kubectl get crd | grep istio
adapters.config.istio.io                    2019-03-24T03:17:08Z
apikeys.config.istio.io                     2019-03-24T03:17:07Z
attributemanifests.config.istio.io          2019-03-24T03:17:07Z
authorizations.config.istio.io              2019-03-24T03:17:07Z
bypasses.config.istio.io                    2019-03-24T03:17:07Z
checknothings.config.istio.io               2019-03-24T03:17:07Z
circonuses.config.istio.io                  2019-03-24T03:17:07Z
cloudwatches.config.istio.io                2019-03-24T03:17:08Z
clusterrbacconfigs.rbac.istio.io            2019-03-24T03:17:07Z
deniers.config.istio.io                     2019-03-24T03:17:07Z
destinationrules.networking.istio.io        2019-03-24T03:17:07Z
dogstatsds.config.istio.io                  2019-03-24T03:17:08Z
edges.config.istio.io                       2019-03-24T03:17:08Z
envoyfilters.networking.istio.io            2019-03-24T03:17:07Z
...
```

 After you deploy Istio's CRDs, you can address Istio resources through istioctl or kubectl, as shown in Example 4-9.

Example 4-9. Using istioctl to display information about Istio gateways

```
$ istioctl get gateway
Command "get" is deprecated, Use `kubectl get` instead (see https://kubernetes.io
```

```
    /docs/tasks/tools/install-kubectl)
No resources found.
```

Notice the message regarding deprecation of certain `istioctl` commands. Be aware that while `istioctl` is still maintained and being enhanced as a CLI to manage Istio, `kubectl` is the preferred method of interaction with Istio's custom resources (see Example 4-10). `istioctl` provides some Istio-specific utilities not found in `kubectl`.

Example 4-10. Using kubectl to display information about Istio gateways

```
$ kubectl get gateway
NAME                AGE
No resources found.
```

As an alternative to looping through the *install/kubernetes/helm/istio-init/files/crd*yaml* manifests, we could apply *istio-demo.yaml*, which has these same CRD manifests included. The *istio-demo.yaml* file also includes all of Istio's control-plane components (not just the CRDs). Within the *install/* folder of your release distribution folder, you'll find installation files for different supported platforms to run Istio. Given that Kubernetes is the platform we've chosen to work with in this book, open the *install/kubernetes/* folder. There, you'll find the *istio-demo.yaml* file, which contains all necessary Istio components (in the form of CRDs, clusteroles, configmaps, services, HPAs, deployments, services, and so on) and a few helpful adapters like Grafana and Prometheus.

Once you register Istio's custom resources with Kubernetes, you can install Istio's control-plane components.

Installing Istio Control-Plane Components

We use the *istio-demo.yaml* specification file, which contains Istio configurations that enable services to operate in mTLS permissive mode. Use of mTLS permissive mode is recommended if you have existing services or applications in your Kubernetes cluster. However, if you're starting with a fresh cluster, security best practices suggest switching to `istio-demo-auth.yaml` to enforce encryption of service traffic between sidecars.

```
$ kubectl apply -f install/kubernetes/istio-demo.yaml
```

Wait a few minutes to let the installation run, the Docker images to properly download, and the deployments to succeed. The application of this extensive YAML file allows Kubernetes to realize many new CRDs.

> ## Install Istio with mTLS Authentication Enforced
>
> When you configure Istio in mTLS permissive mode, it allows a service to accept both plain-text traffic and mTLS traffic, depending on the type of traffic a client sends. mTLS permissive mode facilitates migration of existing services on the service mesh. So, if you have an existing Kubernetes setup with services running you might elect to install Istio with permissive mTLS.
>
> Alternatively, and specifically within this local deployment, you might opt to use *istio-demo-auth.yaml*, which will enforce mTLS authentication between all clients and servers. You might consider that initial deployment of Istio with strict mTLS enforcement configured is most successfully used within a fresh Kubernetes cluster where all workloads will be Istio-enabled. To apply Istio configuration with mTLS authentication enforced, run the following command:
>
> ```
> $ kubectl apply -f install/kubernetes/istio-demo-auth.yaml
> ```
>
> Note the use of `tls.mode: ISTIO_MUTUAL` in the *istio-demo-auth.yaml* file.
>
> Using mTLS permissive mode, service operators can gradually install and configure the Istio service proxies to mutually authenticate requests. When configuration of all services is complete, the service operator can configure Istio to enforce mTLS-only mode. For more information, see "mTLS" on page 98.

Istio's control plane is installed in its own `istio-system` namespace, and from this namespace it manages services running in all other namespaces having services with sidecar proxies; or, in other words, all other namespaces that have services on the mesh. The control plane acts on a cluster-wide basis, which means that it behaves in a single-tenant fashion, as demonstrated in Example 4-11.

Example 4-11. istio-system namespace created for Istio control-plane components

```
$ kubectl get namespaces
NAME           STATUS   AGE
default        Active   49d
docker         Active   49d
istio-system   Active   2m15s
kube-public    Active   49d
kube-system    Active   49d
```

You can verify installation of the control plane into the `istio-system` namespace by using the commands shown in Example 4-12. If the installation is successful, you should see similar output.

Example 4-12. Istio control-plane services and pods running in the istio-system namespace

```
$ kubectl get svc -n istio-system
NAME            TYPE        CLUSTER-IP        EXTERNAL-IP PORT(S)            AGE

grafana         ClusterIP 10.108.237.105  <none>     3000/TCP            11d
istio-citadel ClusterIP 10.108.165.14   <none>     8060/TCP,15014/TCP   11d
istio-egressgateway ClusterIP 10.107.148.169 <none>   80/TCP,443/TCP,15443/TCP 11d
...

$ kubectl get pod -n istio-system
NAME                                        READY   STATUS      RESTARTS  AGE
grafana-57586c685b-jr2pd                    1/1     Running     0         5m45s
istio-citadel-645ffc4999-8j4v6              1/1     Running     0         5m45s
istio-cleanup-secrets-1.1.0-4c9pc           0/1     Completed   0         5m48s
istio-egressgateway-5c7fd57fdb-85g26        1/1     Running     0         5m46s
istio-galley-978f9447f-mj5xj                1/1     Running     0         5m46s
istio-grafana-post-install-1.1.0-g49gh      0/1     Completed   0         5m48s
istio-ingressgateway-8ccdc79bc-8mk4p        1/1     Running     0         5m46s
istio-pilot-649455846-klc8c                 2/2     Running     0         5m45s
istio-policy-7b7d7f644b-sqsp8               2/2     Running     4         5m45s
istio-security-post-install-1.1.0-v4ffp     0/1     Completed   0         5m48s
istio-sidecar-injector-6dcc9d5c64-tklqz     1/1     Running     0         5m45s
istio-telemetry-6d494cd676-n6pkz            2/2     Running     4         5m45s
istio-tracing-656f9fc99c-nn9hd              1/1     Running     0         5m44s
kiali-69d6978b45-7q7ms                      1/1     Running     0         5m45s
prometheus-66c9f5694-2xzpm                  1/1     Running     0         5m45s
```

Wait a second, you're asking, why is there only a single replica of each Istio control-plane component? How is this not a single point of failure? Well...you're right. Single-replica control-plane components are an issue for a *production deployment*. The Istio control plane should be deployed in a high-availability (HA) architecture (with multiple replicas of each component) in any environment for which down time isn't tolerable. Does it bother you that the data plane is inline? What if it fails or loses connection with the control plane? Fortunately, the data plane has some built-in resilience that's able to retain configuration and continue to operate in the event that control-plane components fail or disconnect from the control plane. As you continue through this book, you'll see that Istio is designed to be highly resilient. It needs to be. Failures in distributed systems are near guaranteed.

Thus far, we've deployed only half of the service mesh—the control plane. Prior to deploying the sample application and, consequently, the data plane, you might consider that no proxies are running; however, you would be overlooking the fact that two proxies are already running. Both the ingress and egress gateways are up and running instances of our service proxy. Let's inspect these.

Our simple demo deployment includes an egress gateway for purposes of gaining familiarity with and facilitating exploration of Istio. This optional gateway is disabled by default as of v1.1. If you need to control and secure your outbound traffic through the egress gateway, you'll need to manually enable `gateways.istio-egressgateway.enabled=true` in any non-demo deployment configuration profiles.

Using the `istioctl proxy-status` command allows you to get an overview of your mesh; this is an example of an `istioctl` utility that's not found in `kubectl`, as shown in Example 4-13. If you suspect one of your sidecars isn't receiving configuration or is not synchronized, `proxy-status` will let you know. We get further into using `istioctl` to debug Istio in Chapter 11.

Example 4-13. Confirming Istio ingress and egress gateways have sidecar proxies deployed and synchronized using istioctl proxy-status

```
$ istioctl proxy-status
NAME                     CDS    LDS    EDS      RDS       PILOT          VERSION
istio-egressgateway-...  SYNCED SYNCED SYNCED... NOT SENT istio-pilot-... 1.1.0
istio-ingressgateway-... SYNCED SYNCED SYNCED... NOT SENT istio-pilot-... 1.1.0
```

Understanding how Istio is managing the configuration of Envoy deployed as gateways in the control plane is enlightening in relation to how Envoy instances are managed in the data plane. If you recall, the data plane is composed of intelligent proxies deployed as sidecars alongside application services. Let's deploy our data plane. We'll do that by deploying the Bookinfo sample application.

Deploying the Bookinfo Sample Application

Let's now deploy our first set of services (an application) onto the service mesh. For this, we use Istio's sample application, Bookinfo (*https://oreil.ly/N5voj/*), which is designed to showcase many aspects of the value proposition of service meshes. The Kubernetes manifest files for Bookinfo are found in your release distribution folder at *samples/bookinfo/*. Since we use Bookinfo as the example application throughout this book, let's become more familiar with it.

From left to right in Figure 4-3, users call the `productpage` microservice, which in turn calls the details and reviews microservices to populate the page. The `details` microservice contains book information.

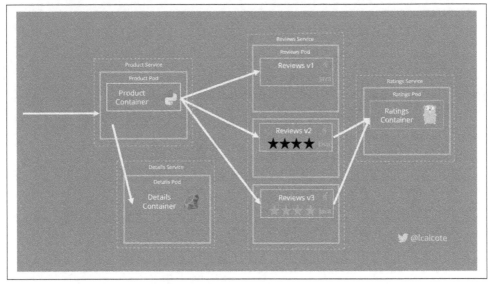

Figure 4-3. Bookinfo, showing separate microservices that show various Istio features

The `reviews` microservice contains book reviews and subsequently calls the `ratings` microservice to retrieve reviews. The `ratings` microservice contains book rankings in the form of a 1- to 5-star book reviews. The `reviews` microservice has three versions:

- `reviews` v1 has no ratings (does not call the `ratings` service)
- `reviews` v2 has ratings of 1 to 5 black stars (calls the `ratings` service)
- `reviews` v3 has ratings of 1 to 5 red stars (calls the `ratings` service)

That each of these application services is written in a different language—Python, Ruby, Java, and Node.js—further demonstrates the value of a service mesh.

 Most service mesh projects include a sample application. They do this so that adopters can quickly come to learn how the service mesh works and demonstrate the value that it provides.

Running the sample with Istio doesn't require making changes to the application. Instead, we simply configure and run the services in an Istio-enabled environment with service proxies as sidecars injected alongside each service. Istio's service proxies can be manually or automatically injected as sidecars to application services (see Figure 4-4). Let's look at how automatic sidecar injection works as we deploy our sample application. (We further examine manual sidecar injection in Chapter 5.)

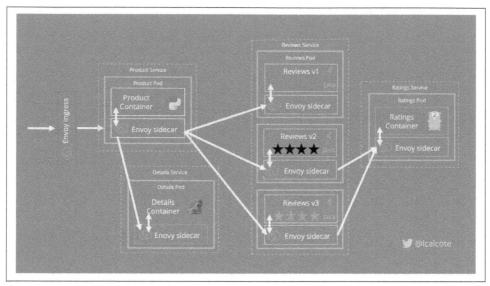

Figure 4-4. Bookinfo deployed on an Istio mesh with service proxies as sidecars

Deploying the Sample App with Automatic Sidecar Injection

To have Envoy deployed as sidecars to each of our services, Istio will deploy a sidecar injector. Chapter 5 looks at the sidecar injector in greater detail. For now, in Example 4-14 let's verify the presence of the sidecar injector deployment and its namespace label used to designate that pods of a particular namespace will automatically have sidecars injected upon deployment (admission).

Example 4-14. Verifying the presence of the Istio sidecar injector

```
$ kubectl -n istio-system get deployment -l istio=sidecar-injector
NAME                     READY  UP-TO-DATE  AVAILABLE  AGE
istio-sidecar-injector   1/1    1           1          82m
```

The `NamespaceSelector` decides whether to run the webhook on an object based on whether the namespace for that object matches the selector (*https://oreil.ly/rncCW*).

Label the default namespace with `istio-injection=enabled`:

```
$ kubectl label namespace default istio-injection=enabled
```

Then confirm which namespaces have the `istio-injection` label:

```
$ kubectl get namespace -L istio-injection
NAME          STATUS  AGE  ISTIO-INJECTION
default       Active  1h   enabled
Docker        Active  1h   enabled
istio-system  Active  1h   disabled
```

```
kube-public    Active    1h
kube-system    Active    1h
```

The *istio-demo.yaml* deployment we ran has automatic injection configured.

Now that we have the sidecar injector with mutating admission webhook in place and the namespace labeled for automatic sidecar injection, we can deploy the sample app. For an in-depth description of Kubernetes mutating admission webhooks, see "Automatic Sidecar Injection" on page 80. Next, give Bookinfo's manifest to Kubernetes for deployment of our sample application:

```
$ kubectl apply -f samples/bookinfo/platform/kube/bookinfo.yaml
```

With the sample application deployed, you can confirm that automatic sidecar injection is working in your environment by inspecting any one of the Bookinfo pods and noting the istio-proxy container as a new addition to the application pod:

```
$ kubectl describe po/productpage-v1-....
...
istio-proxy:
    Container ID:    docker://f28abdf1f0acf92687711488f7fcca8cc5968e2ed39d…
    Image:           docker.io/istio/proxyv2:1.1.7
    Image ID:        docker-pullable://istio/proxyv2@sha256:e6f039115c7d5e…
    Port:            15090/TCP
    Host Port:       0/TCP
    Args:
      proxy
      sidecar
...
```

 Sidecars may be removed from application pods even if the namespace carries the sidecar-injection label. We cover this procedure in Chapter 5.

Networking with the Sample App

Now that the Bookinfo services are up and running, you need to make the application accessible from outside of your Kubernetes cluster; for example, from a browser. We use an Istio Gateway (*https://oreil.ly/iUIwY*) for this purpose. You will need to define the ingress gateway for the application:

```
$ kubectl apply -f samples/bookinfo/networking/bookinfo-gateway.yaml
```

Confirm the gateway has been created:

```
$ kubectl get gateway

NAME                 AGE
bookinfo-gateway     7m
```

To interact with the freshly deployed application, find where the `productpage` has been exposed as a service available to receive requests originating outside of the cluster. This can be seen in Example 4-15.

Example 4-15. Identifying the IP address and port number of the exposed sample application on Istio ingress gateway

```
$ echo "http://$(kubectl get nodes -o template --template='{{range.items}}
    {{range.status.addresses}}{{if eq .type "InternalIP"}}{{.address}}{{end}}{{end}}
    {{end}}'):$(kubectl get svc istio-ingressgateway
    -n istio-system -o jsonpath='{.spec.ports[0].nodePort}')/
    productpage"

http://x.x.x.x:31380/productpage
```

You'll also want to ensure that your applications don't use the same network ports that Istio's components use. Table 4-1 lists the ports used by Istio.

Table 4-1. Network ports used by Istio

Port	Protocol	Used by	Description
8060	HTTP	Citadel	GRPC server
9090	HTTP	Prometheus	Prometheus
9091	HTTP	Mixer	Policy/Telemetry
9093	HTTP	Citadel	TCP server
15000	TCP	Envoy	Envoy admin port (commands/diagnostics)
15001	TCP	Envoy	Envoy
15004	HTTP	Mixer, Pilot	Policy/Telemetry - mTLS
15010	HTTP	Pilot	Pilot service - XDS pilot - discovery
15011	TCP	Pilot	Pilot service - mTLS - Proxy - discovery
15014	HTTP	Citadel, Mixer, Pilot	Control-plane monitoring
15030	TCP	Prometheus	Prometheus
15090	HTTP	Mixer	Proxy
42422	TCP	Mixer	Telemetry - Prometheus

With our application up and accessible, we can begin manipulating service traffic. The ability to access our application is a simple way of confirming how we're affecting the application, but an application's exposure to the mesh is not a requirement for manipulating its traffic.

Uninstalling Istio

Deleting the `istio-system` namespace will *not* uninstall Istio. It's a common mistake to think that it does, but deleting the `istio-system` removes Istio's control-plane components, leaving CRDs, sidecars, and other artifacts resident in your cluster. The logic here is that CRDs contain the runtime configuration set by service operators. Given this, it follows that service operators are better served in being made to explicitly delete the runtime configuration data rather than unexpectedly parts with it. In our case, we're not beholden to our installation, and so uninstalling Istio is as simple as running this command from within your Istio release folder:

```
$ kubectl delete -f install/kubernetes/istio-demo.yaml
```

This will not delete all of the Istio CRDs, mesh configuration, and sample application, however. To delete those, run the following:

```
$ for i in install/kubernetes/helm/istio-init/files/crd*yaml;
    do kubectl delete -f $i; done
$ kubectl delete -f samples/bookinfo/platform/kube/bookinfo.yaml
$ kubectl delete -f samples/bookinfo/networking/bookinfo-gateway.yaml
```

You can verify that Istio and Bookinfo were successfully removed by running the following:

```
$ kubectl get crds
$ kubectl get pods
```

If you still get CRDs after attempting to uninstall, see Chapter 11 for some debugging suggestions.

Helm-Based Installations

Package managers like Helm (without Tiller) or configuration managers like Ansible are generally recommended for facilitating idempotency as a desired practice when deploying Istio in production environments. An Istio operator is in progress to replace the Helm Tiller installation as the project's recommended utility for controlling upgrades.

Install Helm

You will need to have access to a system with Helm installed. Helm can be installed by placing the binary in your PATH, or with your favorite package manager.

1. Download the latest Helm release (*https://oreil.ly/61_6b*) relevant to your OS.

2. Unpack the downloaded file.

3. Locate Helm and move it to its desired location (e.g., */usr/local/bin/helm*).

Or you can add the unpackaged directory to your PATH by navigating to it on the CLI and using the following command:

```
export PATH=$PWD:$PATH
```

To install on your local (macOS) system, alternatively, you can use Homebrew to install, as shown in Example 4-16.

Example 4-16. Installing Helm on macOS with Homebrew

```
$ brew install kubernetes-helm
```

For other systems, see Helm's installation (*https://oreil.ly/UvQm2*) documentation.

With Helm installed, you can proceed with Tiller (Helm install) or without Tiller (Helm template). Tiller is the server-side component of Helm that runs in your cluster. Tiller interacts directly with the Kubernetes API Server to install, upgrade, query, and remove Kubernetes resources. It also stores the objects that represent releases.

Install with Helm Template

Let's briskly walk through a Helm template deployment (without Tiller). Create a namespace for Istio's control-plane components and then install all of Istio's CRDs. Render Istio's core components to a Kubernetes manifest called *istio.yaml* using the following command from the Istio release directory:

```
$ kubectl create namespace istio-system
$ helm template install/kubernetes/helm/istio-init --name istio-init
    --namespace istio-system | kubectl apply -f -
$ helm template install/kubernetes/helm/istio --name istio
    --namespace istio-system | kubectl apply -f -
```

Part of the benefit of using a Helm-based method of deployment is that you can relatively easily customize your Istio configuration by adding one or more `--set <key>=<value>` installation options to the Helm command, like so:

```
$ helm install install/kubernetes/helm/istio --name istio
    --namespace istio-system \
  --set global.controlPlaneSecurityEnabled=true \
  --set mixer.adapters.useAdapterCRDs=false \
  --set grafana.enabled=true --set grafana.security.enabled=true \
  --set tracing.enabled=true \
  --set kiali.enabled=true
```

Istio's installation options (*https://oreil.ly/nf9hk*) highlight how configurable Istio deployments are. Production deployments typically take advantage of a package or configuration manager like Helm or Ansible. Istio deployments initially performed with these tools should also be upgraded to new versions of Istio using that same tool.

Confirming a Helm-Based Installation

Just as when you installed using `kubectl`, Helm-based installations deploy Istio to its own Kubernetes namespace, `istio-system`. To check whether Istio is deployed and to also see all of the pieces that are deployed, run the following:

```
$ kubectl get svc -n istio-system
```

Ensure that these services are running:

```
$ kubectl get pods -n istio-system
```

Uninstalling a Helm-Based Installation

To uninstall Istio after it was deployed using the Helm template, run the following commands to remove Istio from your Kubernetes cluster:

```
$ helm template install/kubernetes/helm/istio --name istio
    --namespace istio-system | kubectl delete -f -
$ kubectl delete -f install/kubernetes/helm/istio-init/files
$ kubectl delete namespace istio-system
```

Other Environments

It's not all about Kubernetes. A number of other platforms are supported for deployment. *Mesh expansion* is the term the Istio community uses to describe the onboarding of existing services onto the service mesh. We won't walk through all of the ways that you can expand the Istio service mesh in this book, but we will note that supported platforms include the following:

- Bare metal and VMs
- Apache Mesos and Cloud Foundry
- Nomad and Consul
- Eureka

Additionally, there are a number of Istio managed-service offerings offered by various public clouds and managed-services vendors.

CHAPTER 5
Service Proxy

You're likely familiar with the differentiation between *forward* and *reverse* proxies. As a refresher, forward proxies focusing on outbound traffic with the aim of improving performance and filtering requests are typically deployed as the interface between users on private networks and their internet requests. Forward proxies commonly improve performance because they can cache static web content and provide a level of security by preventing users from accessing specific categories of websites. If you work in a large organization, you might have a forward proxy between your local machine and the internet, filtering protocols and websites, in accordance with your organization's network use policy.

Conversely, reverse proxies focus on inbound traffic coming from the internet to private networks. They are commonly used to secure and filter HTTP requests, providing load balancing across real (backend) servers. To the extent that forward proxies typically represent user traffic to external servers, reverse proxies are commonly used to represent real servers to users (clients).

As illustrated in Figure 5-1, *reverse proxies* represent themselves as the servers. Depending on the type and configuration, to the client there's little to no difference between the reverse proxy server and the service it's making requests of. Reverse proxies forward requests to one or more real servers, which handle the requests. The response from the proxy server is returned as if it came directly from the real server, leaving the client with no knowledge of the real server(s).

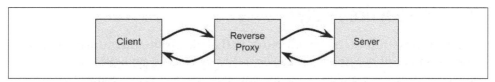

Figure 5-1. Reverse proxies act as intermediates between client and server requests.

This concept isn't that different from how highly resilient three-tiered applications are designed. You want indirection, HA, and load balancing between each of the three tiers. Though these tiers might conventionally be vertically scaled, proxies increase application resiliency since they're inserted in client/server communication to provide additional network services like load balancing, as illustrated in Figure 5-2.

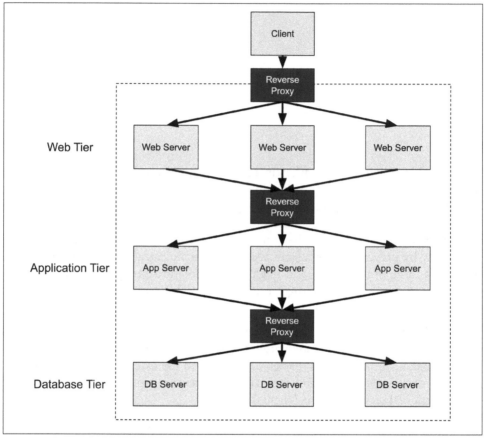

Figure 5-2. Three-tiered application with reverse proxy/load balancer between tiers

Proxies provide a placeholder for a service and control access to it, introducing an additional level of indirection.

What Is a Service Proxy?

Akin to reverse proxies, a *service proxy* is the client-side intermediary transiting requests on behalf of a service. The service proxy enables applications to send and receive messages over a channel as method calls. Service proxy connections can be created as needed or used to maintain open connections to facilitate pooling. Service proxies are transparently inserted, and as applications make service-to-service calls, they're unaware of the data plane's existence. Data planes are responsible for intra-cluster communication as well as inbound (ingress) and outbound (egress) cluster network traffic. Whether traffic is entering the mesh (ingressing) or leaving the mesh (egressing), application service traffic is directed first to the service proxy for handling. In Istio's case, traffic is transparently intercepted using iptables rules and redirected to the service proxy.

An iptables Primer

iptables is a user-space CLI for managing host-based firewalling and packet manipulation in Linux. Netfilter is the Linux kernel module comprising tables, chains, and rules. Commonly, a given iptables environment will contain multiple tables: *Filter*, *NAT*, *Mangle*, and *Raw*. You can define your own tables; if you don't, the *Filter* table is used by default, as shown in Figure 5-3.

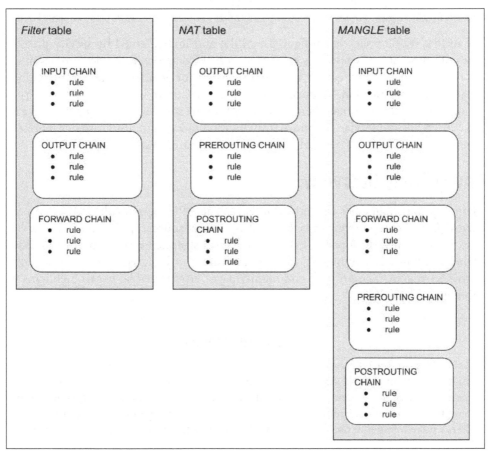

Figure 5-3. iptables tables, chains, and rules

Tables can contain multiple chains. Chains can be built in or user defined, and they can contain multiple rules. Rules match and map packets. You can review the `ipta bles` chains Istio uses (*https://oreil.ly/jA55x*) to redirect traffic to Envoy. `iptables` chains are network namespaced, so changes made within a pod don't affect other pods or the node on which the pod is running.

You can explore and even update the iptables Istio creates. You can see these chains in action and verify the missing `NET_ADMIN` capability of your application and sidecar containers when you `exec` into one of your pod's containers, as shown in Example 5-1.

Example 5-1. Sample output from a container with sidecarred Envoy proxy

```
# iptables -t nat --list
Chain ISTIO_REDIRECT (2 references)
target      prot opt source              destination
REDIRECT    tcp  --  anywhere            anywhere            redir ports 15001
```

Recall that traffic policy is configured by Pilot and implemented by service proxies. The collection of service proxies is referred to as the data plane. Service proxies intercept every packet in the request and are responsible for health checking, routing, load balancing, authentication, authorization, and generation of observable signals. Proxies offer indirection so that clients can point to the same location (e.g., proxy.example.com) while the service can move from location to location; thus, proxies represent a permanent reference. They add resilience to distributed systems.

Envoy Proxy Overview

Living up to its tagline as the universal data-plane API, the versatile and performant Envoy (*https://envoyproxy.io*) has emerged as an open source, application-level service proxy. Envoy was developed at Lyft, where large distributed systems problem needed to be overcome. Envoy has enjoyed broad reuse and integration within the cloud native ecosystem. The project's community page (*https://oreil.ly/-g_eV*) highlights its more prominent uses.

Service Mesh Linguistics

As the lingua franca of the cloud native ecosystem, Go is certainly prevalent, and you might expect that most service mesh projects are written with it. By the nature of their task, data planes must be highly efficient in the interception, introspection, and rewriting of network traffic. Although Go certainly provides high performance, there's no denying that native code (machine code) is the holy grail of performance.

As a data-plane component, Envoy is written in C++ (C++11, specifically) in part to benefit from its performance characteristics. As an emerging language (and something of a C++ competitor), Rust has found use within service meshes. Because of its properties around efficiency (outperforming Go) and memory safety (when written to be so) without garbage collection, Rust has been used for Linkerd2's data-plane component and for nginMesh's Mixer module.

If language use interests you, you might find the service mesh landscape (*https:// oreil.ly/57P0j*) informative. You can also refer to *The Enterprise Path to Service Mesh Architectures* (*https://oreil.ly/2Jw6u*) for more on the subject.

Why Envoy?

Why not use NGINX, a pervasively used and battle-tested proxy? Or Linkerd v1, Conduit, HAProxy, or Traefik? At the time, Envoy was little known and not necessarily the obvious selection. The Linkerd v1 Java Virtual Machine (JVM)–based service proxy, with its resource utilization characteristics, was well suited for node agent deployments but not sidecar deployments (Linkerd v2 has addressed this and moved to a Rust-based service proxy). Envoy was not originally intended as an edge proxy, but was designed to be deployed as a sidecar. Over time, at Lyft, Envoy was migrated to the sidecar pattern.

Deployment model aside, the concept of hot *reloads* versus hot *restarts* was central to the decision that Istio would use Envoy as opposed to NGINX (which was the original proxy under consideration). From its beginning, Envoy's runtime configuration has been API driven, capable of draining and hot reloading its own process with a new process and new configuration (displacing itself). Envoy achieves hot reloading of its processes using shared memory and communication over a Unix Domain Socket (*https://oreil.ly/YpkZ8*) (UDS), an approach that bears similarities to GitHub's tool (*https://oreil.ly/SNdNG*) for zero downtime HAProxy reloads.

Additionally, and uniquely, Envoy offers an Aggregated Discovery Service (ADS) for delivering the data for each xDS API (more on these APIs later).

HTTP/2 and gRPC

Envoy's early support for HTTP/2 and gRPC set it apart from other proxies at the time. HTTP/2 significantly improves on HTTP/1.1 in that HTTP/2 enables request *multiplexing* over a single TCP connection. Proxies that support HTTP/2 enjoy what can be significantly reduced overhead by collapsing what might be many separate connections into one. HTTP/2 allows clients to send multiple parallel requests and load resources preemptively using *server-push*.

Envoy is HTTP/1.1- and HTTP/2-compatible with proxying capability for each protocol on both downstream and upstream. This means that Envoy can accept incoming HTTP/2 connections and proxying to upstream HTTP/2 clusters, but also that Envoy can accept HTTP/1.1 connections and proxy to HTTP/2 (and vice versa).

gRPC is an RPC protocol that uses protocol buffers (protobufs) on top of HTTP/2. Envoy natively supports gRPC (over HTTP/2) and also enables the bridging of an HTTP/1.1 client to gRPC. More than this, Envoy is capable of operating as a gRPC-JSON transcoder. The gRPC-JSON transcoder functionality allows a client to send HTTP/1.1 requests with a JSON payload to Envoy, which translates the request into the corresponding gRPC call and, subsequently, translates the response message back into JSON. These are powerful features (and difficult to get right in an implementation) and that made Envoy stand out from other service proxies.

Envoy in Istio

As an out-of-process proxy, Envoy transparently forms the base unit of the mesh. Akin to proxies in other service meshes, it is the workhorse of Istio, which deploys Envoy sidecarred to application services, as illustrated in Figure 5-4.

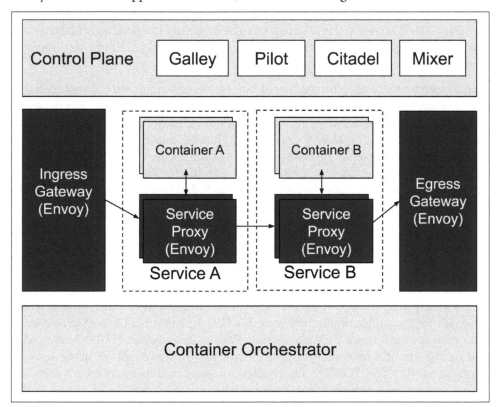

Figure 5-4. Envoy as the Istio service proxy in Istio deployments

Identified as `istio-proxy` in deployment files, Envoy does not require root privileges to run, but runs as user 1337 (nonroot).

Sidecar Injection

Adding a service proxy consists of two things: *sidecar injection* and *network capture*. Sidecar injection—or "sidecarring"—is the method of adding a proxy to a given application. Network capture is the method of directing inbound traffic to the proxy (instead of the application) and outbound traffic to the proxy (instead of directly back to the client or directly to subsequent upstream application services).

Manual Sidecar Injection

You can use `istioctl` as a tool to manually inject the Envoy sidecar definition into Kubernetes manifests. To do so, use `istioctl`'s `kube-inject` capability to manually inject the sidecar into deployment manifests by manipulating the YAML file:

```
$ istioctl kube-inject -f samples/sleep/sleep.yaml | kubectl apply -f -
```

You can update Kubernetes specifications on the fly at the time of applying them to Kubernetes for scheduling. Alternatively, you might use the `istioctl kube-inject` utility, like so:

```
$ kubectl apply -f <(istioctl kube-inject -f <resource.yaml>)
```

If you don't have the source manifests available, you can update an existing Kubernetes deployment to bring its services onto the mesh:

```
$ kubectl get deployment <deployment_name> -o yaml | istioctl kube-inject -f -
    | kubectl apply -f -
```

Let's walk through an example of onboarding an existing application onto the mesh. Let's take a freshly installed copy of Bookinfo, Istio's sample application, as an example of an application already running in Kubernetes but not deployed on the service mesh. We begin by looking at Bookinfo's pods in Example 5-2.

Example 5-2. Bookinfo running off the service mesh

```
$ kubectl get pods
NAME                              READY   STATUS    RESTARTS   AGE
details-v1-69658dcf78-nghss       1/1     Running   0          43m
productpage-v1-6b6798cb84-nzfhd   1/1     Running   0          43m
ratings-v1-6f97d68b6-v6wj6        1/1     Running   0          43m
reviews-v1-7c98dcd6dc-b974c       1/1     Running   0          43m
reviews-v2-6677766d47-2qz2g       1/1     Running   0          43m
reviews-v3-79f9bcc54c-sjndp       1/1     Running   0          43m
```

In Kubernetes, the atomic unit of deployment is an object called a pod. A pod is a collection of containers, so it can be one or more containers deployed atomically together. Looking over Bookinfo's pods in Example 5-2, we see only one container running per pod. When `istioctl kube-inject` is run against Bookinfo's manifests, it adds another container to the Pod specification; however, it does not actually *deploy* anything yet. `istioctl kube-inject` supports modification of Pod-based Kubernetes objects (`Job`, `DaemonSet`, `ReplicaSet`, `Pod`, and `Deployment`) that can be embedded into long YAML files containing other Kubernetes objects. The other Kubernetes objects will be parsed unmodified by `istioctl kube-inject`. Unsupported resources are left unmodified, so it is safe to run `kube-inject` over a single file that contains multiple `Service`, `ConfigMap`, `Deployment`, and so on definitions for a complex application. It is best to do this when the resource is initially created.

You can take the YAML file created by the `kube-inject` command and deploy that directly. To onboard this existing application, we can execute `istioctl kube-inject` against each `Deployment` and have a *rolling update* of that `Deployment` initiated by Kubernetes, as shown in Example 5-3. Let's begin with the `productpage` service.

Example 5-3. Bookinfo's productpage deployment updated to include injection of Istio's sidecar

```
$ kubectl get deployment productpage-v1 -o yaml | istioctl
    kube-inject -f - | kubectl apply -f -
deployment.extensions/productpage-v1 configured
```

Reviewing the Bookinfo pods, we now see that the `productpage` pod has grown to two containers. Istio's sidecar has been successfully injected. The rest of Bookinfo's application services need to be onboarded for Bookinfo as an application to work, as shown in Example 5-4.

Example 5-4. Bookinfo's productpage running on the service mesh

```
$ kubectl get pods
NAME                              READY   STATUS    RESTARTS   AGE
details-v1-69658dcf78-nghss       1/1     Running   0          45m
productpage-v1-64647d4c5f-z95dl   2/2     Running   0          64s
ratings-v1-6f97d68b6-v6wj6        1/1     Running   0          45m
reviews-v1-7c98dcd6dc-b974c       1/1     Running   0          45m
reviews-v2-6677766d47-2qz2g       1/1     Running   0          45m
reviews-v3-79f9bcc54c-sjndp       1/1     Running   0          45m
```

Instead of ad hoc onboarding of a running application, you might prefer to perform this manual injection operation once and save the new manifest file with istio-proxy (Envoy) inserted. You can create a persistent version of the sidecar-injected deployment by outputting the results of `istioctl kube-inject` to a file:

```
$ istioctl kube-inject -f deployment.yaml -o deployment-injected.yaml
```

Or, like so:

```
$ istioctl kube-inject -f deployment.yaml > deployment-injected.yaml
```

As Istio evolves, the default sidecar configuration is subject to change (potentially unannounced or buried in detailed release notes that you might overlook).

istioctl kube-inject is not idempotent

You cannot repeat the istioctl kube-inject operation on the output from a previous kube-inject. The kube-inject operation is not idempotent. For upgrade purposes, if you're using manual injection, we recommend that you keep the original noninjected YAML file so that the data-plane sidecars can be updated.

The --injectConfigFile and --injectConfigMapName parameters can override the sidecar injection template built into istioctl. When used, either of these options override any other default template configuration parameters (e.g., --hub and --tag). You would typically use these options with the file/configmap created with a new Istio release:

```
# Create a persistent version of the deployment with Envoy sidecar
# injected configuration from Kubernetes configmap 'istio-inject'
istioctl kube-inject -f deployment.yaml -o deployment-injected.yaml
    --injectConfigMapName istio-inject
```

Ad Hoc Sidecarring

Sidecar injection is responsible for configuring network capture. You can selectively apply injection and network capture to enable incremental adoption of Istio. Using the Bookinfo sample application as an example, let's take the productpage service as the external-facing service and selectively remove this service (and only this service out of the set of four) from the service mesh. First, let's quickly confirm the presence of its sidecarred service proxy:

```
$ kubectl get pods productpage-8459b4f9cf-tfblj
    -o jsonpath="{.spec.containers[*].image}"
layer5/istio-bookinfo-productpage:v1 docker.io/istio/proxyv2:1.0.5
```

As you can see, productpage container is our application container, whereas the istio/proxy is the service proxy (Envoy) that Istio injected into the pod. To manually onboard and offboard a deployment onto and off of the service mesh, you can manipulate the annotation within its Kubernetes Deployment specification, as shown in Example 5-5.

Example 5-5. Manual removal of a deployment from the mesh

```
$ kubectl patch deployment nginx --type=json --patch='[{"op": "add", "path":
    "/spec/template/metadata/annotations", "value":
    {"sidecar.istio.io/inject": "false"}}]'
deployment.extensions/productpage-v1 patched
```

Open your browser to the `productpage` application; you'll find that it is still served through Istio's ingress gateway but that its pods no longer have sidecars. Hence, the `productpage` app has been removed from the mesh:

```
UNAVAILABLE:upstream connect error or disconnect/reset before headers
```

Automatic Sidecar Injection

Automatic sidecar injection is the magical feeling you get as you go to onramp your services. Automatic sidecar injection means that not only do you not need to change your code, but you don't need to change your Kubernetes manifests either. Depending on your application's configuration, you might or might not need to change any aspect of your application. Automatic sidecar injection in Kubernetes relies on *mutating admission webhooks*. The `istio-sidecar-injector` is added as a mutating webhook configuration resource when Istio is installed on Kubernetes, as demonstrated in Examples 5-6 and 5-7.

Example 5-6. Kubernetes cluster with Istio and Linkerd mutating webhooks registered for each respective service mesh's sidecar injector

```
$ kubectl get mutatingwebhookconfigurations
NAME                                    CREATED AT
istio-sidecar-injector                  2019-04-18T16:35:03Z
linkerd-proxy-injector-webhook-config   2019-04-18T16:48:49Z
```

Example 5-7. The istio-sidecar-injector mutating webhook configuration

```
$ kubectl get mutatingwebhookconfigurations istio-sidecar-injector -o yaml

apiVersion: admissionregistration.k8s.io/v1beta1
kind: MutatingWebhookConfiguration
metadata:
  creationTimestamp: "2019-04-18T16:35:03Z"
  generation: 2
  labels:
    app: sidecarInjectorWebhook
    chart: sidecarInjectorWebhook
    heritage: Tiller
    release: istio
  name: istio-sidecar-injector
  resourceVersion: "192908"
```

```
selfLink: /apis/admissionregistration.k8s.io/v1beta1/
            mutatingwebhookconfigurations/istio-sidecar-injector
uid: eaa85688-61f7-11e9-a968-00505698ee31
webhooks:
- admissionReviewVersions:
  - v1beta1
  clientConfig:
    caBundle: <redacted>
    service:
      name: istio-sidecar-injector
      namespace: istio-system
      path: /inject
  failurePolicy: Fail
  name: sidecar-injector.istio.io
  namespaceSelector:
    matchLabels:
      istio-injection: enabled
  rules:
  - apiGroups:
    - ""
    apiVersions:
    - v1
    operations:
    - CREATE
    resources:
    - pods
    scope: '*'
  sideEffects: Unknown
  timeoutSeconds: 30
```

Having this mutating webhook registered configures Kubernetes to send all pod creation events to the `istio-sidecar-injector` service (in the `istio-system` namespace) if the namespace has the `istio-injection=enabled` label. The injector service then will modify the PodSpec to include *two* additional containers; one for the `init-container` to configure traffic rules, and the other for `istio-proxy` (Envoy) to perform proxying (not many know this). The sidecar injector service adds these two further containers via a template; the template is located in the `istio-sidecar-injector` configmap.

The Kubernetes life cycle allows resources to be customized before they're committed to the etcd store, the "source of truth"; for Kubernetes configuration. When an individual pod is created (either via `kubectl` or a Deployment resource), it goes through this same life cycle, hitting mutating admission webhooks that modify it before it's applied.

Kubernetes labels

Automatic sidecar injection relies on labels to identify which pods to inject Istio's service proxy and initialize as a pod on the data plane. Kubernetes objects such as pods and namespaces may have user-defined labels attached to them. Labels are essentially key/value pairs like you find in other systems that support the concept of tags. The Webhook Admission controller relies on labels to select the namespaces to which they apply. `Istio-injection` is the specific label that Istio uses. You might familiarize yourself with automatic sidecar injection by labeling the `default` namespace with `istio-injection=enabled`:

```
$ kubectl label namespace default istio-injection=enabled
```

Example 5-8 demonstrates confirmation as to which namespaces have the `istio-injection` label.

Example 5-8. Which Kubernetes namespaces carry the istio-injection label?

```
$ kubectl get namespace -L istio-injection
NAME            STATUS    AGE       ISTIO-INJECTION
default         Active    1h        enabled
Docker          Active    1h        enabled
istio-system    Active    1h        disabled
kube-public     Active    1h
kube-system     Active    1h
```

Notice that only the `istio-system` namespace has the `istio-injection` label assigned. With the `istio-injection` label and its value set to disabled, the `istio-system` namespace will not have service proxies automatically injected into their pods upon deployment. This doesn't mean, however, that pods in this namespace can't have service proxies; it just means that service proxies won't be automatically injected.

One caveat: when using the `namespaceSelector`, make sure the namespace(s) you select really have the label you're using. Keep in mind that the built-in namespaces like `default` and `kube-system` don't have labels out of the box. Conversely, the namespace in the metadata section is the actual name of the namespace, not a label:

```
apiVersion: networking.k8s.io/v1
kind: NetworkPolicy
metadata:
  name: test-network-policy
  namespace: default
spec:
  . . .
```

Kubernetes Init Containers

Similar to `cloud-init` for those familiar with VM provisioning, init containers in Kubernetes (*https://oreil.ly/vopoy*) allow you to run temporary containers to perform a task before engaging your primary container(s). Init containers are often used to perform provisioning tasks like bundling assets, performing database migration, or cloning a Git repository into a volume. In Istio's case, init containers are used to set up network filters—iptables—to control the flow of traffic.

Sidecar Resourcing

Istio v1.1 defined default resource limits for its sidecars. Definition of resource limits is essential to being able to autoscale the sidecar. Upon examining the container YAML for a sidecar, you'll notice that the volume is mounted whether you're using mTLS or not, as shown in Example 5-9.

Example 5-9. Sidecar specification found in a Kubernetes pod

```
 . . .
    --controlPlaneAuthPolicy
    MUTUAL_TLS
 . . .
   Mounts:
    /etc/certs/ from istio-certs (ro)
    /etc/istio/proxy from istio-envoy (rw)
 . . .
```

Envoy's Functionality

Like other service proxies, Envoy uses network listeners to ingest traffic. The terms *upstream* and *downstream* describe the direction of a chain of dependent service requests (see Figure 5-5). Which way is which?

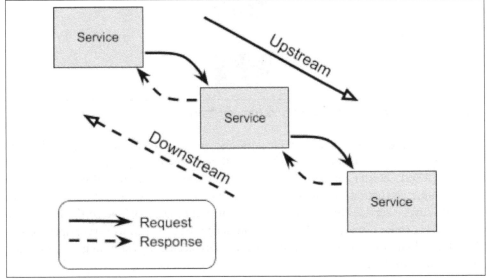

Figure 5-5. Clients are downstream of servers; servers are upstream of clients.

Downstream
> A downstream service initiates requests and receives responses.

Upstream
> An upstream service receives requests and returns responses.

Core Constructs

A *listener* is a named network location (e.g., port, unix domain socket, etc.) that can accept connections from downstream clients. Envoy exposes one or more listeners, which in many cases is an externally exposed port with which external clients can establish a connection. A listener binds to a specific port; physical listeners bind to a port. Virtual listeners are used for forwarding. Listeners can also be optionally configured with a chain of listener filters each of which can be used to manipulate the connection metadata or enable better systems integration without having to incorporate changes in the core.

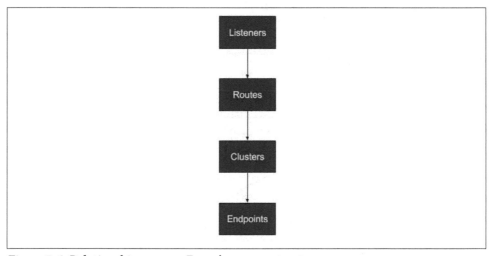

Figure 5-6. Relationships among Envoy's core constructs

You can configure listeners, routes, clusters, and endpoints with static files or dynamically through their respective APIs: listener discovery service (LDS), route discovery service (RDS), cluster discovery service (CDS), and endpoint discovery service (EDS). Static configuration files can be either JSON or YAML formatted. A collective set of discovery services for Envoy's APIs is referred to as xDS. The configuration file specifies `listeners`, `routes`, `clusters`, and `endpoints` as well as server-specific settings like whether to enable the Admin API, where access logs should go, and tracing engine configuration.

It's important to note that Envoy's reference documentation (*https://www.envoyproxy.io/docs*) explicitly distinguishes between v1 and v2 docs.

There are different versions of the Envoy configuration. The initial version (v1) has been deprecated in favor of v2 of the Envoy configuration. Envoy's v1 API and its integration with Istio required that Envoy poll Pilot receive configuration updates. With v2, Envoy holds a long-running gRPC streaming connection to Pilot, where Pilot can push updates as it sees on an open stream. Envoy has had some backward compatibility with the v1 configuration API; however, considering that it will be removed at some point, perhaps it's best to just focus on v2.

Istio Pilot uses Envoy's ADS for dynamic configuration and centralizes route tables, cluster and listener definitions. Pilot can apply the same rules to multiple service proxies, easing the propagation of service proxy configuration updates across your cluster. At runtime, Pilot uses these APIs to push configuration. Pilot efficiently computes one configuration per service. By default, it pushes configuration changes every 10 seconds, but you can configure this setting using `PILOT_DEBOUNCE_MAX`.

They used to be poll based, but Envoy's new APIs are now push based, in order to better scale and, critically, to be able to dictate configuration in a specific order to Envoy. Using gRPC, Envoy establishes a long-lived connection to Pilot. Pilot will push data as it computes changes. Envoy's AggregateADS guarantees order of delivery, allowing you to sequence updates to service proxies. This is a key property of what makes the service mesh resilient.

Certificates and Protecting Traffic

So, what are your default security postures? As a recently configurable option, but still the default setting, Pilot disallows egress traffic to undefined endpoints. Istio's default security posture dictates that, by default, Pilot needs to be informed of which endpoints external to the cluster are acceptable to send traffic to. As soon as Pilot becomes aware of a topology/environment change, it needs to reconfigure each affected service proxy in the data plane.

Depending on the type of configuration change being made Envoy listeners might or might not need to be closed (connections might or might not be dropped). An example of closing connections intentionally in Istio is when a service identity credential (a certificate) is rotated. While this isn't required, Istio will terminate connections on reload of a service's certificate. Envoy's Secret Discovery Service (SDS) provides the mechanism by which you can push secrets (certificates) to each service proxy. Chapter 6 has more details on SDS.

The `pilot-agent` (shown in Examples 5-10 and 5-11) handles restarting Envoy when certificates are rotated (once per hour). Although an existing open connection will reuse an expired certificate, Istio will intentionally close the connection.

Example 5-10. istio-proxy is a multiprocess container with pilot-agent running alongside Envoy

```
$ kubectl exec ratings-v1-7665579b75-2qcsb -c istio-proxy ps
  PID TTY          TIME CMD
    1 ?        00:00:10 pilot-agent
   18 ?        00:00:32 envoy
   70 ?        00:00:00 ps
```

Example 5-11. Verifying that productpage's certificate is valid

```
$ kubectl exec -it $(kubectl get pod | grep productpage | awk '{ print $1 }') -c
    istio-proxy -- cat /etc/certs/cert-chain.pem |
    openssl x509 -text -noout
```

Envoy's connection-handling behavior can be customized in this regard, and you can examine its configuration, as shown in Example 5-12.

Example 5-12. Showing the filename of the Envoy configuration file within the istio-proxy container

```
$ kubectl exec ratings-v1-7665579b75-2qcsb -c istio-proxy ls /etc/istio/proxy
Envoy-rev0.json
```

mTLS connections are established between service proxies, with certificates used to establish mTLS communication. Service mesh deployments with sidecarred service proxies like Istio typically establish pod-local, unencrypted, TCP connections between the application service and sidecar proxy. This means your service (application container) and Envoy use pod-local networking (on the loopback interface) to communicate. Understanding this traffic flow, it follows that the Kubernetes network policy and sidecar-to-app redirection are compatible (underlap). And that application of the Kubernetes network policy between the app and a sidecar is not possible. Only when an application's network traffic exits the pod will it encounter the Kubernetes network policy.

Administration console

Envoy provides an administration view, allowing you to view configuration, stats, logs, and other internal Envoy data. To gain access to a given service proxy's administrative console while running within the data plane of an Istio deployment, follow the instructions in Chapter 11. If you'd like to play around with Envoy's administrative

---

console outside of an Istio service mesh deployment, the simplest way to do so might be to use Docker, as demonstrated in Example 5-13.

Example 5-13. Running Envoy in a Docker container

```
$ docker run --name=proxy -d \
  -p 80:10000 \
  -v $(pwd)/envoy/envoy.yaml:/etc/envoy/envoy.yaml \
  envoyproxy/envoy:latest
```

After opening your browser to http://localhost:15000, you will be presented with a list of endpoints to explore, like the following:

/certs
  Certificates within the Envoy instance

/clusters
  Clusters with which Envoy is configured

/config_dump
  Dumps the actual Envoy configuration

/listeners
  Listeners with which Envoy is configured

/logging
  View and change logging settings

/stats
  Envoy statistics

/stats/prometheus
  Envoy statistics as Prometheus records

On the list of certificates used by `productpage` pod's service proxy, you should see three files (see Example 5-14). One of them should be `productpage`'s private key (`key.pem`).

Example 5-14. Verifying that the key and certificate are correctly mounted in productpage's service proxy

```
$ kubectl exec -it $(kubectl get pod | grep productpage | awk '{ print $1 }') \
    -c istio-proxy -- ls /etc/certs
cert-chain.pem key.pem  root-cert.pem
```

In theory you could use Envoy to create the state of the world; however, Pilot is responsible for configuring Envoy service proxies, the Istio configuration, and service discovery data.

## CHAPTER 6

Security and Identity

Application and system security has for a long time been focused on the network. Historically, we've built hard outer shells (firewalls, VPNs, etc.) to fend off attacks, but once the outer shell is penetrated, an attacker could easily to access many systems. But we've built *defense-in-depth* and applied networking isolation concepts *within* our own trust domain, requiring security administrators to punch holes in the network and set things up *just so*, with these network identities (IP addresses) assigned here with that access there, funneled through these ports here, and so on, just so that our applications could communicate with one another. This approach to security works well when the rate of system change is low, and when change happens over the course of days it's easier to take manual steps or automate the setup and maintenance of networks.

When it comes to container-based systems, however, the rate of change isn't numbered in days, but rather by the second. In highly dynamic environments, traditional network security models break down. The key problem is that traditional network security puts the emphasis on the only identity available to the network: an IP address. An IP address is not a strong indication of the application, and because dynamic environments like Kubernetes can freely reuse IP addresses for different workloads over time, they're not sufficient to use for policy or security.

To address this problem, one of Istio's key features is the ability to issue an identity to every workload in the service mesh. These identities are tied to the workload, not to some particular host (or some particular network identity). This means that you can write policy about service-to-service communication that's robust to changes in deployment and the topology of the system, not bound to the network.

In this chapter, we'll explore the concepts of *identity*, *authorization*, and *authentication* as they relate to service-to-service communication. We also dig into how Istio provides identity to workloads, performs authentication of those identities at runtime, and uses them to authorize service-to-service communication. Let's start with access control.

Access Control

The fundamental question that access control systems answer is: *"can* entity *perform* action *on* object?"* We call this *entity* the "principal." *Action* is some operation the system defines. The *object* is the thing being acted upon by the principal. Using the Unix filesystem as an example, the *actions* "read," "write," or "execute" can be taken on the file *object* by the user principal.

Authentication

Authentication is all about the principal. Authentication is the process of taking some credential (e.g., a certificate), verifying that the credential is valid (i.e., that the credential is authentic), and ensuring that the *entity* in the access control question contains the identity that in fact is representative of the entity. Authorization is all about what *actions* the *entity* can and cannot perform on an *object*.

Authentication (abbreviated *authn* and pronounced "auth-in") is the act of taking a credential from a request and ensuring that it's authentic. In Istio's case, the credential that services use when they communicate with one another is an *X.509 certificate*. Service proxies authenticate the identity of the calling service (and the client mutually authenticates the server) by validating the X.509 certificate provided by the other party using the normal certificate validation process. If the certificate is valid, the identity encoded within the certificate is considered authenticated. Once we've performed authentication, we say that the principal is *authenticated*, calling it an *authenticated principal* to differentiate it from a *principal*, which might or might not be authenticated.

Authorization

Authorization (abbreviated *authz* and pronounced "auth-zee") is the act of answering the question *"is* entity *allowed to perform* action *on* object?"* For example, to run a shell script on Unix, the system checks that the current user (an *authenticated principal*) has the execute permission on the script file. In Istio, authorization of service-to-service communication is configured with RBAC policies, which we cover in detail later in the chapter.

> We also use the abbreviation "auth" to refer to both authn and authz.

When we think about the access control question, "*can* entity *perform* action *on* object?*", it becomes clear that both authentication *and* authorization are required, and one without the other is useless. If we only authenticate credentials, any user can perform any action on any object. All we've done is assert that this user is in fact who they present themselves to be while they do it! Similarly, if we only authorize requests, any user can pretend to be any other user and perform actions on that user's objects; all we've done is make sure *someone* has permission to perform the action in question, not necessarily the caller. One final thing to note is that the question Istio auth answers is a little more specific than "*can* entity *perform* action *on* object?*" More specifically, Istio answers the question: "Can *Service A* perform *action* on *Service B*?" In other words, both *entity* and *object* are identities of services in the mesh.

With the concepts of authentication and authorization in hand, natural next questions are: What are the identities and who are the principals that Istio gives to services? How does the service mesh manage these identities at runtime? How do you write policy about the actions one service can perform on another and how does Istio enforce those policies at runtime? The remainder of this chapter steps through answers to each of these questions.

Identity

Understanding that service meshes span clusters—that services on and off of a service mesh are able to communicate with one another—where does the service mesh begin and end? What would you say is the boundary of a service mesh? Typically, the answers revolve around the concept of *administrative domain*, with the administrative domain being either all things that are configured by one service operator or all things that can communicate with one another as part of the same mesh. Both are popular answers. In our opinion, these types of answers fall short. For example, multiple teams can administer different segments of a mesh and different parts of a mesh might not in fact be allowed to communicate. Instead, we believe the best answer is "a service mesh is a single identity domain." In other words, a single namespace from which every service in the system is allocated an identity.

Identity forms the boundary of a service mesh. Identity is a fundamental function of a service mesh in that all communication stems from identity. Traffic steering and telemetry functions of the service mesh rely on an understanding of how to identify services. Without knowing what you're metering, metrics are useless data.

SPIFFE

Istio implements the *Secure Production Identity Framework for Everyone* (SPIFFE) specification to issue identities. In short, Istio creates an X.509 certificate, which sets the certificate's subject alternative name (SAN) to a uniform resource identifier (URI) that describes the service. Istio defers to the platform for identity attributes. In a

Kubernetes deployment, Istio uses a pod's service account as its identity, encoding it into a URI: `spiffe://ClusterName/ns/Namespace/sa/ServiceAccountName`.

 In Kubernetes, a pod will use the "default" service account for the namespace it's deployed in if the `ServiceAccount` field is not set in the pod specification. This means that all services in the same namespace will share a single identity if service accounts aren't already set up for each service.

SPIFFE is a specification for a framework that can bootstrap and issue identities. SPIRE (the SPIFFE Runtime Environement) is the SPIFFE community's reference implementation, and Citadel (formerly Istio Auth) is a second implementation. The SPIFFE specification describes three concepts:

- An Identity, as a URI, used by services to communicate
- A standard encoding of that Identity into a SPIFFE Verifiable Identity Document (SVID)
- An API for issuing and retrieving SVIDs (the Workload API)

SPIFFE requires that a service's identity be encoded as a URI with the scheme `spiffe`, like: `spiffe://trust-domain/path`. The trust domain is the root of trust of the identity (e.g., an organization, an environment, or a team). The trust domain is the URI's authority field (specifically the host section of the authority). The specification allows the path section of the URI to be anything—a universally unique identifier (UUID), a trust hierarchy, or nothing. On Kubernetes, Istio encodes a service's `ServiceAccount` using the local cluster's name as the trust domain, and creates a path using the `ServiceAccount` name and namespace. For example, the default `ServiceAccount` is encoded as `spiffe://cluster.local/ns/default/sa/default` ("ns" for namespace, "sa" for service account).

SPIFFE also describes how to encode this identity into an X.509 SVID. An X.509 certificate can be verified to prove identity. The specification stipulates that the Identity URI be encoded as the certificate's SAN field. There are three verifications to perform when validating an SVID:

1. Perform normal X.509 validation.
2. Confirm that the certificate is *not* a signing certificate. Signing certificates cannot be used for identification according to the specification.
3. Verify that there is exactly one SAN in the certificate with the SPIFFE scheme.

SPIFFE defines a Workload API, which is an API for issuing and retrieving SVIDs; however, this is where Istio diverges from SPIFFE. Istio implements certificate provisioning using a custom protocol, the *CA Service*, instead. The Citadel Node Agent issues a CSR via that API when a new workload is scheduled; Citadel performs validation on the request and returns an SVID for the workload. Both the SPIFFE Workload API and the CA service accomplish a similar goal (prove some information about the workload to receive an identity for it).

Finally, while the SPIFFE specification does not require it, both SPIRE and Istio issue X.509 SVIDs that are short lived—they expire on the order of an hour after issuance. This is in contrast with traditional usage of X.509 certificates, which tend to be used for HTTPS TLS termination and commonly expire a year or more after issuance.

The benefit of short-lived certificates is that attacks are bounded within that expiry time without requiring certificate revocation (and making revocation easy if you do choose to use it). Suppose that an attacker compromises a workload and steals the workload's SVID; it's only valid across the rest of the trust domain for a short time. If their attack requires an extended period to execute, they must continually extract a valid credential from the workload. As soon as you become aware of the attack, you can use policy to prohibit that identity from accessing other services, stop reissuing certificates for that identity, and even put that certificate into a revocation list. Because the certificates are ephemeral, managing that revocation list is easy—it's a standard practice to remove expired certificates from a certificate revocation list. The list stays small as the certificates expire quickly.

This use of short-lived certificates comes with one big disadvantage, though: it's difficult to issue and rotate certificates on every workload across the fleet on a short interval. We talk about how Istio solves this problem in the next section.

Key Management Architecture

Three components—Citadel, node agents, and Envoy—are the key management architecture, all participating in issuing and rotating SVIDs across an Istio deployment (see also Figure 6-1):

Citadel
> Citadel issues identities to workloads across the deployment by acting as a CA, signing certificate requests that form X.509 SVIDs.

Node agent
> A trusted agent deployed on each node, this agent acts as a broker between Citadel and the Envoy sidecars deployed on the node.

Envoy (service proxy)
> Envoy speaks to the node agent locally to retrieve an identity and presents that identity to other parties at runtime.

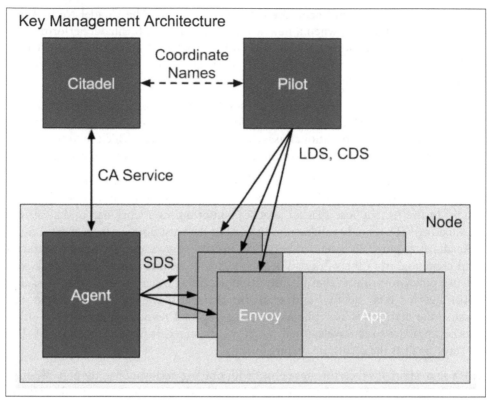

Figure 6-1. Istio's key management architecture and component interactions (see Chapter 5 for more on Envoy xDS APIs)

Citadel

Citadel is responsible for accepting requests for identity, authenticating them, authorizing them, and ultimately issuing a certificate for the identity in question. Citadel itself is composed of several logical components, as shown in Figure 6-2.

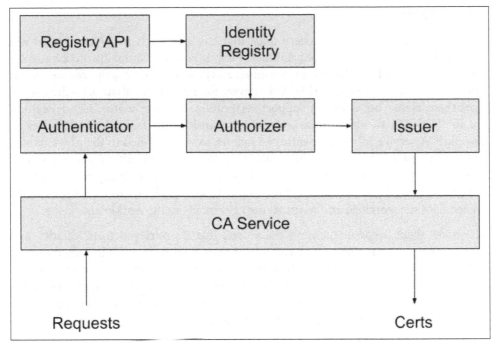

Figure 6-2. Citadel's architecture and internal component interactions

Walking through the CA service certificate provisioning flow from bottom to top, left to right in Figure 6-2, we see the following:

1. Citadel exposes the CA service as its public API to identity requesters. To request an identity, a caller interfaces with the CA service, ultimately sending a CSR to Citadel, which Citadel signs, transforming the CSR into a certificate (an X.509 SVID).

2. When the request is received, it's then fed to an *authenticator*, which verifies the request. The authentication method depends on how Citadel is deployed. For example, in Kubernetes, Pilot is trusted to provide each workload with its service name.

3. After the request is authenticated and the *authorizer* determines whether the requested identity is valid for the authenticated principal to receive. The authorizer consults an Identity Registry, which maps workloads via their authenticated principal to identities to perform authorization.

4. Once a workload is authorized to receive an identity, we need to actually issue it by signing a certificate. The authorizer calls the *issuer* to generate a certificate and make it available to the requestor. Issuers in Citadel today include an in-memory CA as well as HashiCorp Vault.

Node Agents

Node agents are deployed on every node that has workloads to which Citadel will issue identities. It has two responsibilities: First, it acts as a simple protocol adapter between Envoy and Citadel. Envoy consumes a SDS API, which configures the secrets Envoy will serve at runtime. This API is great for issuing key material—the certificates themselves—but does not support verification. In other words, Citadel cannot use the SDS API to authenticate ownership of an identity. Instead, Citadel uses its bespoke CA service API to authenticate requests, as we described in the previous section. Node agents bridge the SDS and CA service on behalf of the workloads deployed on the nodes. This brings us to the second key responsibility of node agents: to be trusted agents on the nodes, able to validate workload environments for Citadel on behalf of the workload and to distribute keys locally to the workloads.

The node agent keeps in memory the secrets that it's retrieved from Citadel, and when they near expiration (e.g., have 25% of their time-to-live [TTL] left) the agent will contact Citadel and attempt to refresh the certificate. We leave a little wiggle room in case Citadel is temporarily inaccessible. When the node agent dies and is restarted by the container orchestrator, it will attempt to retrieve fresh credentials for all workloads on the node. In this way, the node agent remains stateless. Upon receiving a fresh SVID from Citadel, the node agent pushes the certificate to Envoy via SDS. As described in Chapter 5, this triggers Envoy to establish new connections to destination workloads. Envoy will drain the current connections into the new connections and terminate the connections that were using the old (and now potentially expired) certificates.[1]

Relying on the node agent in this way is justified in Istio's security model since the agent is already handling all secrets on the node to begin with; it *must* operate at a higher level of trust than other components on the node for exactly that reason. Therefore, extending that trust to additionally force the agent to validate the execution environment is reasonable. Even if we had Envoy communicate directly with Citadel, we could not trust environmental answers that Envoy provides because it runs in the same trust domain as the application itself (so an attacker compromising the application could just as easily confuse Envoy into giving different or wrong answers to environmental attestation challenges).

Finally, the architectural decision to have workloads communicate with the local node agent and have that node agent communicate with Citadel is important for keeping Citadel scalable. This design binds the number of connections to Citadel

---

1 We don't need to reestablish connections using the new credentials immediately—after all, the TLS session remains valid so long as it was *initiated* before the certificate expires. An established connection will happily continue to use an expired certificate. We choose to reestablish connections to mitigate certain types of credential hijacking attacks. Plus, a little jitter tends to be good for a system!

instances in the system with the number of nodes in the deployment (generally, a smaller number), not with the number of workloads (generally, a larger number). Often in environments like Kubernetes, there is a substantially larger number of workloads than nodes, so this design provides real benefits.

Envoy

The final participant in this whole dance is the service proxy, Envoy. Envoy is configured to communicate with the local node agent as its source for the SDS API. The location of the SDS server can be served to Envoy by Pilot dynamically; however, Istio deployments typically configure this information statically because doing so is less error prone at runtime. Envoy can communicate with the SDS server (the node agent) by resolving some address to the local node or, more commonly, by communicating locally over UDSs.

 Envoy won't overwrite static configuration with configuration from the API, so you can't accidentally push a configuration to Envoy that makes it unable to communicate with the configuration server.

Envoy uses the SVID certificate when it initiates connections to other services in the mesh. Two workloads in the mesh will optionally perform *mTLS* when they communicate. Doing so assures both the client and server of the identity of the other party, allows both to perform authentication and authorization of the communication being initiated, and provides for encryption in transit. mTLS alone isn't enough, though, because we still need something to perform authorization of communication between two identities. We cover both mTLS and authorization of communication later in the chapter.

Pilot

Pilot also plays a minor role in key management. When Pilot pushes configuration to Envoy, including configuration about destination services and how to receive traffic, it needs to reference certificates. It references these certificates by name; therefore, it must coordinate with SDS, which is provided by the node agent. It would not be desirable to force the node agents to communicate with Pilot in addition to Citadel. Instead, Istio components plan on a common naming scheme for secrets ahead of time so that Pilot can unambiguously refer to secrets provisioned by SDS. Further, the primary certificate on all Envoys, the identity SVID, resides at a well-known location (in */etc/certs/*, as described in Chapter 5).

mTLS

With all of the identity certificates (SVIDs) distributed to workloads across the system, how do we actually use them to verify the identity of the servers with which we're communicating and perform authentication and authorization? This is where mTLS comes into play. First, though, a bit of background.

When we think of TLS or SSL (TLS is the new version of SSL), the use case that typically comes to mind is HTTPS. A user wants to use their browser to connect to some web server (e.g., http://wikipedia.org). Their browser (or the OD) will perform a DNS lookup to determine the site's IP address. The browser fires off an HTTPS request to that address and waits for a response from the server (site). When the browser (client) attempts to connect to the server, the server responds by presenting a certificate with the identity (e.g., wikipedia.org) signed by some root of trust that the client trusts. The client validates the certificate, authenticating the identity of the server and allowing the connection to be established. Then, a set of keys are generated for the connection to enable encryption of the data sent by both the client and the server. In other words, TLS is how the client knows it can trust the server, that the server really is controlled by wikipedia.org, and that no one is eavesdropping or otherwise tampering with the data sent by the server.

mTLS is TLS in which both parties, client and server, present certificates to each other. This allows the client to verify the identity of the server, like normal TLS, but it also allows the server to verify the identity of the client attempting to establish the connection. We use mTLS in Istio, where both parties present their SVID to each other. This allows both parties to authenticate the SVID provided by the other and to perform authorization on the connection. In practice, in Istio we perform authorization only on the server side. This makes sense given how you write authorization policy, which we cover in the next section.

Configuring Istio Auth Policies

Istio splits authentication and authorization policy into two sets of configurations. The first, authentication policy, controls how proxies in the mesh communicate with one another (whether or not they require an SVID). The second, authorization policy, requires authentication policy first and configures which identities are allowed to communicate.

Authentication Policy: Configuring mTLS

Adopting mTLS into an existing deployment is challenging because you need to make sure both client and server are provisioned with certificates at the same time (traditional TLS is far simpler given that it requires coordinating only the server deployment). As a result, Istio provides a few knobs to take a deployment not using mTLS and gradually enable it without causing outages for clients.

Authentication policy (`authentication.istio.io/v1alpha1.Policy`) is the primary CRD we use to configure how services in the mesh communicate with one another. Authentication policy allows us to require, make optional, or disable mTLS on a service-by-service, namespace-by-namespace basis. A cluster-scoped variant, Mesh-Policy, applies a default policy to every namespace and service in the mesh.

To enable mTLS for a single service, we create a policy in that service's namespace with that service as the target, requiring mTLS like so:

```
apiVersion: authentication.istio.io/v1alpha1
kind: Policy
metadata:
  name: foo-require-mtls
  namespace: default
spec:
  targets:
  - name: foo.default.svc.cluster.local
  peers:
  - mtls:
      mode: STRICT
```

This policy applies to the `default` namespace and marks TLS as required for talking to service `foo`. Note that because the default mTLS configuration is in STRICT mode, we can simplify this configuration a bit by omitting the redundant fields:

```
apiVersion: authentication.istio.io/v1alpha1
kind: Policy
metadata:
  name: foo-require-mtls
  namespace: default
spec:
  targets:
  - name: foo.default.svc.cluster.local
  peers:
  - mtls: {}
```

Many policy examples on istio.io take this form, omitting the mTLS object because the default behavior is to require STRICT mode.

Of course, just creating this configuration in a cluster could cause outages if the clients don't already have certificates with which to perform mTLS. That's why Istio includes a PERMISSIVE mTLS mode, which allows clients to connect in *either* clear text *or* via mTLS. The following configuration allows clients to contact service `bar` using both mTLS and clear text:

```
apiVersion: authentication.istio.io/v1alpha1
kind: Policy
metadata:
```

```
    name: bar-optional-mtls
    namespace: default
spec:
  targets:
  - name: bar.default.svc.cluster.local
  peers:
  - mtls:
      mode: PERMISSIVE
```

Similarly, we could make mTLS optional across an entire namespace by omitting the `targets` field:

```
apiVersion: authentication.istio.io/v1alpha1
kind: Policy
metadata:
  name: default-namespace-optional-mtls
  namespace: default
spec:
  peers:
  - mtls:
      mode: PERMISSIVE
```

This configuration allows workloads in the mesh to contact any service in the default namespace using either mTLS or clear text. We can also enable or disable mTLS per port on a service. An example of where per-port policy is valuable is the health checks performed by kubelet in Kubernetes deployments. It can be burdensome to provision separate certificates for mTLS connections with kubelets. By writing two `policy` objects, we can exclude the health check port from mTLS while requiring mTLS for all other ports, making integration with existing systems easier, like so:

```
apiVersion: authentication.istio.io/v1alpha1
kind: Policy
metadata:
  name: bar-require-mtls-no-port-81
  namespace: default
spec:
  targets:
  - name: bar.default.svc.cluster.local
  peers:
  - mtls:
      mode: STRICT
---
apiVersion: authentication.istio.io/v1alpha1
kind: Policy
metadata:
  name: bar-require-mtls-no-port-81
  namespace: default
spec:
  targets:
  - name: bar.default.svc.cluster.local
    port:
      name: http-healthcheck
```

```
peers:
- mtls:
    mode: PERMISSIVE
```

Using this same approach, operators can exclude mTLS as a requirement for connections to the http-healthcheck port across the namespace by omitting listing any specific service names in the target field.

To apply the same configuration across all namespaces, we use the `MeshPolicy` resource. This is identical to the `policy` resource in schema but exists at the cluster level. Also, note that the default `MeshPolicy` *must* be named "default" or Istio will not recognize it correctly.

```
apiVersion: authentication.istio.io/v1alpha1
kind: MeshPolicy
metadata:
  name: mesh-wide-optional-mtls
spec:
  peers:
  - mtls:
      mode: PERMISSIVE
```

And, of course, we can make mTLS required across the mesh by setting `mode:` `STRICT` or by omitting the mTLS object entirely:

```
apiVersion: authentication.istio.io/v1alpha1
kind: MeshPolicy
metadata:
  name: mesh-wide-mtls
spec:
  peers:
  - mtls: {}
```

Istio also supports performing end-user authentication via JSON Web Tokens (JWTs). Istio's authentication policy supports setting a rich set of restrictions about the data in the JWT, allowing you to validate nearly all of the fields of the JWT. The following `policy` configures Envoy to require mTLS, but it also requires end-user credentials stored as a JWT in the "x-goog-iap-jwt-assertion" header, issued by Google ("*https://securetoken.google.com*"), verified against Google's public keys ("*https://www.googleapis.com/oauth2/v1/certs*"), for the audience "bar":

```
apiVersion: authentication.istio.io/v1alpha1
kind: Policy
metadata:
  name: end-user-auth
  namespace: default
spec:
  target:
  - name: bar
  peers:
  - mtls: {}
```

```
  origins:
  - jwt:
      issuer: "https://securetoken.google.com"
      audiences:
      - "bar"
      jwksUri: "https://www.googleapis.com/oauth2/v1/certs"
      jwt_headers:
      - "x-goog-iap-jwt-assertion"
  principalBinding: USE_ORIGIN
```

Authorization Policy: Configuring Who Can Talk to Whom

With authentication policy in place, we want to use the identities across the system to control which services can communicate. In other words, we want to describe a service-to-service communication policy. Istio's authorization policy is described using an RBAC system. Like most RBAC systems, it defines two objects that are used together to write policy:

ServiceRole
> Describes a set of actions that can be performed on a set of services by any principal with the role.

ServiceRoleBinding
> Assigns roles to a set of principals. In this context, the principals are the service identities Istio issues. Recall that in Kubernetes deployments, these identities are Kubernetes `ServiceAccounts`.

First, we need to create a `ClusterRBACConfig` (formerly `RBACConfig` prior to v1.1) object, which turns on RBAC in Istio:

```
apiVersion: "rbac.istio.io/v1alpha1"
kind: RBACConfig
metadata:
  name: default
  namespace: istio-system
spec:
  mode: ON
```

This configuration enables RBAC of service-to-service communication across the entire mesh. Like enabling mTLS, this is potentially dangerous to do in a live system, so Istio supports enabling RBAC for service-to-service communication incrementally by changing the `RBACConfig`'s mode. Istio supports four modes:

OFF
> No RBAC required for communication. If no `ClusterRBACConfig` object exists, this is the default behavior of the system.

ON

> RBAC policies are required for communication, and communication not allowed by a policy is forbidden.

ON_WITH_INCLUSION

> RBAC policies are required for communicating with any service in the set of namespaces listed in the policy.

ON_WITH_EXCLUSION

> RBAC policies are required for communicating with any service in the mesh, *except* for services in the set of namespaces listed in the policy.

To roll out RBAC incrementally across the system, first enable RBAC in ON_WITH_INCLUSION mode. As you define policies for each service or namespace, add that service or namespace to the inclusion list. This allows you to enable RBAC service by service (or namespace by namespace), as shown in Example 6-1.

Example 6-1. Stepwise rollout of RBAC policy

```
apiVersion: "rbac.istio.io/v1alpha1"
kind: ClusterRBACConfig
metadata:
  name: default
  namespace: istio-system
spec:
  mode: ON_WITH_INCLUSION
  inclusion:
    services:
    - bar.bar.svc.cluster.local
    namespaces:
    - default
```

The policy in Example 6-1 does not require RBAC policies to communicate with any service in the default namespace other than with the bar service. At some point, more namespaces and services in our system will have RBAC policies than those without; at that point we can swap to an ON_WITH_EXCLUSION policy.

With RBAC enabled for the bar service, we need to write policies. We begin by picking a namespace or service and describing the roles that exist for that service. For our example, we create a ServiceRole that allows read access (HTTP GET requests) to the bar service:

```
apiVersion: "rbac.istio.io/v1alpha1"
kind: ServiceRole
metadata:
  name: bar-viewer
  namespace: default
spec:
```

```
    rules:
    - services:
      - bar.default.cluster.local
      methods:
      - GET
```

We then can use a `ServiceRoleBinding` to assign that role to the service account that the bar service uses, allowing it to call the foo service:

```
apiVersion: "rbac.istio.io/v1alpha1"
kind: ServiceRoleBinding
metadata:
  name: bar-bar-viewer-binding
  namespace: default
spec:
  subjects:
  - properties:
      # the SPIFFE ID of the bar service account in the bar namespace
      source.principal: "cluster.local/ns/bar/sa/bar"
  roleRef:
    kind: ServiceRole
    name: "bar-viewer"
```

Unlike RBAC in applications, permitting or denying users a specific operation, Istio's RBAC is service-to-service focused, specifying which services can connect and communicate with one another. To achieve this, include a key management system, Citadel, to provide an identity for each service in the mesh and allow it to authenticate itself.

Identity forms the boundary of our mesh. With Istio's service proxies carrying individual identities and handling all traffic to and from services, you can use mutual trusted certificates to secure connections and authorize these connections. Istio facilitates incremental adoption of service-to-service mTLS and RBAC.

## CHAPTER 7

Pilot

Pilot is responsible for programming the data plane, ingress and egress gateways, and service proxies in an Istio deployment. Pilot models the environment of a deployment by combining the Istio configuration from Galley and service information from a service registry such as the Kubernetes API server or Consul. Pilot uses this model to generate a configuration for the data plane and pushes that new configuration to the fleet of service proxies connected to it.

Configuring Pilot

To better understand all aspects of the mesh that concern Pilot, let's explore the surface area of Pilot's configuration. As we digest this, understand that Pilot's dependency on Galley for underlying platform and environment information will continue to increase as the Istio project advances in releases. Pilot has three main sources of configuration:

Mesh configuration
    A set of configurations global to the service mesh

Networking configuration
    Th configuration for `ServiceEntries`, `DestinationRules`, `VirtualServices` `VirtualServices`, `Gateways`, and service proxies

Service discovery
    The location and metadata information from registries about the catalog of services resident in one or more underlying platforms

Mesh Configuration

Mesh configuration is a set of global configurations that is static for the installation of the mesh. Mesh configuration is split over three API objects:

MeshConfig (mesh.istio.io/v1alpha1.MeshConfig)
> MeshConfig covers configuring how Istio components communicate with one another, where configuration sources are located, and so on.

ProxyConfig (mesh.istio.io/v1alpha1.ProxyConfig)
> ProxyConfig covers options that are associated with initializing Envoy by tracking where its bootstrap configuration is located, which ports to bind to, and so on.

MeshNetworks (mesh.istio.io/v1alpha1.MeshNetworks)
> MeshNetworks describes a set of networks that the mesh is deployed across with the addresses of the ingress gateways of each network.

MeshConfig is primarily used to configure whether policy and/or telemetry are enabled, where to load configuration, and locality-based load-balancing settings. Mesh Config contains the following exhaustive set of concerns:

- How to use Mixer:
  - The addresses of the policy and telemetry servers
  - Whether policy checks are enabled at runtime
  - Whether to fail open or closed when Mixer Policy is inaccessible or returns an error
  - Whether to perform policy checks on the client side
  - Whether to use session affinity to target the same Mixer Telemetry instance. Session affinity is always enabled for Mixer Policy (performance of the system depends on it!).
- How to configure service proxies for listening:
  - The ports to which to bind to accept traffic (i.e., the port iptables redirects to) and to accept HTTP PROXY requests
  - TCP connection timeout and keepalive settings
  - Access log format, output file, and encoding (JSON or text)
  - Whether to allow all outbound traffic, or restrict outbound traffic to only services that Pilot knows about
  - Where to listen for secrets from Citadel (the SDS API), and how to bootstrap trust (in environments with local machine tokens)

- Whether to support Kubernetes Ingress resources
- The set of configuration sources for all Istio components (e.g., the local filesystem, or Galley) and how to communicate with them (the address, whether to use (Transport Layer Security [TLS], which secrets, etc.)
- Locality-based load-balancing settings—configuration about failover and traffic splits between zones and regions (more on that in Chapter 8)

ProxyConfig is primarily used to provide a custom bootstrap configuration for Envoy. ProxyConfig contains the following exhaustive set of concerns:

- The location of the file with Envoy's bootstrap configuration as well as the location of the Envoy binary itself
- Envoy's service cluster, meaning the name of the service for which this Envoy is sidecar
- Shutdown settings (both connection draining and hot restart)
- The location of Envoy's xDS server (Pilot) and how to communicate with it
- Connection timeout settings
- Which ports should host the proxy's admin server and statsd listener
- Envoy's concurrency (number of worker threads)
- How Envoy binds the socket to intercept traffic (either via iptables REDIRECT or TPROXY)
- The location of the trace collector (i.e., where to send trace data)

MeshNetworks defines a set of named networks, the way to send traffic into that network (its ingress), and that network's locality. Each network is either a Classless Inter-Domain Routing (CIDR) range or a set of endpoints returned by a service registry (e.g., the Kubernetes API server). ServiceEntry, the API object used to define services in Istio, has a set of endpoints. Each endpoint can be labeled with a network so that a ServiceEntry can describe a service deployed across several networks (or clusters). We discuss this momentarily in "Service Discovery" on page 108.

Most values in MeshConfig cannot be updated dynamically, and you must restart the control plane for them to take effect. Similarly, updates to values in ProxyConfig only take effect when you redeploy Envoy (e.g., in Kubernetes, when the pod is rescheduled). MeshNetworks can be updated dynamically at runtime without restarting any control-plane components.

On Kubernetes, most of the configuration in MeshConfig and ProxyConfig is hidden behind options in the Helm installation, although not all of it is exposed via Helm. To fully control the installation, you'll need to postprocess the file output by Helm.

Networking Configuration

Networking configuration is Istio's bread and butter—it's the configuration used to manage how traffic flows through the mesh. We cover each object of the API in depth in Chapter 8 and discuss how these constructs are used together to affect how traffic flows through the mesh. Here we introduce each object but only at a high level so that you can relate Istio's configuration to Envoy's xDS APIs (discussed in Chapter 5) to help you understand Pilot's configuration server and to enable you to debug the system (we talk about both in subsequent sections).

`ServiceEntry` is the centerpiece of Istio's networking APIs. `ServiceEntry` defines a service by its names—the set of hostnames that clients use to call the service. We cover this in more detail in the next section. `DestinationRules` configure how clients communicate with a service: what load-balancing, outlier-detection, circuit-breaking, and connection-pooling strategies to use; which TLS settings to use; and so on. `Vir tualServices` configure how traffic flows to a service: L7 and L4 routing, traffic shaping, retries, timeouts, and so forth. Gateways configure how services are exposed outside of the mesh: what hostnames are routed to which services, how to serve certificates for those hostnames, and more. Service proxies configure how services are exposed inside of the mesh: which services are available to which clients.

Service Discovery

Pilot integrates with various service discovery systems, like the Kubernetes API server, Consul, and Eureka, to discover service and endpoint information about the local environment. Adapters in Pilot work by ingesting service discovery information from their source and synthesizing `ServiceEntry` objects from that data. For example, the integration with Kubernetes uses the Kubernetes SDK to watch the API server for service creation and service endpoint update events. Using this data, Pilot's registry adapter synthesizes a `ServiceEntry` object. That `ServiceEntry` is used to update Pilot's internal model and generate updated configuration for the data plane.

Historically, Pilot registry adapters were implemented in-process in Pilot using Golang. With the introduction of Galley, you now can separate these adapters from Pilot. A service discovery adapter can run as a separate job (or an offline process executed by a CI system, for example) that reads an existing service registry and produces a set of `ServiceEntry` objects from it. You then can feed those `ServiceEntrys` to Galley by providing them as files, pushing them into the Kubernetes API server, or you can implement a *Mesh Config Protocol* server yourself and feed the `ServiceEn trys` to Galley. The *Mesh Config Protocol* and configuration ingestion in general is covered in Chapter 11. For largely static environments (e.g., legacy VM-based deployments with rarely changing IP addresses), generating static `ServiceEntrys` can be an effective way to enable Istio.

ServiceEntrys create a *Service* by tying a set of hostnames together with a set of end-points. Those endpoints can be IP addresses or DNS names. Each endpoint can be individually labeled and tagged with a network, locality, and weight. This allows `Serv iceEntrys` to describe complex network topologies. For example, a service deployed across separate clusters (with different networks) that are geographically disparate (have different localities) can be created and have traffic split among its members by percentage (weights)—or in fact by nearly any feature of the request (see Chapter 8). Because Istio knows the ingress points of remote networks, when selecting a service endpoint in a remote network the service proxy will forward traffic to the remote net-work's ingress. We can even write policies to prefer local endpoints over endpoints in other localities, but automatically failover to other localities if local endpoints are unhealthy. We talk about *locality-based load balancing* a bit more in Chapter 13.

Configuration Serving

From these three configuration sources—mesh configuration, networking configura-tion, and service discovery—Pilot creates a model of the environment and state of a deployment. Asynchronously, as service proxy instances are deployed into the cluster, they connect to Pilot. Pilot groups the service proxies together based on their labels and the service to which the service proxy is sidecarred. Using this model, Pilot gen-erates *Discovery Service* (xDS) responses for each group of connected service proxies (more on the Discovery Service APIs shortly). When a service proxy connects, Pilot sends the current state of the environment and configuration reflecting the environ-ment. Given the generally, dynamic nature of the underlying platform(s), the model is updated with some frequency. Updates to the model require an update of the current set of xDS configurations. When the xDS configuration is changed, Pilot computes the groups of affected service proxies and pushes the updated configuration to them.

Chapter 5 examines the xDS APIs, but let's take a moment to recap and introduce the concepts at a high level so that we can describe how Istio networking configuration manifests as xDS. We can divide service proxy (Envoy) configuration into two main groups:

- Listeners and routes
- Clusters and endpoints

Listeners configure a set of filters (e.g., Envoy's HTTP functionality is delivered by an HTTP filter) and how Envoy attaches those filters to a port. They have two flavors: *physical* and *virtual*. A physical listener is one where Envoy binds to the specified port. A virtual listener accepts traffic from a physical listener, but does not bind to a port (instead some physical listener must direct traffic to it). Routes go alongside lis-teners and configure how that listener directs traffic to a specific cluster (e.g., by matching on HTTP path or Service Name Indication, or SNI). A cluster is a group of endpoints along with information about how to contact these endpoints (TLS settings, load-balancing strategy, connection-pool settings, etc.). A cluster is analogous to a "service" (as an example, one Kubernetes service might manifest as a single cluster). Finally, endpoints are individual network hosts (IP addresses or DNS names) to which Envoy will forward traffic.

Within this configuration, the elements refer to each other by name. So, a listener directs traffic to a named route, a route directs traffic to a named cluster, and the cluster directs traffic to a set of endpoints. Pilot does the bookkeeping to keep these names consistent throughout. We see how these names are useful for debugging the system in the next section.

A Note on "x"

We refer to the Envoy APIs as the *xDS APIs* because each configuration primitive—listener, route, cluster, endpoint—has its own Discovery Service named after it. Each Discovery Service allows for the updating of its resource. Rather than referring individually to the LDS, RDS, CDS, and EDS, we group them together as the *xDS APIs*.

Istio's networking configuration maps to Envoy's API nearly directly:

- Gateways configure physical listeners.
- `VirtualServices` configure both virtual listeners (hostname matches are encoded as separate listeners, and protocol processing is configured via listeners with specific filters per protocol) and routes (HTTP/TLS match conditions, retry and timeout configuration, etc.).
- `ServiceEntrys` create clusters and populate their endpoints.
- `DestinationRules` configure how to communicate with clusters (secrets, load-balancing strategy, circuit breaking and connection pooling, etc.), and create new clusters when they're used to define subsets.

The final piece of Istio networking configuration is the sidecar. It doesn't relate directly to an Envoy configuration primitive itself; instead, Istio uses it to filter what configuration is sent to each group of Envoys.

With this mapping in-hand, let's consider how a commonplace Istio configuration manifests as an Envoy xDS configuration and layout some tips for debugging Istio network configuration.

Debugging and Troubleshooting Pilot

This section focuses on troubleshooting Pilot, as a complement to Chapter 11, which is dedicated to debugging. Istio is a complex system with a lot of moving parts. Until you develop a deep understanding of Istio, it can be difficult to understand why the system behaves in a certain way. (What exacerbates this issue is that often the system is behaving by not serving any traffic!) Fortunately, there's an ever-growing set of tools to help you understand and debug system state. In this section, we give an overview of some tools that are particularly useful for understanding and troubleshooting networking in Istio.

istioctl

`istioctl` has a slew of useful tools for helping understand the state of an Istio deployment, including `istioctl authn` for inspecting the state of mTLS in the mesh, retrieving per-pod metrics, and for inspecting Pilot and Envoy configuration. These last two, `istioctl proxy-config` and `istioctl proxy-status`, are invaluable for understanding the state of network configuration in a deployment.

Unfortunately, many of the following tools (specifically, `proxy-config` and `proxy-status`) are Kubernetes-specific because they currently rely on Kubernetes for their implementation. For example, `istioctl proxy-config` works by using `kubectl exec` to retrieve data from the remote machine.

In the future, equivalent tools will be built for other platforms. Where possible, we describe how the tool is implemented to make it possible for those on non-Kubernetes platforms to follow along. See Chapter 11 for a deeper dive on how `istioctl proxy-config` interacts with Kubernetes.

In support of other platforms (and other service meshes), we also point out where other tools can fill these gaps. Meshery (*https://oreil.ly/c_eJo*) is one example, in which the same `istioctl proxy-config` and `proxy-status` information is provided but graphically presented (for Istio and other service meshes) so that you can see the status of your mesh. Meshery can validate the current state against the *planned state* of your Istio configuration, making deployment dry runs easier to manage, and validate that your configuration changes will have the desired effect.

`istioctl proxy-config <bootstrap | listener | route | cluster> <kubernetes pod>`:: Connects to the specified pod and queries the service proxy's administrative interface to retrieve the current state of the service proxy's configuration. We can retrieve the service proxy's bootstrap configuration (which typically just configures it to talk to Pilot), its listeners, routes, and clusters. `proxy-config` supports an output flag (`--output` or just `-o`), which you can use to print the full body of Envoy's configuration in JSON. In "Tracing Configuration" on page 114, we use this to under-stand how an Istio configuration shows up in the service proxy.

`istioctl proxy-status <Istio service>`
> Connects to Pilot's debug interface and retrieves the xDS status of each connected service proxy instance (if a service name is provided, just the service proxies for that service). This shows whether each service proxy's configuration is up to date with the latest configuration in Pilot, and if not, how far behind the proxy is. This is particularly useful for identifying a configuration that affects only a subset of proxies as the culprit for a problem when troubleshooting.

Troubleshooting Pilot

Pilot exposes a variety of endpoints for understanding its state of the world. Unfortu-nately, they're woefully underdocumented. As of this writing, there are no public docs describing them. These endpoints, all exposed on Pilot with the prefix `/debug/`, return JSON blobs of the various configurations that Pilot holds.

To examine the state of service proxies connected to Pilot, see these endpoints:

`/debug/edsz`
> Prints all of Pilot's set of precomputed EDS responses (i.e., the endpoints it sends to each connected service proxy).

`/debug/adsz`
> Prints the set of listeners, routes, and clusters pushed to each service proxy con-nected to Pilot.

`/debug/cdsz`
> Prints the set of clusters pushed to each service proxy connected to Pilot.

`/debug/synz`
> Prints the status of ADS, CDS, and EDS connections of all service proxies con-nected to pilot. In particular, this shows the last nonce Pilot is working with ver-sus the last nonce Envoy has ACK'd, showing which Envoys are not accepting configuration updates.

To examine Pilot's understanding of the state of the world (its service registries), see these endpoints:

`/debug/registryz`
> Prints the set of services that Pilot knows about across all registries.

`/debug/endpointz[?brief=1]`
> Prints the endpoints for every service that Pilot knows about, including their ports, protocols, service accounts, labels, and so on. If you provide the `brief` flag,

the output will be a human-readable table (as opposed to a JSON blob for the normal version). This is a legacy endpoint and `/debug/endpointShardz` provides strictly more information.

`/debug/endpointShardz`
Prints the endpoints for every service that Pilot knows about, grouped by the registry that provided the endpoint (the "shard," from Pilot's point of view). For example, if the same service exists in both Consul and Kubernetes, endpoints for the service will be grouped into two shards, one each for Consul and Kubernetes. This endpoint provides everything from `/debug/endpoint` and more, including data like the endpoint's network, locality, load-balancer weight, representation in the Envoy xDS configuration, and more.

`/debug/workloadz`
Prints the set of endpoints ("workloads") connected to Pilot, and their metadata (like labels).

`/debug/configz`
Prints the entire set of Istio configuration Pilot knows about. Only validated configurations that Pilot is using to construct its model will be returned. This is useful for understanding situations in which Pilot is not processing a new configuration itself.

You can also find miscellaneous endpoints with higher-level debug information by wading through these endpoints:

`/debug/authenticationz[?proxyID=pod_name.namespace]`
Prints the Istio authentication policy status of the target proxy for each host and port that it's serving, including the name of the authentication policy affecting it; the name of the `DestinationRule` affecting it; whether the port expects mTLS, standard TLS, or plain text; and whether settings across the configuration cause a conflict for this port (a common cause of 500 errors in new Istio deployments).

`/debug/config_dump[?proxyID=pod_name.namespace]`
Prints the listeners, routes, and clusters for the given node; this can be `diff`'d directly against the output of `istioctl proxy-config`.

`/debug/push_status`
Prints the status of each connected endpoint as of Pilot's last push period; includes the status of each connected proxy, when the push period began (and ended), and the identities assigned to each port of each host.

ControlZ

Each Istio control-plane component exposes an administrative interface that you can use to configure fine-grained logging, see information about the process and environment, and view metrics about that instance. Most often used for adjusting log levels, ControlZ allows you to independently and dynamically modify logging levels for each scope at runtime. Istio components use a common logging system with a notion of *scopes*. As an example, Pilot defines scopes for logging about Envoy API connections; so one scope for ADS connections, another for EDS connections, and a third for CDS. For more on ControlZ, see "Introspecting Istio Components" on page 187 in Chapter 11.

Prometheus

Pilot, along with the other Istio control-plane components, hosts a Prometheus endpoint with detailed metrics about their internal state. Istio's default Grafana deployment includes dashboards that use these metrics to chart the state of each Istio control-plane component. You can use these metrics to help debug Pilot's internal state. By default, Pilot hosts its Prometheus endpoint on port 8080 at /metrics (e.g. kubectl exec -it PILOT_POD -n istio-system -c discovery — curl localhost: 8080/metrics).

Tracing Configuration

It can be a difficult task to trace the steps involved in the creation and dispersal of configuration, starting with Pilot and mapping to service proxies. Pilot's debug endpoints (previously described), together with istioctl, are at-hand tools to understand Pilot and any changes within it. In this section, we use these tools to understand the before-and-after of Istio configuration and the resultant xDS configuration pushed to service proxies.

There are far too many permutations of configuration for us to show how they all manifest. Instead, for each major type of configuration we show you some Istio configuration and the Envoy configuration it results in, highlight the main similarities, and outline how other changes to the same Istio configuration will manifest in Envoy so that you can test and see for yourself and use this knowledge to diagnose and solve the majority of Istio issues that you'll come across.

Listeners

Gateways and VirtualServices results in Listeners for Envoy. Gateways result in physical listeners (listeners that bind to a port on the network), whereas VirtualSer vices result in virtual listeners (listeners that do *not* bind to a port, but instead receive traffic from physical listeners). Examples 7-1 and 7-2 demonstrate how the Istio configuration manifests into an xDS configuration by creating a Gateway (see foo-gw.yaml (*https://oreil.ly/8SW3s*) in this book's GitHub repository).

Example 7-1. A Gateway for serving HTTP traffic for subdomains of http://foo.com (using a clean Istio installation)

```
apiVersion: networking.istio.io/v1alpha3
kind: Gateway
metadata:
  name: foo-com-gateway
spec:
  selector:
    istio: ingressgateway
  servers:
  - hosts:
    - "*.foo.com"
    port:
      number: 80
      name: http
      protocol: HTTP
```

Creation of this Istio `Gateway` results in a single HTTP listener on port 80 on our ingress `Gateway` (see Example 7-2).

Example 7-2. Envoy listener (LDS) configuration for the Gateway created in Example 7-1

```
$ istioctl proxy-config listener istio-ingressgateway_PODNAME
                              -o json -n istio-system
[
    {
        "name": "0.0.0.0_80",
        "address": {
            "socketAddress": {
                "address": "0.0.0.0",
                "portValue": 80
            }
        },
        "filterChains": [
            {
                "filters": [
                    {
                        "name": "envoy.http_connection_manager",
...
                        "rds": {
                            "config_source": {
                                "ads": {}
                            },
                            "route_config_name": "http.80"
                        },
...
```

Notice that the newly created filter is listening on address 0.0.0.0. This is the listener used for all HTTP traffic on port 80, no matter what host it's addressed to. If we set up TLS termination for this Gateway, we would then see a new listener created just for the hosts for which we're terminating TLS, whereas the rest would fall into this catchall listener. Let's bind a VirtualService to this Gateway as demonstrated in Example 7-3 (see foo-vs.yaml (*https://oreil.ly/OZqjU*) in this book's GitHub repository).

Example 7-3. A VirtualService that binds to the Gateway from Example 7-1 and creates virtual listeners in Envoy

```
apiVersion: networking.istio.io/v1alpha3
kind: VirtualService
metadata:
 name: foo-default
spec:
 hosts:
 - bar.foo.com
 gateways:
 - foo-com-gateway
 http:
 - route:
   - destination:
       host: bar.foo.svc.cluster.local
```

To see how it manifests as virtual listeners, see Example 7-4:

Example 7-4. Envoy listener (LDS) configuration for the VirtualService in Example 7-3 —no change from the configuration seen in Example 7-2; all the action is in the routes!

```
$ istioctl proxy-config listener istio-ingressgateway_PODNAME -o json
[
    {
        "name": "0.0.0.0_80",
        "address": {
            "socketAddress": {
                "address": "0.0.0.0",
                "portValue": 80
            }
        },
        "filterChains": [
            {
                "filters": [
                    {
                        "name": "envoy.http_connection_manager",
...
                        "rds": {
                            "config_source": {
                                "ads": {}
```

```
                  },
                  "route_config_name": "http.80"
          },
...
```

Looking at the configuration in Example 7-4, we don't see any change in the listener. That's because the listener on IP 0.0.0.0 is a catchall—all HTTP traffic on port 80. That's not how TLS will be configured in the listener, however. If we created a `Gateway` that configures TLS, instead, we'd see a new listener created for just the hosts in the section with TLS. The rest would fall through to the default listener. Instead, for HTTP, all of the action happens in routes. Other protocols—for example, TCP—push more of the logic to the listener. Experiment by defining a few `Gateways` with different protocols to see how they manifest as listeners. For ideas and examples, see this book's GitHub repository (*https://oreil.ly/istio-up-and-running*).

You should also notice the Mixer configuration in the listeners. The Mixer configuration in Envoy appears in both listeners (where we set source attributes) and also in routes (where we set destination attributes). Using the `MeshConfig` to disable Mixer *checks* will result in a slightly different configuration, as will the disabling of Mixer *reports*. If you disable both *checks* and *reports*, you'll see the Mixer configuration disappear entirely from Envoy.

We also recommend that you try different protocols for the ports (or list a single `Gateway` with many ports with various protocols) to see how this results in different filters. Configuring different TLS settings within the `Gateway` also results in changes to the generated listener configuration. You'll always see a protocol-specific filter configured in the listener for each protocol you use (for HTTP, this is the `http_connection_manager` and its `router`; for MongoDB, it's another; for TCP, yet another one; etc.). We also recommend trying different combinations of hosts in the `Gateway` and `VirtualService` to see how they interact. We cover at length how the two work together—how you *bind* `VirtualServices` to `Gateways`—in Chapter 8.

Routes

We've seen how `VirtualServices` result in the creation of listeners (or don't, as in our example!). Most of the configuration you specify in `VirtualServices` actually manifest as Routes in Envoy. Routes come in different flavors with a set of routes per protocol that Envoy supports.

We can list the routes Envoy currently has by using our existing `VirtualService` from Example 7-3. This route is pretty simple, because our `VirtualService` just forwards traffic to a single destination service, as shown in Example 7-5. This example shows the default Retry Policy and the embedded Mixer configuration (which is used for reporting telemetry back to Mixer).

Example 7-5. Envoy route (RDS) configuration for the VirtualService in Example 7-3

```
$ istioctl proxy-config route istio-ingressgateway_PODNAME -o json
[
    {
        "name": "0.0.0.0_80",
        "virtualHosts": [
            {
                "name": "bar.foo.com:80",
                "domains": [
                    "bar.foo.com",
                    "bar.foo.com:80"
                ],
                "routes": [
                    {
                        "match": {
                            "prefix": "/"
                        },
                        "route": {
                            "cluster": "outbound|8000||bar.foo.svc.cluster.local",
                            "timeout": "0s",
                            "retryPolicy": {
                                "retryOn": "connect-failure,refused-stream,
                                unavailable,cancelled,resource-exhausted,
                                retriable-status-codes","numRetries": 2,
                                "retryHostPredicate": [
                                    {
                                        "name":
                                        "envoy.retry_host_predicates.previous_hosts"
                                    }
                                ],
                                "hostSelectionRetryMaxAttempts": "3",
                                "retriableStatusCodes": [
                                    503
                                ]
                            }
                        },
...
```

We can update our route to include some match conditions to see how this results in different routes for Envoy, as shown in Example 7-6 (see foo-routes.yaml (*https://oreil.ly/bbevw*) in this book's GitHub repository).

Example 7-6. A VirtualService routing /whiz to the whiz service

```
apiVersion: networking.istio.io/v1alpha3
kind: VirtualService
metadata:
 name: foo-default
spec:
```

```
hosts:
- bar.foo.com
gateways:
- foo-com-gateway
http:
- match:
  - uri:
      prefix: /whiz
  route:
  - destination:
      host: whiz.foo.svc.cluster.local
- route:
  - destination:
      host: bar.foo.svc.cluster.local
```

Similarly, we can add retries, split traffic among several destinations, inject faults, and more. All of these options in VirtualServices manifest as routes in Envoy (see Example 7-7).

Example 7-7. Envoy route (RDS) configuration for the VirtualService in Example 7-6

```
$ istioctl proxy-config route istio-ingressgateway_PODNAME -o json
[
    {
        "name": "http.80",
        "virtualHosts": [
            {
                "name": "bar.foo.com:80",
                "domains": [
                    "bar.foo.com",
                    "bar.foo.com:80"
                ],
                "routes": [
                    {
                        "match": {
                            "prefix": "/whiz"
                        },
                        "route": {
                            "cluster": "outbound|80||whiz.foo.svc.cluster.local",
...
                    {
                        "match": {
                            "prefix": "/"
                        },
                        "route": {
                            "cluster": "outbound|80||bar.foo.svc.cluster.local",
...
```

Now, we see how our URI match manifests as a route with a prefix match. The route for "/" that we had before remains, as well, but it comes after our new match. Matches in Envoy are performed in order, and that order matches the order in your `Virtual Service`.

Clusters

If we use `istioctl` to look at clusters, as well, we can see that Istio generates a cluster for each service and port in the mesh. We can create a new `ServiceEntry` like the one in Example 7-8 ourselves to see a new cluster appear in Envoy, as shown in Example 7-9 (see some-domain-se.yaml (*https://oreil.ly/8F4cu*) in the GitHub repository for this book).

Example 7-8. A ServiceEntry for some.domain.com with a static IP address

```
apiVersion: networking.istio.io/v1alpha3
kind: ServiceEntry
metadata:
  name: http-server
spec:
  hosts:
  - some.domain.com
  ports:
  - number: 80
    name: http
    protocol: http
  resolution: STATIC
  endpoints:
  - address: 2.2.2.2
```

Example 7-9. Envoy cluster (CDS) configuration for the ServiceEntry in Example 7-8

```
$ istioctl proxy-config cluster istio-ingressgateway_PODNAME -o json
[
...
    {
        "name": "outbound|80||some.domain.com",
        "type": "EDS",
        "edsClusterConfig": {
            "edsConfig": {
                "ads": {}
            },
            "serviceName": "outbound|80||some.domain.com"
        },
        "connectTimeout": "10s",
        "circuitBreakers": {
            "thresholds": [
                {
                    "maxRetries": 1024
                }
            ]
```

```
      }
    },
  ...
```

This results in a single cluster, `outbound|80||some.domain.com`. Notice how Istio encodes inbound versus outbound in the cluster name as well as the port.

We can add new ports (with different protocols) to the `ServiceEntry` to see how this results in new clusters being generated. The other tool we can use that generates and updates clusters in Istio is a `DestinationRule`. By creating subsets, we generate new clusters (seeExamples 7-10 and 7-11), and by updating load-balancing and TLS settings, we affect the configuration within the cluster itself (see some-domain-dest.yaml (*https://oreil.ly/fh1tx*) in this book's GitHub repository).

Example 7-10. A DestinationRule for some.domain.com that splits it into two subsets

```
apiVersion: networking.istio.io/v1alpha3
kind: DestinationRule
metadata:
  name: some-domain-com
spec:
  host: some.domain.com
  subsets:
  - name: v1
    labels:
      version: v1
  - name: v2
    labels:
      version: v2
```

Example 7-11. Envoy cluster (CDS) configuration for the DestinationRule in Example 7-10

```
$ istioctl proxy-config cluster istio-ingressgateway_PODNAME -o json
[
...
    {
        "name": "outbound|80||some.domain.com",
...
    },
    {
        "name": "outbound|80|v1|some.domain.com",
...
        "metadata": {
            "filterMetadata": {
                "istio": {
                    "config": "/apis/networking/v1alpha3/namespaces/default
                    /destination-rule/some-domain-com"
                }
```

```
            }
        }
    },
    {
        "name": "outbound|80|v2|some.domain.com",
...
    },
...
```

Notice that we still have our original cluster, `outbound|80||some.domain.com`, but that we got a new cluster for each Subset we defined, as well. Istio annotates the Envoy configuration with the rule that resulted in it being created to help debug.

In this chapter, we covered Pilot: its basic model, the sources of configuration it consumes to produce a model of the mesh, how it uses that model of the mesh to push configuration to Envoys, how to debug it, and finally how to understand the transformation Pilot performs from Istio configuration to Envoy's. With this information in hand you should be equipped to debug and resolve the vast majority of issues new and intermediate Istio users face.

## CHAPTER 8

Traffic Management

Among the core capabilities of all service meshes is traffic management, and as such, it's generally a deep functional area. This is certainly the case for Istio. With traffic management as our topic of study in this chapter, we begin our exploration of Istio's capabilities in the context of how requests flow through the system, becoming familiar with Istio's networking APIs as we go. We look at how you can use those APIs to configure traffic flow, enabling you to do things like canary new deployments, set timeout and retry policies that are consistent across all of your services, and, finally, test your application's failure modes with controllable, repeatable fault injection.

Understanding How Traffic Flows in Istio

To understand how Istio's networking APIs work, it's important to understand how requests actually flow through Istio. Pilot, as we learned in the previous chapter, understands the topology of the service mesh, and uses this knowledge, along with additional Istio networking configurations that *you* provide, to configure the mesh's service proxies. See Chapter 7 for more on the kind of configuration that Pilot pushes to service proxies.

As the data-plane service proxy, Envoy intercepts all incoming and outgoing requests at runtime (as traffic flows through the service mesh). This interception is done *transparently* via iptables rules or a Berkeley Packet Filter (BPF) program that routes all network traffic, in and out through Envoy. Envoy inspects the request and uses the request's hostname, SNI, or service virtual IP address to determine the request's *target* (the service to which the client *is intending* to send a request). Envoy applies that target's routing rules to determine the request's *destination* (the service to which the service proxy *is actually* going to send the request). Having determined the destination, Envoy applies the destination's rules. Destination rules include load-balancing strategy, which is used to pick an *endpoint* (the endpoint is the address of a worker supporting the destination service). Services generally have more than one worker available to process requests. Requests can be balanced across those workers. Finally, Envoy forwards the intercepted request to the endpoint.

A number of items of note are worth further illumination. First, it's desirable to have your applications speak *cleartext* (communicate without encryption) to the sidecarred service proxy and let the service proxy handle transport security. For example, your application can speak HTTP to the sidecar and let the sidecar handle the upgrade to HTTPS. This allows the service proxy to gather L7 metadata about requests, which allows Istio to generate L7 metrics *and* manipulate traffic based on L7 policy. Without the service proxy performing TLS termination, Istio can generate metrics for and apply policy on only the L4 segment of the request, restricting policy to contents of the IP packet and TCP header (essentially, a source and destination address and port number). Second, we get to perform client-side load balancing rather than relying on traditional load balancing via reverse proxies. Client-side load balancing means that we can establish network connections directly from clients to servers while still maintaining a resilient, well-behaved system. That in turn enables more efficient network topologies with fewer hops than traditional systems that depend on reverse proxies.

Typically, Pilot has detailed endpoint information about services in the registry, which it pushes directly to the service proxies. So, unless you configure the service proxy to do otherwise, at runtime it selects an endpoint from a static set of endpoints pushed to it by Pilot and does not perform dynamic address resolution (e.g., via DNS) at runtime. Therefore, the only things Istio can route traffic to are hostnames in Istio's service registry. There is an installation option in newer versions of Istio (set to "off" by default in 1.1) that changes this behavior and allows Envoy to forward traffic to unknown services that are not modeled in Istio, so long as the application provides an IP address.

In the next section, we discuss *hostnames*, which are the core of Istio's networking model, and how Istio's networking APIs allow you to create hostnames to describe workloads and control how traffic flows to them.

Understanding Istio's Networking APIs

Applications address services by name (e.g., by hostname resolved via DNS) to avoid the fragility of addressing services by IP address (an address that might not be initially known, that might change at any time, is difficult to remember, and might modulate between v4 and v6 addresses depending on its environment). Consequently, Istio's network configuration has adopted a *name-centric model*, in which:

- Gateways (*https://oreil.ly/uPLZa*) expose names.
- VirtualServices (*https://oreil.ly/_qE97*) configure and route names.

- DestinationRules (*https://oreil.ly/rj42r*) describe how to communicate with the workloads behind a name.
- ServiceEntrys (*https://oreil.ly/tyvAq*) enable the creation of new names.

Application requests initiate with the call to the service's name, as shown in Figure 8-1.

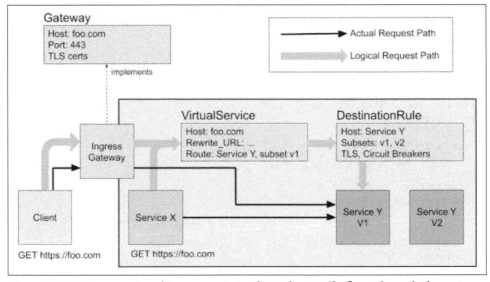

Figure 8-1. Istio core networking concepts implicated as traffic flows through the system

ServiceEntry

ServiceEntrys are how you manually add/remove service listings in Istio's service registry. Entries in the service registry can receive traffic by name and be targeted by other Istio configurations. At their simplest, you can use them to give a name to an IP address, as demonstrated in Example 8-1 (see static-se.yaml (*https://oreil.ly/Us7jl*) in the GitHub repository for this book).

Example 8-1. An example of an Istio ServiceEntry

```
apiVersion: networking.istio.io/v1alpha3
kind: ServiceEntry
metadata:
  name: http-server
spec:
  hosts:
  - some.domain.com
  ports:
  - number: 80
    name: http
```

```
    protocol: http
  resolution: STATIC
  endpoints:
  - address: 2.2.2.2
```

Given the ServiceEntry in Example 8-1, service proxies in the mesh will forward requests to some.domain.com to the IP address 2.2.2.2. As Example 8-2 shows, you can use ServiceEntrys to elevate a name that's addressable via DNS into a name addressable in Istio (see dns-se.yaml (*https://oreil.ly/cEc5k*) in the GitHub repository for this book).

Example 8-2. An Istio ServiceEntry with resolution value set to DNS

```
apiVersion: networking.istio.io/v1alpha3
kind: ServiceEntry
metadata:
  name: external-svc-dns
spec:
  hosts:
  - foo.bar.com
  location: MESH_EXTERNAL
  ports:
  - number: 443
    name: https
    protocol: HTTP
  resolution: DNS
  endpoints:
  - address: baz.com
```

The ServiceEntry defined in Example 8-2 causes service proxies to forward requests to foo.bar.com to baz.com to use DNS to resolve to endpoints. In this example, because we declare that the service is outside the mesh (location: MESH_EXTERNAL) service proxies won't attempt to use mTLS to communicate with it.

All service registries with which Istio integrates (Kubernetes, Consul, Eureka, etc.) work by transforming their data into a ServiceEntry. For example, a Kubernetes service with one pod (and therefore one endpoint) maps directly into a ServiceEntry with a host and an IP address endpoint, as illustrated in Example 8-3 (see svc-endpoint.yaml (*https://oreil.ly/TNaWH*) in this book's GitHub repository).

Example 8-3. Underlying platform services, Kubernetes example

```
apiVersion: v1
kind: Service
metadata:
  name: my-service
spec:
  selector:
```

```
    app: MyApp
  ports:
  - protocol: TCP
    port: 80
- - -
apiVersion: v1
kind: Endpoints
metadata:
  name: my-service
subsets:
  - addresses:
      - ip: 1.2.3.4
    ports:
      - port: 80
```

This becomes the ServiceEntry shown in Example 8-4 (see k8s-se.yaml (*https://oreil.ly/LLawn*) in the GitHub repository for this book).

Example 8-4. Kubernetes service and endpoint manifested as a ServiceEntry

```
apiVersion: networking.istio.io/v1alpha3
kind: ServiceEntry
metadata:
  name: k8s-my-service
spec:
  hosts:
  # The names an application can use in k8s to target this service
  - my-service
  - my-service.default
  - my-service.default.svc.cluster.local
  ports:
  - number: 80
    name: http
    protocol: HTTP
  resolution: STATIC
  endpoints:
  - address: 1.2.3.4
```

> ServiceEntrys created by platform adapters don't appear directly in Istio's configuration (i.e., you cannot istioctl get them). Rather, you can only istioctl get ServiceEntrys that you have created.

Note that Istio does not populate DNS entries based on ServiceEntrys. This means that Example 8-1, which gives the address 2.2.2.2 the name some.domain.com, will not allow an application to resolve some.domain.com to 2.2.2.2 via DNS. This is a departure from systems like Kubernetes, for which declaring a service also creates DNS entries for that service that an application can use at runtime. There is a core

DNS plug-in for Istio that generates DNS records from `Istio ServiceEntrys`, which you can use to populate DNS for Istio services in environments outside of Kubernetes or when you want to model things that are not Kubernetes services.

Finally, as Example 8-5 demonstrates, you can use `ServiceEntrys` to create virtual IP addresses (VIPs), mapping an IP address to a name that you can configure via Istio's other networking APIs.

Example 8-5. Using a ServiceEntry to create a virtual IP address

```
apiVersion: networking.istio.io/v1alpha3
kind: ServiceEntry
metadata:
  name: http-server
spec:
  hosts:
  - my-tcp-service.internal
  addresses:
  - 1.2.3.4
  ports:
  - number: 975
    name: tcp
    protocol: TCP
  resolution: DNS
  endpoints:
  - address: foo.com
```

This declares `1.2.3.4` as a VIP with the name `my-tcp-service.internal`. All traffic to that VIP on port 975 will be forwarded to an IP address for `foo.com` resolved via DNS. Of course, we can configure the endpoints for a VIP just like any other `Service Entry`, deferring to DNS or configuring a set of addresses explicitly. Other Istio configurations can use the name `my-tcp-service.internal` to describe traffic for this service. Again, though, understand that Istio will not set up DNS entries external to the service mesh (or in the case of Kubernetes, external to the cluster), so that `my-tcp-service.internal` resolves to the address `1.2.3.4` for applications. You must configure DNS to do that, or the application must address `1.2.3.4` directly itself.

DestinationRule

`DestinationRules`, a little counterintuitively, are really all about configuring clients. They allow a service operator to describe how a client in the mesh should call their service, including the following:

- Subsets of the service (e.g., v1 and v2)
- The load-balancing strategy the client should use
- The conditions to use to mark endpoints of the service as unhealthy

- L4 and L7 connection pool settings
- TLS settings for the server

We cover client-side load balancing, load-balancing strategy, and outlier detection in detail in the section "Resiliency" on page 150 later in this chapter.

Connection pool settings

With `DestinationRules`, we can configure low-level connection pool settings like the number of TCP connections allowed to each destination host, the maximum number of outstanding HTTP1, HTTP2, or gRPC requests allowed to each destination host, and the maximum number of retries that can be outstanding across all of the destination's endpoints. Example 8-6 shows a `DestinationRule` that allows a maximum of four TCP connections per destination endpoint and a maximum of 1,000 concurrent HTTP2 requests over those four TCP connections.

Example 8-6. A DestinationRule configuring low-level connection pool settings

```
apiVersion: networking.istio.io/v1alpha3
kind: DestinationRule
metadata:
  name: foo-default
spec:
  host: foo.default.svc.cluster.local
  trafficPolicy:
    connectionPool:
      tcp:
        maxConnections: 4
      http:
        http2MaxRequests: 1000
```

TLS settings

`DestinationRules` can describe how a sidecar should secure the connection with a destination endpoint. Four modes are supported:

DISABLED
    Disables TLS for the TCP connection

SIMPLE
    Originates a TLS connection to the destination endpoint

MUTUAL
    Establishes a mTLS connection to the destination endpoint

ISTIO_MUTUAL
    Asks if mTLS is using Istio-provisioned certificates

Enabling mTLS across the mesh via Istio's mesh configuration is a shorthand for setting Istio mTLS as the value for all destinations in the mesh. For example, we can use a `DestinationRule` to allow connecting to an HTTPS website outside the mesh, as shown in Example 8-7 (see egress-destrule.yaml (*https://oreil.ly/o7aNe*) in the GitHub repository for this book).

Example 8-7. Allowing outbound traffic to http://google.com domain to egress mesh

```
apiVersion: networking.istio.io/v1alpha3
kind: DestinationRule
metadata:
  name: google.com
spec:
  host: "*.google.com"
  trafficPolicy:
    tls:
      mode: SIMPLE
```

Or, we can describe connecting to another server with mTLS, as illustrated in Example 8-8.

Example 8-8. DestinationRule enforcing use of mTLS

```
apiVersion: networking.istio.io/v1alpha3
kind: DestinationRule
metadata:
  name: remote-a-ingress
spec:
  host: ingress.a.remote.cluster
  trafficPolicy:
    tls:
      mode: MUTUAL
      clientCertificate: /etc/certs/remote-cluster-a.pem
      privateKey: /etc/certs/client_private_key_cluster_a.pem
      caCertificates: /etc/certs/rootcacerts.pem
```

You can use a `DestinationRule` like the one in Example 8-7 together with a `Service Entry` for `ingress.a.remote.cluster` to route traffic across trust domains (e.g., separate clusters) over the internet, securely, with no VPN or other overlay networks. We cover zero-VPN networking and other topics in Chapter 13.

Subsets

Finally, `DestinationRules` allow you to split a single service into subsets based on labels. You also can separately configure for each subset all of the features we described thus far of what a `DestinationRule` allows you to configure. For example, we could split a service into two subsets based on the version and the use of a `Vir`

`tualService` to perform a canary release to the new version, gradually shifting all of the traffic to the new version. As presented in Example 8-9, foo has two versions: v1 and v2. Each version of the foo service has its own load-balancing policy distinctly defined.

Example 8-9. Traffic splitting, using subsets

```
apiVersion: networking.istio.io/v1alpha3
kind: DestinationRule
metadata:
  name: foo-default
spec:
  host: foo.default.svc.cluster.local
  subsets:
  - name: v1
    labels:
      version: v1
    trafficPolicy:
      loadBalancer:
        simple: ROUND_ROBIN
  - name: v2
    labels:
      version: v2
    trafficPolicy:
      loadBalancer:
        simple: LEAST_CONN
```

We cover `VirtualServices` in more detail in the next section.

VirtualService

A `VirtualService` describes how traffic addressed to a name flows to a set of destinations, as shown in Example 8-10.

Example 8-10. A simple VirtualService

```
apiVersion: networking.istio.io/v1alpha3
kind: VirtualService
metadata:
  name: foo-identity
spec:
  hosts:
  - foo.default.svc.cluster.local
  http:
  - route:
    - destination:
        host: foo.default.svc.cluster.local
```

The `VirtualService` in Example 8-10 forwards traffic addressed to `foo.default.svc.cluster.local` to the destination `foo.default.svc.cluster.local`. Pilot implicitly generates a `VirtualService` (like the one in the example) to pair with every service's `ServiceEntry`.

Of course, we can do many more interesting things with `VirtualServices` than that. For example, we can define HTTP endpoints for a service and have Envoy deliver 404s errors (on the client side) for invalid paths without calling the remote server, as demonstrated in Example 8-11.

Example 8-11. A VirtualService with path-based matching

```
apiVersion: networking.istio.io/v1alpha3
kind: VirtualService
metadata:
  name: foo-apiserver
spec:
  hosts:
  - foo.default.svc.cluster.local
  http:
  - match:
    - uri:
        prefix: "/api"
    route:
    - destination:
        host: apiserver.foo.svc.cluster.local
```

Clients calling `foo.default.svc.cluster.local/api/…` are directed to a set of API servers at the destination `apiserver.foo.svc.cluster.local`, and any other URI will result in Envoy not finding a destination in that request and responding to the application with a 404 error. This is why Pilot creates an implicit `VirtualService` for every `ServiceEntry`. So, even though an explicit catch-all destination isn't explicitly defined, any unmatched path in the `DestinationRule` results in a 404, forming an implicit catch-all.

You can use `VirtualServices` to target very specific segments of traffic and direct them to different destinations. For example, a `VirtualService` can match requests by header values, the port a caller is attempting to connect to, or the labels on the client's workload (e.g., labels on the client's pod in Kubernetes) and send matching traffic to a different destination (e.g., a new version of a service) than all of the unmatched traffic. We cover these use cases in detail in the section "Traffic Steering and Routing" on page 144 later in this chapter. A simple example is sending a fraction of traffic to the new version of a service (see Example 8-12), allowing a quick rollback in the case of a bad deployment.

Example 8-12. Splitting traffic between VirtualService subsets

```
apiVersion: networking.istio.io/v1alpha3
kind: VirtualService
metadata:
  name: foo-apiserver
spec:
  hosts:
  - foo.default.svc.cluster.local
  http:
  - match:
    - uri:
        prefix: "/api"
    route:
    - destination:
        host: apiserver.foo.svc.cluster.local
        subset: v1
      weight: 90
    - destination:
        host: apiserver.foo.svc.cluster.local
        subset: v2
      weight: 10
```

It's important to note that within a VirtualService, the match conditions are checked at runtime in the order in which they appear. This means that the most specific match clauses should appear first, and less-specific clauses later. For safety, a "default" route, with no match conditions, should be provided. Because, again, a request that does not match any condition of a VirtualService will result in a 404 for the sender (or some "connection-refused" error for non-HTTP protocols).

Hosts

We say that a VirtualService *claims* a name: a hostname can appear in at most one VirtualService, though a VirtualService can claim many hostnames. This can cause problems when a single name, like apis.foo.com, is used to host many services that route by path—for example, apis.foo.com/bars or apis.foo.com/bazs—because many teams must edit a single VirtualService apis.foo.com. One solution to this problem is to use a set of tiered VirtualServices. The top-level VirtualService splits up requests into logical services by path prefix and is a resource shared by every team (similar to a Kubernetes Ingress resource). Then a VirtualService for each of the logical services in the top-level VirtualService can describe traffic for that block of requests. You can repeatedly apply this pattern to delegate management of smaller and smaller segments of traffic.

For example, consider a shared VirtualService with business logic for multiple teams, like the one in Example 8-13.

Example 8-13. A monolithic VirtualService definition

```
apiVersion: networking.istio.io/v1alpha3
kind: VirtualService
metadata:
  name: foo-apiserver
spec:
  hosts:
  - apis.foo.com
  http:
  - match:
    - uri:
        prefix: "/bars/newMethod"
    route:
    - destination:
        host: bar.foo.svc.cluster.local
        subset: v2
  - match:
    - uri:
        prefix: "/bars"
    route:
    - destination:
        host: bar.foo.svc.cluster.local
        subset: v1
  - match:
    - uri:
        prefix: "/bazs/legacy/rest/path"
    route:
    - destination:
        host: monolith.legacy.svc.cluster.remote
    retries:
      attempts: 3
      perTryTimeout: 2s
  - match:
    - uri:
        prefix: "/bazs"
    route:
    - destination:
        host: baz.foo.svc.cluster.local
```

This `VirtualService` definition can be decomposed into separate `VirtualServices` (shown in Example 8-14) owned by the appropriate teams.

Example 8-14. VirtualServices split into independent definitions to facilitate independent change management

```
apiVersion: networking.istio.io/v1alpha3
kind: VirtualService
metadata:
  name: foo-svc-shared
spec:
```

```
  hosts:
  - apis.foo.com
  http:
  - match:
    - uri:
        prefix: "/bars"
    route:
    - destination:
        host: bar.foo.svc.cluster.local
  - match:
    - uri:
        prefix: "/bazs"
    route:
    - destination:
        host: baz.foo.svc.cluster.local
---
apiVersion: networking.istio.io/v1alpha3
kind: VirtualService
metadata:
  Name: foo-bars-svc
spec:
  hosts:
  - bar.foo.svc.cluster.local
  http:
  - match:
    - uri:
        prefix: "/bars/newMethod"
    route:
    - destination:
        host: bar.foo.svc.cluster.local
        subset: v2
  route:
  - destination:
      host: bar.foo.svc.cluster.local
      subset: v1
---
apiVersion: networking.istio.io/v1alpha3
kind: VirtualService
metadata:
  Name: foo-bazs-svc
spec:
  hosts:
  - baz.foo.svc.cluster.local
  http:
  - match:
    - uri:
        prefix: "/bazs/legacy/rest/path"
    route:
    - destination:
        host: monolith.legacy.svc.cluster.remote
      retries:
        attempts: 3
```

```
      perTryTimeout: 2s
  route:
  - destination:
      host: baz.foo.svc.cluster.local
```

 As described in "Decoupling at Layer 5" on page 10 in Chapter 1, service meshes dramatically facilitate the practice of decoupling service teams (developers, operators, etc.), and as such they are a key way to improve the speed at which teams can move, reduce the scope of risk teams face when managing changes, clarify responsibility between roles, and facilitate accountability over specific aspects of service delivery.

Example 8-14 is a specific example of how you can conscientiously approach clarifying lines of responsibility and thoroughly decoupling service teams within your service mesh configuration at L5.

Finally, `VirtualServices` can claim a set of hostnames described by a wildcard pattern. In other words, a `VirtualService` can claim a host like `*.com`. When choosing the configuration, the most specific host will always apply: for a request to `baz.foo.com`, the `VirtualService` for `baz.foo.com` applies, and the `VirtualSer vices` for `*.foo.com` and `*.com` are ignored. Note, though, that no `VirtualService` can claim "*" (the wildcard host).

Gateway

Gateways are concerned with exposing names over trust boundaries. Suppose that you have a `webserver.foo.svc.cluster.local` service deployed in your mesh that serves your website, `foo.com`. You can expose that webserver to the public internet using a `Gateway` to map from your internal name, `webserver.foo.svc.clus ter.local`, to your public name, `foo.com`. You also need to know on what port to expose the public name, and the protocol with which to expose it, as shown in Example 8-15.

Example 8-15. A simple Gateway definition, exposing HTTP/80

```
apiVersion: networking.istio.io/v1alpha3
kind: Gateway
metadata:
  name: foo-com-gateway
spec:
  selector:
    app: gateway-workloads
  servers:
  - hosts:
    - foo.com
```

```
  port:
    number: 80
    name: http
    protocol: HTTP
```

For secure transmissions just mapping between the names isn't enough, though. A
Gateway must be able to prove to callers that it owns the name, too. You can do this
by configuring the Gateway to serve a certificate for *http://foo.com*, as shown in
Example 8-16 (see gw-https.yaml (*https://oreil.ly/DLkkP*) in this book's GitHub repository).

Example 8-16. Gateway serving a certificate for foo.com

```
apiVersion: networking.istio.io/v1alpha3
kind: Gateway
metadata:
  name: foo-com-gateway
spec:
  selector:
    app: gateway-workloads
  servers:
  - hosts:
    - foo.com
    port:
      number: 443
      name: https
      protocol: HTTPS
    tls:
      mode: SIMPLE # Enables HTTPS on this port
      serverCertificate: /etc/certs/foo-com-public.pem
      privateKey: /etc/certs/foo-com-privatekey.pem
```

Both foo-com-public.pem and foo-com-privatekey.pem in Example 8-16 are long-
lived certificates for foo.com such as you would get from a CA like Let's Encrypt.
Unfortunately, Istio doesn't handle these types of certificates today, so you need to
mount any certificates that a Gateway must serve into the workload's filesystem. Also,
note that we updated both the port and protocol to match. We could keep serving
foo.com over HTTP on port 80 in addition to HTTPS/443, as shown in
Example 8-17, if we wanted to.

Example 8-17. A Gateway simultaneously serving HTTP/80 and HTTPS/443

```
apiVersion: networking.istio.io/v1alpha3
kind: Gateway
metadata:
  name: foo-com-gateway
spec:
  selector:
```

```
    app: gateway-workloads
  servers:
  - hosts:
    - foo.com
    port:
      number: 80
      name: http
      protocol: HTTP
  - hosts:
    - foo.com
    port:
      number: 443
      name: https
      protocol: HTTPS
    tls:
      mode: SIMPLE # Enables HTTPS on this port
      serverCertificate: /etc/certs/foo-com-public.pem
      privateKey: /etc/certs/foo-com-privatekey.pem
```

But based on security best practices, we're better off configuring our `Gateway` to perform an HTTPS upgrade, as shown in Example 8-18 (see gw-https-upgrade.yaml (*https://oreil.ly/2lf6g*) in the GitHub repository for this book).

Example 8-18. A Gateway configured to upgrade inbound HTTP/80 connections to secure HTTPS/443 connections

```
apiVersion: networking.istio.io/v1alpha3
kind: Gateway
metadata:
  name: foo-com-gateway
spec:
  selector:
    app: gateway-workloads
  servers:
  - hosts:
    - foo.com
    port:
      number: 80
      name: http
      protocol: HTTP
    tls:
      httpsRedirect: true # Sends 301 redirect for http requests
  - hosts:
    - foo.com
    port:
      number: 443
      name: https
      protocol: HTTPS
    tls:
      mode: SIMPLE # Enables HTTPS on this port
```

```
    serverCertificate: /etc/certs/foo-com-public.pem
    privateKey: /etc/certs/foo-com-privatekey.pem
```

Our examples demonstrate commonly used HTTP(S) and ports 80 and 443; however, Gateways can expose any protocol over any port. When Istio is controlling the Gate way implementation, the Gateway will listen to all ports listed in its configuration.

So far, none of these Gateways map foo.com to any service in our mesh! For that, we need to *bind* a VirtualService to our Gateway, as shown in Example 8-19 (see foo-vs.yaml (*https://oreil.ly/aRbTM*) in this book's GitHub repository).

Example 8-19. A VirtualService binding foo.com to Gateway

```
apiVersion: networking.istio.io/v1alpha3
kind: VirtualService
metadata:
  name: foo-com-virtual-service
spec:
  hosts:
  - foo.com
  gateways:
  - foo-com-gateway
  http:
  - route:
    - destination:
        host: webserver.foo.svc.cluster.local
```

We cover the rules for binding VirtualServices to Gateways in the section "Binding VirtualServices to Gateways" on page 141, but this raises an important point: Gate ways configure L4 behavior, not L7 behavior. What we mean by that is that a Gateway describes ports to bind to, what protocols to expose on those ports, and the names (and proof of those names through certificates) to serve on those ports. But, Virtual Services describe L7 behavior. L7 behavior here being how to map from some name (i.e., foo.com) to different applications and workloads.

Decoupling L4 from L7 behavior was a design goal for Istio. This allows patterns like providing a single Gateway that many teams can reuse, as shown in Example 8-20 (see gw-to-vses.yaml (*https://oreil.ly/n3YT0*) in the GitHub repository for this book).

Example 8-20. A single Gateway used by multiple VirtualServices

```
apiVersion: networking.istio.io/v1alpha3
kind: Gateway
metadata:
  name: foo-com-gateway
spec:
  selector:
```

```
      app: gateway-workloads
    servers:
    - hosts:
      - *.foo.com
      port:
        number: 80
        name: http
        protocol: HTTP
- - -
apiVersion: networking.istio.io/v1alpha3
kind: VirtualService
metadata:
  name: foo-com-virtual-service
spec:
  hosts:
  - api.foo.com
  gateways:
  - foo-com-gateway
  http:
  - route:
    - destination:
        host: api.foo.svc.cluster.local
- - -
apiVersion: networking.istio.io/v1alpha3
kind: VirtualService
metadata:
  name: foo-com-virtual-service
spec:
  hosts:
  - www.foo.com
  gateways:
  - foo-com-gateway
  http:
  - route:
    - destination:
        host: webserver.foo.svc.cluster.local
```

More important, this decoupling of L4 and L7 behavior means that you can use a Gateway to model network interfaces in Istio (e.g., network appliances or nonflat L3 networks). Finally, you can use Gateways to build mTLS tunnels between parts of a mesh deployed on separate L3 networks. For example, you can use them to establish secure connections between Istio deployments across separate cloud provider availability zones, over the public internet, without the need for a VPN.

Finally, you can use Gateways to model arbitrary network interfaces—regardless of whether that interface is under Istio's control. So, even though a network interface might be represented by Istio, the behavior of the network service behind the Gateway representing the interface might or might not be under Istio's control. For example, if you're using a Gateway to model an externally provided load balancer, maybe in your cloud deployment, the Istio configuration cannot affect the decisions made by that load balancer. Workloads that belong to a `Gateway` are described by the "selector" field on the `Gateway` object. Workloads with labels matching the selector are treated like `Gateway`s in Istio. When Istio controls the `Gateway` implementation (i.e., when the `Gateway` is an Envoy), we can *bind* `VirtualService`s to the `Gateway` to take advantage of `VirtualService` features at ingress and egress points in our cluster.

Binding VirtualServices to Gateways

We say a `VirtualService` *binds* to a `Gateway` if the following are true:

- The `VirtualService` lists the `Gateway`'s name in its gateways field
- At least one host *claimed* by the `VirtualService` is *exposed* by the `Gateway`

The hosts in a `Gateway`'s configuration are similar to those in a `VirtualService`, with a few subtle differences. Distinctively, `Gateway`s do not claim hostnames like `Virtual Services` do. Instead, a `Gateway` *exposes* a name, allowing a `VirtualService` to configure traffic for that name by binding to that `Gateway`. For example, any number of `Gateway`s can exist exposing the name `foo.com`, but a single `VirtualService` must configure traffic for them across all `Gateway`s. The host field of a `Gateway` accepts wildcard hostnames in the same way the `VirtualService` does, but `Gateway`s *do* allow the wildcard hostname "*".

Let's explore a bit, first looking at two `Gateway`s differing in their `hosts` configuration: `foo-gateway` and the `wildcard-gateway` (see gw-examples.yaml (*https://oreil.ly/ AuyOE*) in this book's GitHub repository). First the `foo-gateway` example:

```
apiVersion: networking.istio.io/v1alpha3
kind: Gateway
metadata:
 name: foo-gateway
spec:
 selector:
   app: my-gateway-impl
 servers:
 - hosts:
   - foo.com
   port:
     number: 80
     name: http
     protocol: HTTP
```

And here is the `wildcard-gateway` example:

```
apiVersion: networking.istio.io/v1alpha3
kind: Gateway
metadata:
 name: wildcard-gateway
spec:
```

```
  selector:
    app: my-gateway-impl
  servers:
  - hosts:
    - *.com
    port:
      number: 80
      name: http
      protocol: HTTP
```

Now let's look at how the following VirtualServices bind (or don't bind, as the case may be) to the Gateways (see vs-examples.yaml (*https://oreil.ly/eSWbt*) in the GitHub repository for this book).

The following example binds to "foo-gateway" because the Gateway name in the VirtualService matches, and because the VirtualService claims the host "foo.com" which is exposed by "foo-gateway." So requests to "foo.com" received on port 80 by this Gateway will be routed to port 7777 of the "foo" service in namespace "default."

This also doesn't bind to "wildcard-gateway"; the hosts match but the VirtualService does not list the Gateway "wildcard-gateway" as a target:

```
apiVersion: networking.istio.io/v1alpha3
kind: VirtualService
metadata:
 name: foo-default
spec:
 hosts:
 - foo.com
 gateways:
 - foo-gateway
 http:
 - route:
   - destination:
       host: foo.default.svc.cluster.local
```

The next example binds to "foo-gateway" because the Gateway name in the VirtualService matches, and because the VirtualService claims the host "foo.com" which is exposed by "foo-gateway". Only the name "foo.com" is visible to callers of the Gateway even though the VirtualService claims the name "foo.super.secret.internal.name" too.

Does not bind to "wildcard-gateway": the hosts match but the VirtualService does not list the Gateway "wildcard-gateway" as a target:

```
apiVersion: networking.istio.io/v1alpha3
kind: VirtualService
metadata:
 name: foo-default
spec:
 hosts:
```

```
  - foo.com
  - foo.super.secret.internal.name
 gateways:
 - foo-gateway
 http:
 - route:
    - destination:
        host: foo.default.svc.cluster.local
```

The following example doesn't bind to either `Gateway`: while the `VirtualService` lists both `Gateways`, the hostname the `VirtualService` claims, "foo.super.secret.internal.name", is not exposed by either `Gateway` so they will not accept requests for those names:

```
apiVersion: networking.istio.io/v1alpha3
kind: VirtualService
metadata:
 name: foo-internal
spec:
 hosts:
 - foo.super.secret.internal.name
 gateways:
 - foo-gateway
 - wildcard-gateway
 http:
 - route:
    - destination:
        host: foo.default.svc.cluster.local
```

The final example binds to "foo-gateway" because the `Gateway` name in the `Virtual Service` matches, and because the `VirtualService` claims the host "foo.com" which is exposed by "foo-gateway".

Also, it binds to "wildcard-gateway" because the `Gateway` name in the `VirtualSer vice` matches, and because the `VirtualService` claims the host "foo.com" which is exposed by "wildcard-gateway" (because "foo.com" matches the wildcard "*.com"):

```
apiVersion: networking.istio.io/v1alpha3
kind: VirtualService
metadata:
 name: foo-internal
spec:
 hosts:
 - foo.com
 gateways:
 - foo-gateway
 - wildcard-gateway
 http:
 - route:
    - destination:
        host: foo.default.svc.cluster.local
```

The mesh Gateway

There's a special, implicit `Gateway` in every Istio deployment called the *mesh* `Gateway`. This kind of `Gateway` has workloads that are represented by every service proxy in the mesh and exposes the wildcard host on every port. When a `VirtualService` doesn't list any `Gateways`, it automatically applies to the mesh `Gateway`; that is, all of the sidecars in the mesh. A `VirtualService` always binds to *either* the mesh gateway *or* the gateways listed in its `gateways` field. A common tripping hazard using `VirtualServices` is when we try to update a `VirtualService` being used within the mesh to bind to a specific `Gateway`, displacing the mesh `Gateway`. On pushing that resource, its configuration no longer applies to sidecars, which causes errors. For this kind of update, include the "mesh" gateway specifically in the list of `Gateways` to bind to.

Traffic Steering and Routing

We can use the APIs described earlier in many different ways to affect traffic flow in our deployment. In this section, we cover some of the most common use cases like using `VirtualServices` to make routing decisions based on the following:

- Request attributes like the URI
- Headers
- The request's scheme
- The request's target port

Or, you can use `VirtualServices` to implement *canary* and *blue/green* deployment strategies between services.

How Do You Deploy New Service Versions Safely?

Kubernetes will do a 50/50 traffic split between the old and new versions of your service. Istio service proxy destination rules allow you, as the service operator, to provide granular traffic steering (or you can use environment variables in a VM).

Istio ignores Kubernetes services because these services can implement only round-robin load balancing. When your application tries to do this, it finds two subsets of your service, identified by labels, which you can use to carve up a service. There are a set of environment variables that Istio sends.

Envoy doesn't care whether one subset runs on containers and another on VMs. Content-based traffic steering happens local to Envoy.

Routing with request metadata

One of Istio's most powerful features is its ability to perform traffic routing based on request metadata like the request's URI, its headers, the source or destination IP addresses, and other metadata about the request. The one key limitation is that Istio will not perform routing based on the *body* of the request.

The section "VirtualService" on page 131, earlier in the chapter, extensively covers routing based on URI prefixes extensively. You can perform similar routing on exact URI matches and regexes, as shown in Example 8-21.

Example 8-21. Path-based matching in a VirtualService

```
apiVersion: networking.istio.io/v1alpha3
kind: VirtualService
metadata:
  Name: foo-bars-svc
spec:
  hosts:
  - bar.foo.svc.cluster.local
  http:
  - match:
    - uri:
        exact: "/assets/static/style.css"
    route:
    - destination:
        host: webserver.frontend.svc.cluster.local
  - match:
    - uri:
        # Match requests like "/foo/132:myCustomMethod"
        regex: "/foo/\\d+:myCustomMethod"
    route:
    - destination:
        host: bar.foo.svc.cluster.local
        subset: v3
  - route:
    - destination:
        host: bar.foo.svc.cluster.local
        subset: v2
```

We can also route based on headers or cookie values, as shown in Example 8-22.

Example 8-22. Redirecting requests based on the presence of a value in a cookie

```
apiVersion: networking.istio.io/v1alpha3
kind: VirtualService
metadata:
  Name: dev-webserver
spec:
  hosts:
```

```
    - webserver.company.com
  http:
  - match:
    - headers:
        cookie:
          environment: "dev"
    route:
    - destination:
        host: webserver.dev.svc.cluster.local
  - route:
    - destination:
        host: webserver.prod.svc.cluster.local
```

Of course, Istio supports routing requests for TCP services as well, using L4 request metadata like destination subnet and target port (see Example 8-23). For TLS TCP services, you can use the SNI to perform routing just like the host header in HTTP.

Example 8-23. Directing requests based on L4 information

```
apiVersion: networking.istio.io/v1alpha3
kind: VirtualService
metadata:
  Name: dev-api-server
spec:
  hosts:
  - api.company.com
  tcp:
  - match:
    - port: 9090
      destinationSubnets:
      - 10.128.0.0/16
    route:
    - destination:
        host: database.test.svc.cluster.local
  - match:
    - port: 9090
    route:
    - destination:
        host: database.prod.svc.cluster.local
  tls:
  - match:
    - sniHosts:
      - example.api.company.com
    route:
    - destination:
        host: example.prod.svc.cluster.local
```

See Istio's website (*https://istio.io/*) for a full reference on all available match conditions and their syntax.

Blue/green deployments

In a *blue/green* deployment, two versions, old and new, of an application are deployed side by side, and user traffic is flipped from the old set to the new. This allows for a quick fallback to the previously working version if something goes wrong, because all that's required is reverting user traffic back to the old set from the new (as opposed to a deployment strategy such as a rolling update, in which to roll back to the previous version we must first redeploy the previous version's binary).

Istio's networking APIs make it pretty easy to do blue/green deployments. We declare two *subsets* for our service using a `DestinationRule` and then we use a `VirtualSer vice` to direct traffic to one subset or the other, as shown in Example 8-24.

 Rather than use "blue/green" in our `DestinationRule`, we refer to subsets by the version of the application they represent. This is both easier for developers to understand (because it talks about parts of their service in terms of versions they control) and less prone to errors (avoiding, "Hey, before I deploy, is blue or green the active set?"-type outages). This phrasing also makes it easier to transition to other deployment strategies like canary deployments.

Example 8-24. Defining subsets using a DestinationRule

```
apiVersion: networking.istio.io/v1alpha3
kind: DestinationRule
metadata:
  name: foo-default
spec:
  host: foo.default.svc.cluster.local
  subsets:
  - name: v1
    labels:
      version: v1
  - name: v2
    labels:
      version: v2
```

Then, we can write a `VirtualService` that directs all traffic in the cluster targeting our service to a single subset of the service, as demonstrated in Example 8-25.

Example 8-25. Directing requests based on subset label v1

```
apiVersion: networking.istio.io/v1alpha3
kind: VirtualService
metadata:
  name: foo-blue-green-virtual-service
spec:
  hosts:
```

```
    - foo.default.svc.cluster.local
  http:
  - route:
    - destination:
        host: foo.default.svc.cluster.local
        subset: v1
```

To flip to the other set, you simply update the VirtualService to target subset v2, as shown in Example 8-26.

Example 8-26. Directing requests based on subset label v2

```
apiVersion: networking.istio.io/v1alpha3
kind: VirtualService
metadata:
  name: foo-blue-green-virtual-service
spec:
  hosts:
  - foo.default.svc.cluster.local
  http:
  - route:
    - destination:
        host: foo.default.svc.cluster.local
        subset: v2
```

Of course, you can combine this with Gateways to perform blue/green deployments for users consuming your service via a Gateway in addition to the services in your mesh.

Canary deployments

A *canary* deployment is the practice of sending a small portion of traffic to newly deployed workloads, gradually ramping up until all traffic flows the new workloads. The goal is to verify that a new workload is healthy (up, running, and not returning errors) before sending all traffic to it. It's similar to a blue/green deployment in that it allows a fast fallback to known-healthy workloads, but improves on that method by sending only a portion of traffic, rather than all of it, to the new workloads. Overall, this reduces the amount of *error budget* (a metric allocating a specific amount of service interruption that is allowed within a given time period) that you might spend performing a deployment.

Canary-based deployments also tend to require resource capacity for updates. A true blue/green deployment requires double the resource capacity of a standard deployment (to have both a *full* blue and a *full* green deployment). Canaries can be combined with in-place binary rollout strategies to get the rollback safety of a blue/green deployment while only requiring a constant amount of additional resources (spare capacity to schedule just a small number of additional workloads).

A new workload can be canaried in a variety of ways. You can use the full set of matches outlined in the section "Routing with request metadata" on page 145 to send small portions of traffic to a new backend. However, the simplest canary deployment is a percentage-based traffic split. We can start by sending 5% of traffic to the new version, gradually pushing new `VirtualService` configurations, ramping traffic up to 100% to the new version, as shown in Example 8-27 (see canary-shift.yaml (*https:// oreil.ly/fwGh-*) in the GitHub repository for this book).

Example 8-27. A canary deployment using percentage-based traffic shifting

```
apiVersion: networking.istio.io/v1alpha3
kind: VirtualService
metadata:
  name: foo-canary-virtual-service
spec:
  hosts:
  - foo.default.svc.cluster.local
  tcp:
  - route:
    - destination:
        host: foo.default.svc.cluster.local
        subset: v2
      weight: 5
    - destination:
        host: foo.default.svc.cluster.local
        subset: v1
      weight: 95
```

Another common pattern is to canary a new deployment to a set of trusted test users like the service team itself or a set of customers who have opted into experimental features. You can use Istio to set a "trusted-tester" cookie, for example, which at routing time can divert requests in that specific session to different workloads as opposed to workloads serviced by requests without this cookie, as shown in Example 8-28 (see canary-cookie.yaml (*https://oreil.ly/8mCg9*) in the GitHub repository for this book).

Example 8-28. A canary deployment using a cookie

```
apiVersion: networking.istio.io/v1alpha3
kind: VirtualService
metadata:
  name: foo-canary-virtual-service
spec:
  hosts:
  - foo.default.svc.cluster.local
  http:
  - match:
    - headers:
        cookie:
```

```
        trusted-tester: "true"
  route:
  - destination:
      host: foo.default.svc.cluster.local
      subset: test
- route:
  - destination:
      host: foo.default.svc.cluster.local
      subset: v1
```

Of course, take care when using caller-supplied values (like cookies) to perform routing: ideally all services in your cluster should perform authentication and authorization on all requests. This ensures that even if a caller fakes data to trigger routing behavior, they cannot access data they wouldn't be able to otherwise (and in fact, implementing authentication and authorization via Istio is a powerful way to ensure that all services in your cluster do this correctly).

Resiliency

A resilient system is one that can maintain good performance for its users (i.e., staying within its SLOs) while coping with failures in the downstream systems on which it depends. Istio provides a lot of features to help build more resilient applications; most important being client-side load balancing, circuit breaking via outlier detection, automatic retry, and request timeouts. Istio also provides tools to inject faults into applications, allowing you to build programmatic, reproducible tests of your system's resiliency.

Load-Balancing Strategy

Client-side load balancing is an incredibly valuable tool for building resilient systems. By allowing clients to communicate directly with servers without going through reverse proxies, we remove points of failure while still keeping a well-behaved system. Further, it allows clients to adjust their behavior dynamically based on responses from servers; for example, to stop sending requests to endpoints that return more errors than other endpoints of the same service (we cover this feature, outlier detection, more in the next section). DestinationRules allow you to define the load-balancing strategy clients use to select backends to call. As Example 8-29 shows, we can configure clients to use a simple round-robin load-balancing strategy (see round-robin.yaml (*https://oreil.ly/cQC7Y*) in this book's GitHub repository).

Example 8-29. A simple round-robin load-balancing configuration

```
apiVersion: networking.istio.io/v1alpha3
kind: DestinationRule
metadata:
```

```
  name: foo-default
spec:
  host: foo.default.svc.cluster.local
  trafficPolicy:
    loadBalancer:
      simple: ROUND_ROBIN
```

This `DestinationRule` sends traffic round robin across the endpoints of the service `foo.default.svc.cluster.local`. A `ServiceEntry` defines what those endpoints are (or how to discover them at runtime; e.g., via DNS). It's important to note that a `DestinationRule` applies only to hosts in Istio's service registry. If a `ServiceEntry` does not exist for a host, the `DestinationRule` is ignored.

More complex load-balancing strategies such as consistent hash-based load balancing are also supported. The following `DestinationRule` configures load balancing based on a hash of the caller's IP address (you also can use HTTP headers and cookies with consistent load balancing), as shown in Example 8-30.

Example 8-30. Facilitating sticky sessions based on source IP address

```
apiVersion: networking.istio.io/v1alpha3
kind: DestinationRule
metadata:
  name: foo-default
spec:
  host: foo.default.svc.cluster.local
  trafficPolicy:
    loadBalancer:
      consistentHash:
        useSourceIp: true
```

Outlier Detection

Circuit breaking is a pattern of protecting calls (e.g., network calls to a remote service) behind a "circuit breaker." If the protected call returns too many errors, we "trip" the circuit breaker and return errors to the caller without executing the protected call. This can be used to mitigate several classes of failure, including cascading failures. In load balancing, to "lame-duck" an endpoint is to remove it from the "active" load-balancing set so that no traffic is sent to it for some period of time. Lame-ducking is one method that we can use to implement the circuit-breaker pattern.

Outlier detection is a means of triggering lame-ducking of endpoints that are sending bad responses. We can detect when an individual endpoint is an outlier compared to the rest of the endpoints in our "active" load-balancing set (i.e., returning more errors than other endpoints of the service) and remove the bad endpoint from our "active" load-balancing set, as demonstrated here:

```
apiVersion: networking.istio.io/v1alpha3
kind: DestinationRule
metadata:
  name: foo-default
spec:
  host: foo.default.svc.cluster.local
  trafficPolicy:
    outlierDetection:
      consecutiveErrors: 5
      interval: 1m
      baseEjectionTime: 3m
```

The `DestinationRule` here configures the sidecar to eject any endpoint that has had five consecutive errors from the load-balancing set for at least three minutes. The sidecar scans the set of all endpoints each minute to decide whether any endpoints should be ejected or whether ejected endpoints can be returned back to the load-balancing set. Remember that outlier detection is per client because any server could return bad results to only a specific client (e.g., if there's a network partition between them, but not between the server and its other clients).

Retries

Every system has transient failures: network buffers overflow, a server shutting down drops a request, a downstream system fails, and so on. We use retries—sending the same request to a different endpoint of the same service—to mitigate the impact of transient failures. However, poor retry policies are a frequent secondary cause of outages: "Something went wrong, and client retries made it worse," is a common refrain. Often this is because retries are hardcoded into applications (e.g., as a `for` loop around the network call) and therefore are difficult to change. Istio gives you the ability to configure retries globally for all services in your mesh. More significant, it allows you to control those retry strategies at runtime via configuration, so you can change client behavior on the fly, as shown in the following:

```
apiVersion: networking.istio.io/v1alpha3
kind: VirtualService
metadata:
  name: foo-default
spec:
  hosts:
  - foo.com
  gateways:
  - foo-gateway
  http:
  - route:
    - destination:
        host: foo.default.svc.cluster.local
    retries:
      attempts: 3
      perTryTimeout: 500ms
```

The retry policy defined in a `VirtualService` works in concert with the connection pool settings defined in the destination's `DestinationRule` to control the total number of concurrent outstanding retries to the destination. You can read more about that in the section "DestinationRule" on page 128 earlier in the chapter.

Timeouts

Timeouts are important for building systems with consistent behavior. By attaching deadlines to requests, we're able to abandon requests taking too long and free server resources. We're also able to control our tail latency much more finely, because we know the longest that we'll wait for any particular request in computing our response for a client. You can attach a timeout to any HTTP route in a `VirtualService`, as shown in Example 8-31 (see timeout.yaml (*https://oreil.ly/8A8U6*) in the GitHub repository for this book).

Example 8-31. A simple timeout for a VirtualService

```
apiVersion: networking.istio.io/v1alpha3
kind: VirtualService
metadata:
  name: foo-default
spec:
  hosts:
  - foo.com
  gateways:
  - foo-gateway
  http:
  - route:
    - destination:
        host: foo.default.svc.cluster.local
    timeout: 1s
```

When used with a retry, the timeout represents the total time that the client will spend waiting for a server to return a result. Example 8-32 demonstrates the configuration of a per-try-timeout, which controls the timeout of each individual attempt (see per-try-timeout.yaml (*https://oreil.ly/gzixs*) in the GitHub repository for this book).

Example 8-32. A VirtualService with a timeout per retry configured

```
apiVersion: networking.istio.io/v1alpha3
kind: VirtualService
metadata:
  name: foo-default
spec:
  hosts:
  - foo.com
```

```
gateways:
- foo-gateway
http:
- route:
  - destination:
      host: foo.default.svc.cluster.local
  timeout: 2s
  retries:
    attempts: 3
    perTryTimeout: 500ms
```

The VirtualService in Example 8-32 configures our client to wait at most two seconds, retrying three times, at 500-ms timeouts each. We add in some slack time to allow for randomized waits between retries.

Fault Injection

Fault injection is an incredibly powerful way to test and build reliable distributed applications. Companies like Netflix have taken this to the extreme, coining the term "chaos engineering" to describe the practice of injecting faults into running production systems to ensure that the systems are built to be reliable and tolerant of environmental failures.

Istio allows you to configure faults for HTTP traffic, injecting arbitrary delays or returning specific response codes (e.g., 500) for some percentage of traffic:

```
apiVersion: networking.istio.io/v1alpha3
kind: VirtualService
metadata:
  name: foo-default
spec:
  hosts:
  - foo.default.svc.cluster.local
  http:
  - route:
    - destination:
        host: foo.default.svc.cluster.local
    fault:
      delay:
        fixedDelay: 5s
        percentage: 100
```

For example, the VirtualService in the preceding example injects a five-second delay for all traffic calling the foo service. This is a great way to reliably test things like how a UI behaves on a bad network when its backends are far away. It's also valuable for testing that applications set timeouts on their requests.

Replying to clients with specific response codes, like a 429 or a 500, is also great for testing. For example, it can be challenging to programmatically test how your application behaves when a third-party service that it depends on begins to fail. Using

Istio, you can write a set of reliable end-to-end tests of your application's behavior in the presence of failures of its dependencies, such as the following:

```
apiVersion: networking.istio.io/v1alpha3
kind: VirtualService
metadata:
  name: foo-default
spec:
  hosts:
  - foo.default.svc.cluster.local
  http:
  - route:
    - destination:
        host: foo.default.svc.cluster.local
    fault:
      abort:
        httpStatus: 500
        percentage: 10
```

For example, we can simulate 10% of requests to some backend failing at runtime with a 500 response code.

Ingress and Egress

Gateways represent *network trust boundaries* in a deployment. In other words, we typically use Gateways to model proxies on the edge of the network that control ingress and egress of traffic into and out of the network (in an environment like Kubernetes, which provides a flat network to pods, the network spans the entire cluster). Together, Gateways and VirtualServices can precisely control how traffic enters and exits the mesh. Even better, when Istio is deployed with Policy enabled, you can apply policy to traffic as it enters or leaves the mesh.

Ingress

The section "Gateway" on page 136 earlier in the chapter covers how hostnames are "exposed" over a Gateway by *binding* a VirtualService to that Gateway. After a VirtualService is bound to a Gateway, all of the normal VirtualService functionality we described in the previous sections, such as retries, fault injection, or traffic steering, can be applied to traffic at ingress. In many ways, the ingress Gateway acts as the "external-to-cluster, client-side service proxy."

One thing Istio can't control, though, is how client traffic gets *to* the ingress proxies. A common pattern in Kubernetes environments is to model Istio's ingress proxies as a NodePort service and then let the platform handle provisioning public IP addresses, DNS records, and so on.

Egress

In the same way we think about ingress proxies as a sort of "external-to-cluster, client-side service proxy," egress proxies act as a sort of "internal-to-cluster, server-side service proxy." With a combination of `ServiceEntries`, `DestinationRules`, `VirtualServices`, and `Gateways`, we can trap outbound traffic and redirect it to egress proxies where we're free to apply policy.

Let's an egress `Gateway` example. Here, we assume that Istio has been deployed with `istio-egressgateway.istio-system.svc.cluster.local` as the egress proxy. That in place, we start by modeling the external destination we're trying to reach, for example. Example 8-33 uses *https://wikipedia.org* as a `ServiceEntry` (see se-egress-gw.yaml (*https://oreil.ly/8NYdX*) in this book's GitHub repository).

Example 8-33. A ServiceEntry mapped to an egress Gateway

```
apiVersion: networking.istio.io/v1alpha3
kind: ServiceEntry
metadata:
  name: https-wikipedia-org
spec:
  hosts:
  - wikipedia.org
  ports:
  - number: 443
    name: https
    protocol: HTTPS
  location: MESH_EXTERNAL
  resolution: DNS
  endpoints:
  - address: istio-egressgateway.istio-system.svc.cluster.local
    ports:
      http: 443
```

As shown in Example 8-34, next we can configure an egress `Gateway` to accept traffic for `wikipedia.org` (see egress-gw-wiki.yaml (*https://oreil.ly/_bYos*) in the GitHub repository for this book).

Example 8-34. An egress Gateway configured to accept outbound traffic addressed to wikipedia.org

```
apiVersion: networking.istio.io/v1alpha3
kind: Gateway
metadata:
  name: https-wikipedia-org-egress
spec:
  selector:
    istio: egressgateway
```

```
  servers:
  - port:
      number: 443
      name: https-wikipedia-org-egress-443
      protocol: TLS # Mark as TLS as we are passing HTTPS through.
    hosts:
    - wikipedia.org
    tls:
      mode: PASSTHROUGH
```

We have a problem, though. We want our egress Gateway to use DNS to get an address for wikipedia.org and forward the request, but we've configured all of the proxies in the mesh to resolve wikipedia.org to the egress Gateway (so the proxy will forward the message back to itself, or drop it). To fix this, we need to take advantage of the fact that we can bind VirtualServices to Gateways and route traffic going to wikipedia.org to a fake name we create; for example, egress-wikipedia-org:

```
apiVersion: networking.istio.io/v1alpha3
kind: VirtualService
metadata:
  name: egress-wikipedia-org
spec:
  hosts:
  - wikipedia.org
  gateways:
  - https-wikipedia-org-egress
  tls:
  - match:
    - ports: 443
      sniHosts:
      - wikipedia.org
    route:
    - destination:
        host: egress-wikipedia-org
```

Then, we use a ServiceEntry to resolve egress-wikipedia-org via DNS as wikipedia.org:

```
apiVersion: networking.istio.io/v1alpha3
kind: ServiceEntry
metadata:
  name: egress-https-wikipedia-org
spec:
  hosts:
  - egress-wikipedia-org
  ports:
  - number: 443
    name: https
    protocol: HTTPS
  location: MESH_EXTERNAL
  resolution: DNS
```

```
  endpoints:
  - address: wikipedia.org
    ports:
      http: 443
```

With this in place, we force traffic to an external site through a dedicated egress Gate
way deployment. By default, Istio allows routing of traffic to destinations that do not
have a ServiceEntry. As a security best practice, this default setting should be inver-
ted and services outside of the mesh should explicitly be whitelisted by creating service entries for them. To enable egress to an external service without going through
an egress proxy, just create an identity ServiceEntry for it:

```
apiVersion: networking.istio.io/v1alpha3
kind: ServiceEntry
metadata:
  name: egress-https-wikipedia-org
spec:
  hosts:
  - wikipedia.org
  ports:
  - number: 443
    name: https
    protocol: HTTPS
  location: MESH_EXTERNAL
  resolution: DNS
  endpoints:
  - address: istio-egressgateway.istio-system.svc.cluster.local
    ports:
      http: 443
```

We've seen the full power of Istio's networking APIs, and there are a ton of features—
overwhelmingly so. The important thing to remember is that you can approach
things *incrementally*. Pick one feature that's valuable to you today. Apply a small configuration to your service and get comfortable with it. *Then*, reach for the next feature
that solves your next problem.

CHAPTER 9

Mixer and Policies in the Mesh

Of the various ways in which you can use Mixer, we can divide its responsibilities into two categories: telemetry and policy enforcement. As you look at the APIs that Mixer exposes, these areas of responsibilities become more concretely obvious in that Mixer has two main APIs: check (for precondition tests) and report (for collecting telemetry). Reflecting these two areas of focus is the fact that by default Istio deployments have two Mixer pods running in the control plane—one Mixer pod for telemetry and another for policy enforcement.

Given its role as an aggregation point for telemetry, Mixer is often described as an attribute-processing engine because it ingests telemetric attributes from service proxies and transforms and funnels them to external systems (through adapters). Considering its role as a policy evaluator, Mixer is also described as a (second level) cache in that it responds to requests to check on traffic policy and caches evaluation results. Mixer ingests different configurations from different sources and mingles them together.

Architecture

Residing in the control plane, Mixer liaises between the data plane and the management plane. Contrary to how Mixer appears in Figure 9-1, it is not one single point of failure, because Istio's default configuration includes a set of pod replicas for HA (a HorizontalPodAutoscaler). Mixer is a stateless component, using caching and buffering techniques along with a hardened design with the intention of having 99.999% availability.

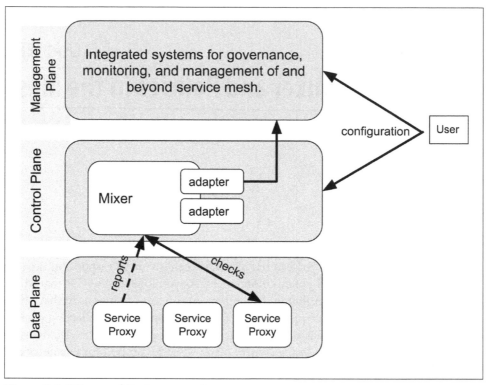

Figure 9-1. Mixer architecture overview

Mixer is referred to as a single entity because even though the API surface is split by responsibility, both functions run the same binary using the same Docker image. They are just provisioned to behave differently based on the function that instance is to handle—*policy* or *telemetry*. Separating into multiple deployments allows for each area of responsibility to scale independently and not have one affecting the performance of the other. The load characteristics of applying policy versus generating telemetry differs and so optimizing their runtime is helpful. In this way, not only can you scale them independently, you can track resource usage terms of how much is dedicated to telemetry versus policy. Not exactly neighbors, these siblings can still be noisy to each other; though it's up to you whether to combine and deploy them as one unit if you desire to optimize resources use based on your environment's load placed on Mixer. You could combine both into a single deployment.

Mixer acts as the central point for telemetry processing, policy evaluation, *and* extensibility. Mixer achieves high extensibility by having a general-purpose plug-in model. Mixer plug-ins are known as *adapters*. Any number of adapters can be running in an Istio deployment. Adapters expand Mixer's two areas of responsibility:

Policy evaluation (checks)
Adapters can add precondition checking (e.g., ACLs, authentication) and quota management (e.g., rate limits).

Telemetry collection (reports)
Adapters can add metrics (e.g., request traffic statistics), logs, and traces (i.e., performance or other context carried across services).

Service proxies interact with Mixer through a client library. Depending on whether Mixer receives request attributes on its check or report API, a decision is to be made about whether a request is authorized to proceed (a precondition check) or whether request attributes are telemetry to be routed for post-request analysis.

Enforcing Policy

The check API exposed by istio-policy handles policies of different types such as that of authentication and quota. Performance and availability of the check API is important when you consider that the check API is consulted inline (synchronously) when the service proxy is processing each request. Based on the request attributes presented, the check API validates whether a given request is in or out of compliance with the active policies configured in Mixer. Ultimately, the Mixer adapters determine whether specific policies' conditions are met. Some adapters validate policy conditions against backend systems, whereas some process checks within the adapter itself (e.g., blacklists, quotas).

> Quotas can be an arbitrary dimension of a request. So, for example, they might enforce a quota by way of rate limiting based on API token or IP address.

As an attribute-processing engine, Mixer transforms attributes into requests to specific backends via adapters, which massage the attributes into a format specific to a backend system for evaluation. Backend systems that adapters can interface with could be a policy engine or API management system, for example. These systems evaluate the check request, responding affirmatively or negatively to the request based on various conditions. There is a growing list of third-party adapters created for Mixer, many times contributed by third parties who represent a specific backend system.

Let's look again at Mixer's architecture, this time in the context of how istio-policy goes about receiving check requests, evaluating policy, and responding with a result. istio-policy exposes a check API with a fixed set of parameters, as shown in Figure 9-2.

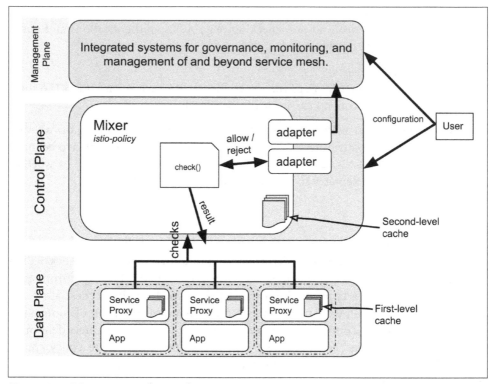

Figure 9-2. Mixer istio-policy architecture overview

Service proxies call Mixer before each request to perform precondition checks and after each request to report telemetry. Check results from Mixer are cached in service proxies. Acting as a first-level cache, service proxies are able to answer a relatively large percentage of precondition checks from their local cache. In turn, as much as anything else, Mixer acts as a cache. The role it plays as a second-level cache for policy results is critical to mitigating the volume of policy check traffic to and evaluation overhead in Mixer.

Well-designed caches are key to enabling conscientiousness to security practices in distributed systems. Ideally, requests between services are authenticated and authorized at every single hop through the chain of upstream services (one request implicating any number of requests to other services in the process of responding to the request). Traditionally, authentication and authorization is performed on the service edge by something like an API gateway. The common pattern is that after a request is authenticated and authorized at the edge, requests to other services in this chain of requests are assumed safe, not subsequently verified.

Ideally, distributed systems have policy applied at every point in the service chain, not just at the edge. This is how we attain consistency of security throughout our distributed system. This presents a real problem to Istio Mixer, our authentication service, however. If every single service is calling Mixer, one request that implicates eight services, for example, means that eight different authorization requests would be sent to Mixer for consideration. Mixer and service proxies need to effectively operate a distributed cache.

Understanding How Mixer Policies Work

You might ask, is policy enforcement enabled? To eliminate unnecessary overhead, the default installation profile for Istio v1.1 and later has policy enforcement disabled by default. Policy is controlled in two places:

- Within Mixer Policy—`mixer.policy.enabled`. By default, this is disabled. Only when it's enabled does the second configuration item take effect.

- Within `global.disablePolicyChecks`—controls whether Mixer policy will be checked. Disables Mixer Policy checks when this configuration item is set to `true`. Pilot will need to be restarted for any changes to this configuration item to take effect.

To install Istio with policy enforcement on, use the `--set global.disablePolicy Checks=false` Helm install option. Or if you have already deployed your Istio service mesh, you might want to first confirm whether policy enforcement is enabled or disabled:

```
$ kubectl -n istio-system get cm istio -o jsonpath="{@.data.mesh}" |
    grep disablePolicyChecks
```

Mixer's configuration describes which adapters are being used and how they operate. Different adapters will map request attributes into adapter inputs based on their specific use cases and backend integration. Each adapter is called with specific inputs.

Reporting Telemetry

Telemetry is generated as and when a request (network traffic) is received by the data plane's service proxies. For each request received, there is an array of metadata that can be captured. This metadata provides context and accountable details of each request and is captured in the form of attributes. Mixer continually receives and processes these request attributes (telemetry). In Figure 9-3, `istio-telemetry` exposes a `report` API with a potentially long list of attributes that varies by adapter.

Reports are generated as Envoy is processing requests and are sent asynchronously to Mixer's `report` API (exposed by `istio-telemetry`) out of band of the request. Envoy buffers outgoing telemetry such that Mixer is called only after having processed many requests (a configurable buffer size). It is within `istio-telemetry` that Mixer synthesizes attributes and pushes to a telemetry backend via one or more adapters.

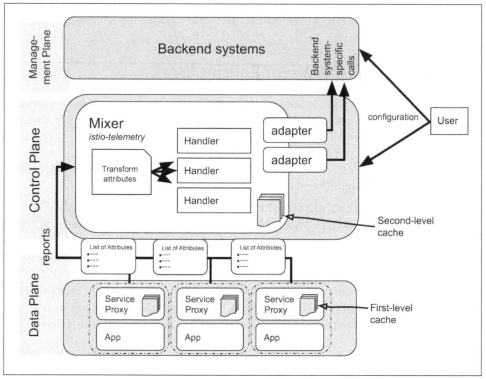

Figure 9-3. Mixer istio-telemetry architecture overview: every individual service proxy has a report buffer where it batches telemetry that it flushes periodically to Mixer's report API.

 In Istio's v1.x architecture, adapters are built into the Mixer binary. Whether they are enabled, though, is configurable.

As noted, telemetry reports are generated as a service proxy processes requests. Requests come in the form of client–server interactions. Consider that requests are created by a client and sent to a service, which in turn can initiate a request (as a client) to another service (server). Both client and server services are capable of sending telemetry reports about any given request that they have handled. The default configuration of Istio releases after version 1.1 is to only have the server send the telemetry report so that only one report will be sent in. This is configurable, however, to the extent that both client and server-side request reports are desired.

Attributes

Attributes are a key concept with Mixer and are essentially collections of typed, name/value tuples. They provide a flexible and extensible mechanism for transferring information from service proxies to Mixer. Attributes can describe request traffic and their context, enabling a mesh operator with granular control in determining what bits of request information should be involved in policy checks and distilled into collected telemetry. Attributes are fundamental to how operators experience Istio, showing up in configuration and logs.

Attribute values are many and varied depending on which adapters are present and enabled. Values can be strings, ints, floats, Bools, timestamps, durations, IP addresses, raw bytes, string maps, and so on. There is an extensible vocabulary of known attributes; Table 9-1 highlights a small sample of the attributes that are sent to Mixer engine at runtime. The complete set of attributes that Istio knows about is fixed at the time of deployment, but versioned from Istio release to release. For an exhaustive list, visit Istio's Attribute Vocabulary page (*https://oreil.ly/zGWf5*).

Table 9-1. Examples of attributes sent to Mixer

Name	Type	Description	Kubernetes example
source.uid	string	Platform-specific unique identifier for the source workload instance.	kubernetes://redis-master-2353460263-1ecey.my-namespace
source.ip	ip_address	Source workload instance IP address.	10.0.0.117
source.labels	map[string, string]	A map of key/value pairs attached to the source instance.	version ≥ v1
source.name	string	Source workload instance name.	redis-master-2353460263-1ecey
source.name space	string	Source workload instance namespace.	my-namespace
source.princi pal	string	Authority under which the source workload instance is running.	service-account-foo
source.owner	string	Reference to the workload controlling the source workload instance.	kubernetes://apis/extensions/v1beta1/namespaces/istio-system/deployments/istio-policy

Sending Reports

Service proxies send information to Mixer about requests and responses in the form of attributes (typed key/value pairs). Mixer transforms attribute sets into structured values, according to an operator-supplied configuration. Mixer dispatches the derived values to a set of adapters, according to the operator-supplied configuration. Adapters publish telemetry data to backend systems, making it available for further consumption and analysis. Attributes are primarily generated by service proxies; however, Mixer adapters also can produce attributes.

Checking Caches

After Mixer makes an initial policy verdict, the attribute protocol comes into play. Envoy and Mixer use well-known attributes to describe the policy used to evaluate service requests. When Mixer makes a verdict on a request, it computes a hash key using these attributes. Envoy uses these same attributes, reducing the overhead on request latencies since both Mixer and Envoy operate as caches once verdicts are delivered. Mixer creates a hash key using the attribute keys. A goal of Envoy's configuration is to strike the balance of cache hits with superfluous sets of hash keys.

Check caches include a TTL value indicating the maximum amount of time a cached check result should be trusted. Caches need to be refreshed as Mixer's configuration is bound to change over time, or in turn, backend that Mixer consults when deciding a check result may equally as likely change and cause service proxies to need their check cache refreshed. Again, in this way, the service proxies function as first-level caches and Mixer functions as a second-level shared cache.

Adapters

In Istio's v1.x architecture, adapters are built into the Mixer binary. Whether they are enabled, though, is configurable. Istio Mixer configuration activates adapters. The only penalty paid for inactive adapters is for the footprint of the adapter bits. Multiple adapters of the same or different type can be running simultaneously. Adapters can be chained so that policy can be defined across them. You can compile your own Mixer with your own adapters. Currently, Mixer architecture accounts for in-process adapters, although, a gRPC interface for out-of-process adapters has been released in alpha in v1.0.

Adapters enable Mixer to expose a single consistent API, independent of the infrastructure backends in use. Most adapters consult external, remote backends, whereas others are self-contained, providing functionality entirely within Mixer (also known as *baby backends*). Baby backends are configured in Istio via adapter-level configuration. As an example, the list adapter provides simple whitelist or blacklist checks. You can configure List adapters directly with the list to check or you can provide them with a URL (could be a filepath) from which the list should be fetched. Lists are checked at runtime matching lists of strings, IP addresses, or regular expression (regex) patterns inclusively or exclusively.

In-Process Adapters

In-process adapters are written in Go and compiled into the Mixer process. Again, whether the adapter is implicated based on whether they are configured to be enacted through a handler, instance, and rule(s). Each of the adapters that follow is built into the Mixer binary, hence each Istio release:

Precondition checks
    denier, listchecker, memquota, opa, rbac, redisquota

Telemetry
    circonus, cloudwatch, dogstatsd, fluentd, prometheus, solarwinds, stack
    driver, statsd, stdio

Attribute generation
    kubernetesenv

To create a new in-process adapter, vendors implement a set of Golang interfaces and submit their adapter for review and consideration of inclusion in the Istio project.

Out-of-Process Adapters

Adapters were initially built into the main as in-process adapters but are moving to an out-of-process model in which adapter code isn't kept in the Istio project, but kept and managed separately with the vendor. Out-of-process adapters interface via a gRPC service that implements template infrastructure backend protocol and runs outside the Mixer process (can be coprocess adapter or backend service). In moving to an out-of-process adapter model, Istio eliminates the need for custom Mixer builds to include or exclude specific adapters. Adapter authors are empowered to write their adapters in the language of their choice given the abstraction through gRPC. In moving to an out-of-process model, no longer will Mixer share a common fate with its adapters, which will run independently in their own process(es).

Creating a Mixer Policy and Using Adapters

As an operator, the sequence of steps undertaken to apply policy to Istio flows like so:

* Apply policy to Kubernetes. Policies go into kube-api server.
* Galley will pull them and either:
  — Push them to Pilot to realize them as an Envoy configuration, or
  — Push them to Mixer to prepare its dynamic dispatch in preparation for service proxies calling in to retrieve and implement these policies

---

Istio configuration lives in the Kubernetes API server. From Mixer's perspective, the Kubernetes API server is the configuration database. From Pilot's perspective, it's the service discovery mechanism. That the same source of truth is referenced for both configuration and service discovery is merely an artifact of Kubernetes, not an Istio requirement that these be one-and-the-same source. Istio can just the same use Consul as service discovery and kube-api server for configuration database.

Mixer Configuration

Service operators control all operational and policy aspects of a Mixer deployment by manipulating configuration resources. Configuring Mixer includes describing which adapters are to be used, how they should operate, which request attributes to map to which adapter's inputs, and when a particular adapter is invoked with specific inputs. Mixer configuration is manipulated and represented through Kubernetes custom resources—rules, handlers, instances, and adapters.

adapters encapsulate the logic necessary to interface with backends. Adapter configuration schema is specified by adapter packages. Configuration contains operational parameters needed by the adapter code to do work. A handler is an instantiation of an adapter—a configured adapter. Handlers can receive data (attributes). An instance is an object full of request data. Instances are a set of structured request attributes with well-known fields. Instances map request attributes to values that are passed to adapter code. Attribute mapping is controlled via attribute expressions.

As an example of an attribute expression, consider the Prometheus instance for requestduration in Example 9-1. In this example, requestduration is configured to return a response.code of 200 in the absence of a response.code. If destination.service isn't present, the report will simply fail.

Example 9-1. Prometheus instance example

```
$ kubectl -n istio-system get metrics requestduration -o yaml
apiVersion: config.istio.io/v1alpha2
kind: metric
metadata:
  name: requestduration
  namespace: istio-system
spec:
  dimensions:
    destination_app: destination.labels["app"] | "unknown"
    destination_principal: destination.principal | "unknown"
    destination_service: destination.service.host | "unknown"
    destination_service_name: destination.service.name | "unknown"
    request_protocol: api.protocol | context.protocol | "unknown"
    response_code: response.code | 200
...
```

Rules specify when a particular `handler` is invoked with a specific `instance`, and map handlers and instances to each other. Rules essentially enforce that when a given condition is true, it's given a particular `handler` specific `instances` (request attributes).

Rules contain a match predicate attribute expression and a list of actions to perform if the predicate evaluates to true. Rules evaluate to true for all requests if a match isn't specified. This behavior is valuable when accounting for quota enforcement, as demonstrated in Example 9-2, in this rule snippet for a `memquota` adapter (a *precondition check* type adapter). In the following example, a rule with no match condition perpetually evaluates to true each time it is evaluated, and therefore, increments the `requestcount.quota`:

Example 9-2. A rule with no match condition

```
...
spec:
  actions:
  - handler: handler.memquota
    instances:
    - requestcount.quota
...
```

Open Policy Agent Adapter

The Open Policy Agent (OPA) is a general-purpose policy engine used to offload authorization decisions. OPA uses Rego as its declarative policy language. It is implemented in Go and can be deployed as a library or as a daemon.

Mixer's OPA adapter is a *check* type adapter. The Mixer security model for *check* type adapters is to fail closed to ensure security is maintained. Any random policy that you can do with OPA, you can do with the OPA Mixer adapter. The adapter bundles up the OPA runtime. Attributes get fed to the Rego language engine for processing by what is a full OPA instance in the adapter.

Consider this example set of configurations for an OPA adapter's rule, handler, and instance, as presented in Examples 9-3 through 9-5.

Example 9-3. Sample OPA rule configuration

```
apiVersion: config.istio.io/v1alpha2
kind: rule
metadata:
  name: authz
spec:
  actions:
  - handler: opa-handler
```

```
    instances:
    - authz-instance
```

Example 9-4. Sample OPA instance configuration

```
apiVersion: config.istio/v1alpha2
kind: authz
metadata:
  name: authz-instance
spec:
  subject:
    user: source.uid | ""
  action:
    namespace: target.namespace | "default"
    service: target.service | ""
    path: target.path | ""
    method: request.method | ""
```

Example 9-5. Sample OPA handler configuration

```
apiVersion: config.istio.io/v1alpha2
kind: opa
metadata:
  name: opa-handler
spec:
  checkMethod: authz.allow
  policy: |
    package authz
    default allow = false
    allow { is_read }
    is_read { input.action.method = "GET" }
```

Which Policies Come from Pilot and Which Go Through Mixer?

Policies that affect traffic are defined in Pilot. Policies that call for enforcement of authentication and authorization on the request go through Mixer. If a policy needs to consult an external system to make a decision, it goes through Mixer.

Prometheus Adapter

The Prometheus adapter is built into the Mixer binary and enabled by default with a metrics expiration duration of 10 minutes. The Prometheus adapter defines a custom resource; *metrics*, as shown in Example 9-6.

Example 9-6. List of metrics tracked on Istio components made available to Prometheus

```
$ kubectl -n istio-system get metrics
NAME                      AGE
```

```
requestcount            25h
requestduration         25h
requestsize             25h
responsesize            25h
tcpbytereceived         25h
tcpbytesent             25h
tcpconnectionsclosed    25h
tcpconnectionsopened    25h
```

The Prometheus handler needs to know the specific dimensions and type of metrics. This is called an `instance` in general, but there are a few special `instances` that have a proper name; `metric` is one of those. Typically, an adapter is built to expect certain instances. We can see in Example 9-7 the set of instances that the Prometheus adapter consumes.

Example 9-7. Example set of instances that the Prometheus adapter consumes

```
$ kubectl -n istio-system get metrics tcpbytereceived -o yaml

apiVersion: config.istio.io/v1alpha2
kind: metric
metadata:
  labels:
    app: mixer
    release: istio
  name: tcpbytereceived
  namespace: istio-system
spec:
  dimensions:
    connection_security_policy: conditional((context.reporter.kind | "inbound") ==
      "outbound", "unknown", conditional(connection.mtls | false, "mutual_tls",
      "none"))
    destination_app: destination.labels["app"] | "unknown"
    destination_principal: destination.principal | "unknown"
    destination_service: destination.service.host | "unknown"
    destination_service_name: destination.service.name | "unknown"
    destination_service_namespace: destination.service.namespace | "unknown"
    destination_version: destination.labels["version"] | "unknown"
    destination_workload: destination.workload.name | "unknown"
    destination_workload_namespace: destination.workload.namespace | "unknown"
    reporter: conditional((context.reporter.kind | "inbound") == "outbound",
      "source", "destination")
    response_flags: context.proxy_error_code | "-"
    source_app: source.labels["app"] | "unknown"
    source_principal: source.principal | "unknown"
    source_version: source.labels["version"] | "unknown"
    source_workload: source.workload.name | "unknown"
    source_workload_namespace: source.workload.namespace | "unknown"
  monitored_resource_type: '"UNSPECIFIED"'
  value: connection.received.bytes | 0
```

Mixer needs to know when to generate this metric data and send it to Prometheus. This is defined as a rule. Every rule has a match condition that is evaluated; if the match is true, the rule is triggered. For example, we could use the match to receive only HTTP data, only TCP data, and so on. Prometheus does exactly this, as shown in Example 9-8, and defines a rule for each set of protocols for which it has metric descriptions.

Example 9-8. List of Mixer rules

```
$ kubectl -n istio-system get rules
NAME                      AGE
kubeattrgenrulerule       25h
promhttp                  25h
promtcp                   25h
promtcpconnectionclosed   25h
promtcpconnectionopen     25h
stdio                     25h
stdiotcp                  25h
tcpkubeattrgenrulerule    25h
```

And, again, let's inspect one to see what it looks like:

```
$ kubectl -n istio-system get rules promtcpconnectionopen -o yaml

apiVersion: config.istio.io/v1alpha2
kind: rule
metadata:
  annotations:
  ...
  generation: 1
  name: promtcpconnectionopen
  namespace: istio-system
spec:
  actions:
  - handler: prometheus
    instances:
    - tcpconnectionsopened.metric
    match: context.protocol == "tcp" && ((connection.event | "na") == "open")
```

In Chapter 10, all of these metrics are exposed to backends for analysis, visualization, alerting and so on.

Mixer: A Design Under Revision

The Mixer v1 architecture's strengths are its flexible adapter model, powerful capabilities, and the fact that it isolates the mesh from backend details and backend failures. The v1 architecture acts as a second-level cache for precondition check results. Despite arguments that Mixer increases your SLOs by enabling higher mesh availability and reduces latency through aggressive use of shared multilevel caches, some

---

believe it falls short, however. Doubts have been cast over the management overhead involved, request latency overhead incurred, and concerns over being a single point of failure. Its ease of use has been questioned as well. From early in the project (v0.3) maintainers have identified these concerns and spoken to them (*https://oreil.ly/ BQexz*).

Still to be determined, is if Mixer's v2 architecture is positioned to move much of Mixer's functionality into Envoy filters, which are generally written in C++. However, an HTTP Lua filter is available to allow Lua scripts to be run (using LuaJIT) during request and response flows. Filters can be written in other languages through gRPC extensions.

As our multiple personality control-plane component, Mixer enables service operator control over policy decisions and telemetry dispatch based on configuration and acts as the point of integration between Istio and infrastructure backends. Through two services (`istio-policy` and `istio-telemetry`), Mixer provides the following core features:

- Precondition checking (ACLs, authentication)
- Quota management (rate limits)
- Telemetry reporting (metrics, logs, traces)

Mixer's performance overhead can be quite high depending on how you configure your Istio deployment. Mixer provides aggressive caching and reduces observed latencies, and offers mediation for service operators to control policy enforcement and telemetry collection. With its backend abstractions, it reduces systemic complexity and the adapter model enables backend mobility.

## CHAPTER 10

Telemetry

Critical to running microservices is the ability to reason over their behavior. Not only does this include the triumvirate of logs, metrics, and traces, but critically needed visualization, troubleshooting, and debugging, as well. In Chapter 2, we covered how service meshes, in general, and Istio, specifically, provide for uniform observability. In this chapter, we survey specifics of the various signals and tools available to monitor services running on Istio. We discuss troubleshooting and debugging in Chapter 11.

Mixer (described in Chapter 9) plays a key role in collecting and coalescing telemetry generated by service proxies. Service proxies generate telemetry at runtime based on traffic they process, and buffer this telemetry before flushing it to Mixer for further processing. Half of Mixer's job is amassing, translating, and transmitting these important signals (the other half being authorization). Routing of these various signals is entirely dependent on which and what type of adapters that Mixer is running. Let's dig into Mixer's adapters.

 As mentioned in Chapter 4, Bookinfo is Istio's canonical sample application, and we use it as the example application throughout this chapter.

Adapter Models

As described in Chapter 9, adapters integrate Mixer with different infrastructure backends that deliver core functionality, such as logging, monitoring, quotas, access control list checking, and more. Operators have a choice of the number and type of adapters deployed, opting for those that integrate with existing backends or those that provide value unto their own. Mixer supports have multiple of the same type simultaneously enabled (e.g., two logging adapters to send logs to two different backends). There is a special case of attribute-producing adapters that always run first before either telemetry or policy adapters. The kubernetesenv is the most prominent example of one of these types. It extracts information from a Kubernetes environment and produces attributes that can be used in downstream adapters.

Telemetry adapters also execute in parallel. There's a bit more complexity with regard to batching, but logically, Mixer dispatches adapter calls in parallel and waits for them to complete. Two of the same types of adapters can be deployed at the same time.

Reporting Telemetry

As a refresher from Chapter 2, Istio supports three forms of telemetry (metrics, logs, traces), which can transmit a diverse set of insights between them. Telemetry is reported from the data plane to the control plane. Service proxy reports contain *attributes* (see Chapter 9 for more on attributes). Context attributes provide the ability to distinguish between HTTP and TCP protocols within policies.

As attributes are generated by service proxies, telemetry reports are sent at three different points in time:

- When the connection is established (initial report)
- Periodically, while the connection is alive (periodical report)
- When the connection is closed (final report)

The default interval for periodical reports is 10 seconds. It's recommended that this interval should not be in subseconds.

Metrics

Service metrics are collected by the sidecar service proxies that send telemetry reports to the istio-telemetry Mixer service. Mixer has any number and type of adapters loaded. A Mixer adapter based on the metric adapter template can be used to collect and process metrics forwarded to it by Mixer. Let's walk through how adapters are configured in general and then use the Prometheus Mixer adapter as an example.

Configuring Mixer to Collect Metrics

Telemetry (and policy) is configured using three types of resources:

Handlers
    These determine the set of adapters that are being used and how they operate. Providing a logging adapter with the IP address for the remote syslog server is an example of handler configuration.

Instances

These describe how to map request attributes (generated by the service proxy) to adapter inputs (where an adapter will receive the generated telemetry). Instances represent a chunk of data on which one or more adapters will operate. For example, an operator might decide to generate `request_bytes` metric instances from an attribute such as `destination_workload`.

Rules

These identify when a specific adapter is invoked and which instances it is given (what telemetry is funneled to it). Rules consist of a match expression and actions. The match expression controls when to invoke an adapter, whereas the actions determine the set of instances to give the adapter.

To use the Prometheus Mixer adapter, we need to have a Prometheus server deployed either on the same Kubernetes cluster or elsewhere that is capable of scraping metrics from the Prometheus Mixer adapter. There are many ways to deploy Prometheus, either on Kubernetes or outside, the details of which are beyond the scope of this book.

Setting Up Metrics Collection and Querying for Metrics

To configure and use the Prometheus Mixer adapter, we need to do the following:

1. Create a `metric` instance that configures metrics that Istio will generate and collect, and configure a Prometheus handler to collect the metrics, assign appropriate labels, and make it available for a Prometheus instance to scrape, as shown in Example 10-1 (network traffic; see the full configuration in this section (*https:// oreil.ly/GcDZ5*) of this book's GitHub repository).

Example 10-1. Step 1: An excerpt from the Prometheus handler and the requests_total metric it tracks across various labels

```
apiVersion: "config.istio.io/v1alpha2"
kind: handler
metadata:
  name: prometheus
  namespace: istio-system
spec:
  compiledAdapter: prometheus
  params:
    metrics:
    - name: requests_total
      instance_name: requestcount.metric.istio-system
      kind: COUNTER
      label_names:2
      - reporter
```

```
       - source_app
       - source_namespace
       - source_principal
       - source_workload
       - source_workload_namespace
       - source_version
       - destination_app
       - destination_namespace
       - destination_principal
       - destination_workload
       - destination_workload_namespace
       - destination_version
       - destination_service
       - destination_service_name
       - destination_service_namespace
       - request_protocol
       - response_code
       - connection_mtls
```

2. Update Prometheus to scrape metrics from the Prometheus Mixer adapter, and create Istio `rules` that will forward the metrics collected by Istio Mixer to the Prometheus Mixer adapter with the configured labels, as demonstrated in Example 10-2.

Example 10-2. Step 2: A rule to match HTTP traffic and take action to forward metrics to the Prometheus handler

```
apiVersion: "config.istio.io/v1alpha2"
kind: rule
metadata:
 name: promhttp
 namespace: istio-system
 labels:
   app: mixer
   chart: mixer
   heritage: Tiller
   release: istio
spec:
 match: (context.protocol == "http" || context.protocol == "grpc") &&
        (match((request.useragent | "-"), "kube-probe*") == false)
 actions:
 - handler: prometheus
   instances:
   - requestcount.metric
   - requestduration.metric
   - requestsize.metric
   - responsesize.metric
```

Traces

Distributed traces are arguably the most insightful of the telemetry information gleaned from the service mesh, giving you insight into difficult-to-answer questions like "Why is my service slow?" Zipkin and Jaeger are both bundled into Istio releases and available as popular, open source distributed tracing systems for storing, aggregating, and interpreting trace data.

Generating trace spans

The Istio service proxy, Envoy, is responsible for generating the initial trace headers and doing so in an OpenTelemetry–compatible way. OpenTelemetry (formerly an OpenTracing–compatible way) is a language-neutral specification for distributed tracing. The `x-request-id` header is generated and used by Envoy to uniquely identify a request as well as perform stable access logging and tracing. Envoy propagates the `x-request-id` to all the services the request interacts with and incorporates the unique request ID into log messages it generates, as well. Thus, if you search for the unique `request-id` in a system like Kibana, you will see logs from all the services for that particular request.

Propagating trace headers

This is one area where Istio's capabilities might be oversold. The service proxy is a sidecar to your application, and so has a lot of context about the requests coming in and out of your application. Because of this, it doesn't have what it needs to eliminate the need for the application to be completely freed of the responsibility of instrumentation. Your application requires a thin-client library to collect and propagate a small set of HTTP headers, including the following:

- `x-request-id`
- `x-b3-traceid`
- `x-b3-spanid`
- `x-b3-parentspanid`
- `x-b3-sampled`
- `x-b3-flags`
- `x-ot-span-context`

Each service in our sample application, Bookinfo, is instrumented to propagate these HTTP trace headers. As such, we need to be able to use Jaeger (for example) as a distributed tracing system to explore latencies between and within the various "hops" in our application requests. Example 10-3 presents a simple Go program with an A function to listen to HTTP requests, extract the trace headers, and print them to stdout (see the example code (*https://oreil.ly/zg-4Q*) for this, available in this book's GitHub repository).

Example 10-3. A simple Go program to print trace headers

```go
package main

import (
    "fmt"
    "log"
    "net/http"
)

func tracingMiddleware(next http.HandlerFunc) http.HandlerFunc {
    incomingHeaders := []string{
        "x-request-id",
        "x-b3-traceid",
        "x-b3-spanid",
        "x-b3-parentspanid",
        "x-b3-sampled",
        "x-b3-flags",
        "x-ot-span-context",
    }

    return func(w http.ResponseWriter, r *http.Request) {
        for _, th := range incomingHeaders {
            w.Header().Set(th, r.Header.Get(th))
        }
        next.ServeHTTP(w, r)
    }
}

func main() {
    http.HandleFunc("/", tracingMiddleware(func(w http.ResponseWriter,
                        r *http.Request) {
        fmt.Fprintf(w, "Hello headers, %v", r.Header)
    }))

    log.Fatal(http.ListenAndServe(":8081", nil))
}
```

Disabling Tracing

The sampling of request traces does incur cost in terms of performance overhead. As shown by Meshery (*https://oreil.ly/WsTUW*) in Figure 10-1, there is a significant difference between sampling traces at a rate of 1% versus a rate of 100%.

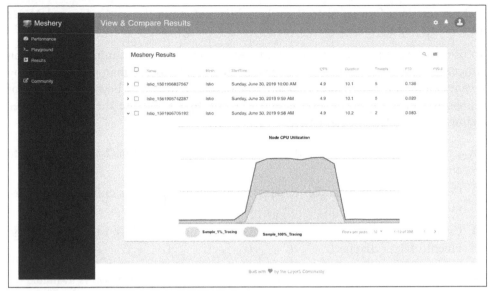

Figure 10-1. The difference in average node CPU use between two performance tests

The simplest way to run your Istio mesh without tracing being enabled at all is to not enable it when installing the service mesh. Thus, your Helm chart looks like the following:

```
--set tracing.enabled=false
```

The `default` and `minimal` Istio configuration profiles don't enable tracing when installing Istio. If you deployed with tracing on and now wish to disable tracing, assuming that your control plane is installed in the `istio-system` namespace, run the following:

```
$TRACING_POD=`kubectl get po -n <istio namespace> | grep istio-tracing
              | awk `{print $1}`
$ kubectl delete pod $TRACING_POD -n <istio namespace>
$ kubectl delete services tracing zipkin   -n <istio namespace>
```

Remove references of the Zipkin URL from the Mixer deployment:

```
$ kubectl -n istio-system edit deployment istio-telemetry
```

Now, manually remove instances of `trace_zipkin_url` from the file and save it.

Logs

Service access logs are crucial in recording particulars of service access information. Mixer's native `logentry` adapter is a foundational adapter. You can use community-contributed Mixer adapters based on the `logentry` Mixer adapter template to collect and process logs forwarded to it by Istio Mixer. Among those, the Fluentd Mixer adapter is a popular choice.

To use the Fluentd adapter, we need a Fluentd daemon to be running and listening either on the same Kubernetes cluster or elsewhere. (There are many ways to deploy Fluentd either on Kubernetes or outside, the details of which are beyond the scope of this book.) As with other Mixer adapters, to configure and use the Fluentd Mixer adapter, we need to do the following:

1. Create a `logentry` instance that configures a log stream that Istio will generate and collect.

2. Configure a Fluentd handler to pass the collected logs to a listening Fluentd daemon.

3. Create an Istio rule that forwards the log stream collected by Istio Mixer to the Fluentd Mixer adapter.

The sample configuration in Example 10-4 assumes a fluentd daemon is available on `localhost:24224`.

Example 10-4. A logging Mixer adapter configuration

```
apiVersion: "config.istio.io/v1alpha2"
kind: logentry
metadata:
  name: istiolog
  namespace: istio-system
spec:
  severity: '"warning"'
  timestamp: request.time
  variables:
    source: source.labels["app"] | source.service | "unknown"
    user: source.user | "unknown"
    destination: destination.labels["app"] | destination.service | "unknown"
    responseCode: response.code | 0
    responseSize: response.size | 0
    latency: response.duration | "0ms"
  monitored_resource_type: '"UNSPECIFIED"'
---
# Configuration for a fluentd handler
apiVersion: "config.istio.io/v1alpha2"
kind: fluentd
metadata:
  name: handler
  namespace: istio-system
spec:
  address: "localhost:24224"
  integerDuration: n
---
```

```
# Rule to send logentry instances to the fluentd handler
apiVersion: "config.istio.io/v1alpha2"
kind: rule
metadata:
  name: istiologtofluentd
  namespace: istio-system
spec:
  match: "true" # Match for all requests
  actions:
   - handler: handler.fluentd
     instances:
     - istiolog.logentry
```

This global default logging level is set to "Info," but you can set the desired severity level in the configuration for instances. Beyond severity levels, you can configure match conditions to log only when requests don't complete successfully. For non-200 responses, you could edit the match condition, as demonstrated in Example 10-5.

Example 10-5. An example of configuration matching

```
apiVersion: "config.istio.io/v1alpha2"
kind: instance
metadata:
  name: requestcount
  namespace: {{ .Release.Namespace }}
  labels:
    app: {{ template "mixer.name" . }}
    chart: {{ template "mixer.chart" . }}
    heritage: {{ .Release.Service }}
    release: {{ .Release.Name }}
spec:
  compiledTemplate: metric
  params:
    value: "1"
    dimensions:
      reporter: conditional((context.reporter.kind | "inbound") == "outbound",
          "source", "destination")
      source_workload: source.workload.name | "unknown"
      source_workload_namespace: source.workload.namespace | "unknown"
      source_principal: source.principal | "unknown"
      source_app: source.labels["app"] | "unknown"
      source_version: source.labels["version"] | "unknown"
      destination_workload: destination.workload.name | "unknown"
      destination_workload_namespace: destination.workload.namespace | "unknown"
      destination_principal: destination.principal | "unknown"
      destination_app: destination.labels["app"] | "unknown"
      destination_version: destination.labels["version"] | "unknown"
      destination_service: destination.service.host | "unknown"
      destination_service_name: destination.service.name | "unknown"
      destination_service_namespace: destination.service.namespace | "unknown"
      request_protocol: api.protocol | context.protocol | "unknown"
```

```
response_code: response.code | 200
response_flags: context.proxy_error_code | "-"
permissive_response_code: rbac.permissive.response_code | "none"
permissive_response_policyid: rbac.permissive.effective_policy_id | "none"
connection_security_policy: conditional((context.reporter.kind | "inbound")
    == "outbound", "unknown", conditional(connection.mtls | false,
    "mutual_tls", "none"))
monitored_resource_type: '"UNSPECIFIED"'
```

 Istio has tentatively started adding sampling support (and experimented with things like errors-only logging), but we haven't turned that into any real recommendation at this point. This is an action item for a future release, it seems.

Metrics

Top-line service performance is easily gleaned from the metrics visualized through charting and dashboarding tools. Grafana is a popular, open source metrics visualization tool used to query, analyze, and alert on metrics. Grafana is not deployed as a Mixer adapter, but is included in the default Istio deployment as an add-on and is configured to read metrics from Prometheus. Prometheus is a time-series database and collection toolkit. The Istio deployment of Grafana comes with predefined dashboards. Metrics shown in the Istio dashboards in Grafana are dependent upon Prometheus running in the environment. Here are some of the items that packaged dashboards include:

Mesh Summary View
> Provides global summary view of the service mesh and shows HTTP/gRPC and TCP workloads.

Individual Services View
> Provides metrics about requests and responses for each individual service within the mesh (HTTP/gRPC and TCP). Also, gives metrics about client and service workloads for this service.

Individual Workloads View
> Provides metrics about requests and responses for each individual workload within the mesh (HTTP/gRPC and TCP). Also, gives metrics about inbound workloads and outbound services for this workload.

Visualization

As one of the more insightful telemetric capabilities (a little like taking the blinders off), topology visualization is a key aspect to understanding your deployment. Formerly, Istio had a rudimentary solution for this need called ServiceGraph, which exposed the following endpoints:

- */force/forcegraph.html*, an interactive *D3.js* visualization
- */dotviz*, a static Graphviz visualization
- */dotgraph*, a DOT serialization
- */d3graph*, a JSON serialization for D3 visualization
- */graph*, a generic JSON serialization

ServiceGraph has been replaced by Kiali (*https://www.kiali.io*), installed as an add-on and used in the web-based GUI to view service graphs of the mesh and your Istio configuration objects. Focused on real-time traffic flow, Vistio (*https://oreil.ly/YpvqZ*) is another application that helps you visualize the traffic of your cluster from Prometheus data.

Service meshes are uniquely positioned as a foundational component in the buildout of an observable system. Data-plane proxies sit in the request path and can observe important qualities of the system and report on them. There's a cost to telemetry, so weigh the trade-off. Projects like Kiali Istio help visualize either configuration or traffic flows through Istio.

## CHAPTER 11

Debugging Istio

Like any other software, operating Istio can mean troubleshooting and debugging from time to time. Istio and other open source tooling provides logging, introspection, and debugging to assist in component management.

Introspecting Istio Components

Istio components have been designed to incorporate a common introspection package called ControlZ (ctrlz (*https://oreil.ly/9yY2K*)). ControlZ is a flexible introspection framework that makes it easy to inspect and manipulate the internal state of a running Istio component. ControlZ offers an administrative UI, to which components provide access by opening a port (9876 by default) that can be accessed from a web browser or via REST for access and control from external tools. The simple UI of the ControlZ introspection framework gives an interactive view into the state of the Istio component.

Mixer, Pilot, Citadel, and Galley are built with the `ctlz` package included, whereas gateways are not. Gateways do not implement the ControlZ administrative UI, because these are Envoy instances that instead implement Envoy's administrative console. When Mixer, Pilot, Citadel, and Galley components start, a message is logged indicating the IP address and port to connect to in order to interact with ControlZ. ControlZ is designed around the idea of "topics." A topic corresponds to the different sections of the UI. There are a set of built-in topics representing the core introspection functionality, and each control-plane component that uses ControlZ can add new topics specialized for their purpose.

By default, ControlZ runs on port 9876. You can override this default port by using the `--ctrlz_port` and `--ctrlz_address` command-line options when starting a component to control the specific address and port where ControlZ will be exposed.

To access the ControlZ interface of one of the control-plane components, use kubectl to port forward from your localhost to the remote ControlZ port.

```
$ kubectl port-forward -n istio-system istio-pilot-74cb7cd5f9-lbndc 9876:9876
```

Open your browser to http://localhost:9876 to remotely access ControlZ, as illustrated in Figure 11-1.

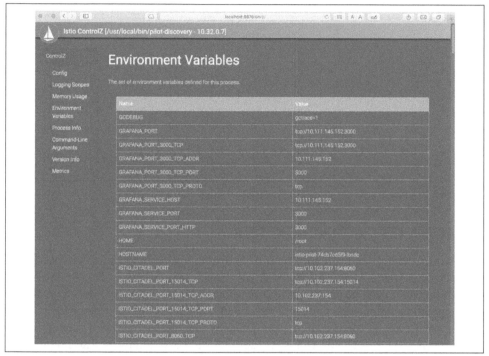

Figure 11-1. ControlZ introspection of Pilot

ControlZ implements Istio's introspection facility. As components integrate with ControlZ, they automatically gain an IP port that allows operators to visualize and control a number of aspects of each process, including controlling logging scopes, viewing command-line options, memory use, and more. Additionally, the port implements a REST API allowing access and control over the same state.

The ControlZ administrative interface is primarily useful for enabling more detailed logs during troubleshooting. Other tools, like the management-plane Meshery, are commonly used as a more capable point of control for managing Istio's life cycle and workloads on the mesh. Let's walk through a management-plane example.

Troubleshooting with a Management Plane

Recall from Chapter 1 that the management plane resides a level above the control plane and operates across multiple homogeneous and heterogeneous service mesh clusters. Among other uses, a management plane can perform workload and mesh configuration validation—whether in preparation for onboarding a workload onto the mesh or in continuously vetting their configuration as you update to new versions of components running your control and data planes or new versions of your applications. Let's walk through a vetting exercise to run a series of checks against your existing workload configuration (and your service mesh configuration). To do so, install and start Meshery (*https://oreil.ly/xubaa*) by downloading its CLI management tool, mesheryctl, using the commands shown in Example 11-1.

Example 11-1. Steps to locally installing the Meshery management plane

```
$ sudo curl -L https://git.io/mesheryctl -o /usr/local/bin/mesheryctl
$ sudo chmod a+x /usr/local/bin/mesheryctl
$ mesheryctl start
```

For ongoing validation of your configuration, install Meshery in your cluster(s). If the Meshery UI doesn't load automatically, open it at http://localhost:9081. Depending on your environment, Meshery will automatically connect your cluster(s), analyze your mesh and workload configuration, and highlight divergence from configuration best practices or suggest remediation to problem areas of your deployment, as depicted in Figure 11-2.

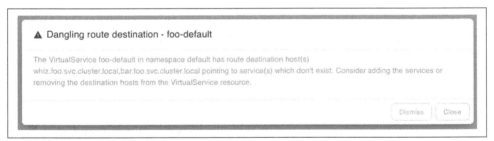

Figure 11-2. Meshery identifying orphaned service mesh configurations

Parlaying with kubectl

As noted in the context of troubleshooting Pilot in Chapter 7, Meshery and istioctl are powerful tools in assessing the synchronization of and coordination between Istio's control-plane components and its data-plane service proxies. In Kubernetes environments, Meshery and istioctl both use kubectl exec under the hood. The invocation of kubectl exec involves execution over one of two HTTP streaming protocols from your local kubectl CLI to the Kubernetes API server on to the kube let local to the node running the service proxy being interrogated by either Meshery or the istioctl command.

The specific mechanics of these two HTTP streaming protocols depend on which version of Kubernetes and which container runtime you're using; the Kubernetes API server supports the SPDY protocol (now deprecated) and HTTP/2 WebSockets. (If WebSockets are unfamiliar, simply think of WebSockets as a protocol that transforms HTTP into a bidirectional byte-streaming protocol.) On top of that stream, the Kubernetes API server introduces an additional multiplexed streaming protocol. The reason for this is that, for many use cases, it is quite useful for the API server to be able to service multiple independent byte streams. Consider, for example, executing a command within a container. In this case, there are actually three streams that need to be maintained: stdin, stderr, and stdout.

When invoked, kubectl exec performs a sequence of actions. Initially, it issues an HTTP POST request to the Kubernetes API server at

    /api/v1/namespaces/$NAMESPACE/pods/$NAME/exec

with a query string defining the command(s) to execute in which container and whether to establish multiplexed bidirectional streaming of stdin, stdout, and stderr:

    ?command=<command-syntax>&container=<name>&stderr=true&stdout=true

These query parameters are self-explanatory, indicating the command to run, if stdin should be enabled, if stdout should be enabled, if stderr should be enabled, and the container's name. Using these query string parameters, a WebSocket connection is established and kube-apiserver will start streaming data between Meshery/istioctl and the respective kubelet, as shown in Figure 11-3.

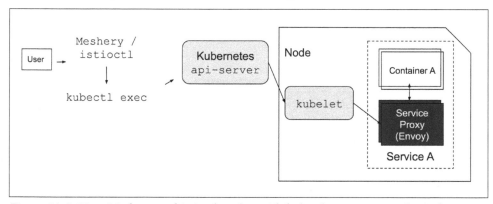

Figure 11-3. How Meshery and istioctl parlay with kubectl to retrieve mesh configuration from service proxies

When you write to the WebSocket, the data will be passed to standard input (`stdin`) and on the receiving end of the WebSocket will be standard output (`stdout`) and error (`stderr`). The API defines a simple protocol to multiplex `stdout` and `stderr` over a single connection. Every message passed through the WebSocket is prefixed by a single byte that defines which stream the message belongs to (see Table 11-1).

Table 11-1. Basic streaming protocol channels used for kubectl exec/attach/logs/proxy

Channel	Purpose	Description
0	stdin	The stdin stream for writing to the process. Data is not read from this stream.
1	stdout	The stdout output stream for reading stdout from the process. Data should not be written to this stream.
2	stderr	The stderr output stream for reading stderr from the process. Data should not be written to this stream.

The `kube-apiserver` establishes a connection to the `kubelet` located on the node where the pod in question resides. From there, the `kubelet` generates a short-lived token and issues a redirect to the container runtime interface (CRI). The CRI handles the `kubectl exec` request and issues a `docker exec` API call. The basic protocol channels of `stdin`, `stdout`, and `stderr` are specified as input, output, and error to the `docker exec` API call, respectively. `kubectl exec/attach/logs/proxy` might require long-running connections to the `kube-apiserver` since any of these commands might need data streamed over time rather than an immediate, one-time response.

Workload Preparedness

Not only might Istio's component be experiencing an issue, but so could your freshly meshed application. As your existing services are onboarded to the service mesh, you'll need to confirm the compatibility of your application and Istio. There are some compatibility concerns to review, as follows.

Application Configuration

Avoid UID 1337. Ensure that your pods do not run applications as a user with the user ID (UID) value of 1337. The Istio service proxy uses 1337 as its UID. You'll need to avoid this conflict.

Network Traffic and Ports

HTTP/1.1 or HTTP/2.0 is required. Applications must use either the HTTP/1.1 or HTTP/2.0 protocols for all its HTTP traffic; HTTP/1.0 is not supported.

Service ports must be named. To use Istio's traffic routing, ensure each service has port name key/value pairs following this syntax: `name: <protocol>[-<suffix>]`. The value used for `<protocol>` should match one of the following types (strings):

- `grpc`
- `http`
- `http2`
- `https`
- `mongo`
- `redis`
- `tcp`
- `tls`
- `udp`

By default, Istio will treat traffic as TCP. Unless the port explicitly uses `udp` to signify UDP traffic, or unless the beginning of a service's port name doesn't match one of these prefixes, Istio will treat traffic on the port as TCP. Consequently, traffic on unnamed ports is treated as TCP, as well. Examples of valid port names are `http2-myservice` or `http2`; however, `http2myservice` is not valid.

 This behavior is akin to that of Kubernetes in that its services use TCP as the default protocol for services, but you can also use any other supported protocol (TCP, UDP, HTTPS, proxy, SCTP). Because many services need to expose more than one port, Kubernetes supports multiple port definitions on a service object. Each port definition can have the same or a different protocol. However, Kubernetes doesn't mandate that two different services referring to the same pod port have the same protocol defined.

Pods must include an explicit list of the ports on which each container listens. Use a `containerPortconfiguration` in the container specification for each port. Any unlisted ports bypass the Istio proxy.

Services and Deployments

Associate all pods to at least one service. Whether it exposes a port or not, all pods must belong to at least one Kubernetes service. For pods belonging to multiple Kubernetes services, ensure that each service defines the same type of protocol when referencing the same port number (for instance, HTTP and TCP).

Meaningful telemetry with Kubernetes labels. With app and version labels deployments, we recommend adding an explicit app label and version label. Add the labels to the deployment specification of pods deployed using the Kubernetes Deployment. The app and version labels add contextual information to the telemetry Istio collects:

An app label
Each deployment specification should have a distinct app label with a meaningful value.

A version label
Indicates the version of the application corresponding to the particular deployment.

These labels are helpful as context propagated in distributed traces.

Pods

Pod configuration must allow NET_ADMIN capability. If your cluster enforces pod security policies, pods must allow the NET_ADMIN capability. As described in Chapter 5, while injecting the service proxy sidecar, Istio uses an init container to manipulate the iptables rules of the pod in order to intercept requests to application containers. Although the service proxy sidecar does not require root to run, the short-lived init container does require `cap_net_admin` privileges to install iptables rules in each pod just prior to starting the pod's primary containers onboard to the service mesh.

Manipulating iptables rules is an action that requires elevated access through the NET_ADMIN capability in the Linux kernel. Pods that have this kernel-level capability enabled can manipulate with the networking configuration of the other pods as well as can manipulate networking configuration on their host node. Most Kubernetes operators avoid allowing tenant pods to have this capability or at least those that operate a shared-tenant cluster.

If you use the Istio CNI Plugin (*https://oreil.ly/G4TK0*), the NET_ADMIN capability requirement does not apply, because the CNI plug-in (a privileged pod) will perform administrative functions on behalf of the `istio-init` container. The following shows a check as to whether pod security policies are enabled in your cluster:

```
$ kubectl get psp
No resources found.
```

This example shows a cluster that has no pod security policies defined. If your cluster does have pod security policies defined, look for NET_ADMIN or * in the list of capabilities of the allowed policies for your given service account. Unless a Kubernetes service account is specified in your pods' deployment, the pods run as the `default` service account in the namespace in which the pods are deployed. To check which capabilities are allowed for the service account of your pods, run the following command:

```
$ for psp in $(kubectl get psp -o
    jsonpath="{range .items[*]}{@.metadata.name}{'\n'}{end}");
    do if [ $(kubectl auth can-i use psp/$psp --as=system:serviceaccount:<your
    namespace>:<your service account>) = yes ]; then kubectl get psp/$psp
    --no-headers -o=custom-columns=NAME:.metadata.name,CAPS:.spec.allowed
    Capabilities; fi; done
```

For more on the NET_ADMIN capability, see Istio's Required Pod Capabilities page (*https://oreil.ly/33bCH*).

Istio Installation, Upgrade, and Uninstall

As with many installation mechanisms and configurable options, there are many choices to be made when considering an installation. More than that, over time you'll need to upgrade deployments, and at some point, you'll need to uninstall given that your service mesh deployment follows the life cycle of the application(s) it serves.

Installation

Simply rerun your deployment script. Initial installation challenges are sometimes overcome by reapplying your installation YAML file to your Kubernetes cluster (rerunning your installation commands). Whether due to network traffic loss or scheduled resources (e.g., CRDs) not yet having been fully instantiated by kube-api, sometimes you'll find that not all Istio components have instantiated successfully the first time you applied them to the cluster.

In that event, you might see a message like this:

```
unable to recognize "install/kubernetes/istio-demo-auth.yaml": no
    matches for kind
```

You will need to ensure that CRDs have been applied by running the following command:

```
$ kubectl apply -f install/kubernetes/helm/istio/templates/crds.yamlt
```

Upgrade

Istio upgrades can follow various paths. Let's look at two of those paths: Helm with Tiller, and without Tiller.

Helm with Tiller

If your installation was performed using helm install (with Tiller), like this

```
$ helm install install/kubernetes/helm/istio --name istio
    --namespace istio-system
```

You might choose to use `helm upgrade` to upgrade your Istio deployment, like so:

```
$ helm upgrade istio install/kubernetes/helm/istio
    --namespace istio-system
```

Helm without Tiller

If you installed Istio using a Helm template (without Tiller), understand that the Helm upgrade command works only when Tiller is installed. From here, you have two choices. You can use Helm to install the source version, installing Tiller in the process, and then use the Hhelm upgrade command. Or you can use the same Helm template process you used to install Istio to also upgrade Istio, like so:

```
$ helm template install/kubernetes/helm/istio --name istio --namespace
    istio-system > istio.yaml
$ kubectl apply -f istio.yaml
```

The `helm template install` (upgrade) process takes advantage of Kubernetes rolling update process and will upgrade all deployments and configmaps to the new version. Using this approach, you can roll back if needed by applying the YAML files from the old version.

Uninstallation

Istio might not uninstall cleanly, leaving residual artifacts of its presence. You might find the following artifacts deposited.

Residual CRDs

If you have uninstalled Istio, but its CRDs remain, you can iteratively delete each individual CRD, like so:

```
$ for i in install/kubernetes/helm/istio-init/files/crd*yaml;
    do kubectl delete -f $i; done
```

Depending on your installation profile, your deployment will have a different number of Istio CRDs. Here's how to verify removal of Istio's CRDs:

```
$ kubectl get crds | grep istio
```

When all CRDs have been successfully removed the result set should be empty.

Troubleshooting Mixer

Following is the command to enable debug logging for Mixer:

```
$ kubectl edit deployment -n istio-system istio-mixer
# Add to args list:
    - --log_output_level=debug
```

You can access Mixer logs via a `kubectl logs` command, as follows:

For the `istio-policy` service:

```
kubectl -n istio-system logs $(kubectl -n istio-system get pods -lapp=policy
    -o jsonpath='{.items[0].metadata.name}') -c mixer
```

For the `istio-telemetry` service:

```
kubectl -n istio-system logs $(kubectl -n istio-system get pods
    -lapp=telemetry -o jsonpath='{.items[0].metadata.name}') -c mixer
```

Using ControlZ (ctrlz)

Alternatively, you can turn on Mixer debugging using ControlZ on Mixer on port 9876. To do so, port forward to ControlZ:

```
$ kubectl --namespace istio-system port-forward istio-[policy/telemetry]-<pod#>
    9876:9876
```

Open your browser to http://localhost:9876.

Troubleshooting Pilot

You can query Pilot's registration API for a list of hosts and IP addresses to retrieve the overall mesh configuration and endpoint information. The response should be a large JSON that looks similar to this:

```
$ kubectl run -i --rm --restart=never dummy --image=tutum/curl:alpine -n
    istio-system --command \
-- curl -v 'http://istio-pilot.istio-system:8080/v1/registration'
```

This book's GitHub repository contains example output (*https://oreil.ly/iJD2W*) from Pilot's registration API.

To gather Pilot's logs, run the following:

```
$ kubectl logs -n istio-system -listio=pilot -c discovery
```

See this book's GitHub repository for example logs (*https://oreil.ly/1b5W6*) from Pilot's discovery container.

Ensure that `pilot-discovery discovery` service is running:

```
$ kubectl -n istio-system exec -it istio-pilot-644ff8f78d-p757j -c discovery sh -
# ps -ax
  PID TTY      STAT   TIME COMMAND
    1 ?        Ssl    72:49 /usr/local/bin/pilot-discovery discovery...
```

Debugging Galley

As of Istio v1.1, Galley's two core areas of responsibility are syntactical and semantic validation of user-authored Istio configurations and acting as the primary configuration registry. Galley uses the MCP (*https://oreil.ly/DkCL9*) to interact with components.

As the primary configuration ingestion and distribution mechanism within Istio, Galley needs to validate user-provided configuration and uses a Kubernetes Admission Controller, as shown in Figure 11-4.

```
$ kubectl get validatingwebhookconfigurations
NAME                              CREATED AT
istio-galley                      2019-06-11T15:33:21Z
```

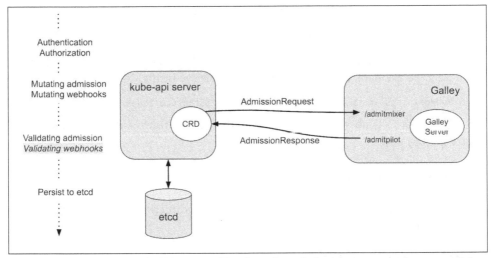

Figure 11-4. Galley's two validating webhooks: pilot.validation.istio.io and mixer.validation.istio.io

The `istio-galley` service has two webhooks served on port 443:

`/admitpilot`
Responsible for validating configurations consumed by Pilot (e.g., `VirtualSer vice`, Authentication)

`/admitmixer`
Responsible for validating configurations consumed by Mixer

Both Webhooks are scoped to all `namespaces` and, as such, the `namespaceSelector` for each `pilot.validation.istio.io` and `mixer.validation.istio.io` should be an empty set.

```
$ kubectl get validatingwebhookconfiguration istio-galley -o yaml
```

See this book's GitHub repository for example output (*https://oreil.ly/6PWBG*) of a
healthy `istio-galley` validating Webhook configuration with empty namespace set.

No such hosts for service "istio-galley." If you're unable to create or update configuration, you might find that Galley is not functioning correctly. Standard troubleshooting procedure applies to Galley in terms of first verifying the status of its pod:

```
$ kubectl -n istio-system get pod -listio=galley
NAME                            READY   STATUS    RESTARTS   AGE
istio-galley-74c6547b94-4vw58   1/1     Running   0          14h
```

No endpoints available for service "istio-galley." And next, a similar verification of its
endpoints is needed:

```
$ kubectl -n istio-system get endpoints istio-galley
NAME           ENDPOINTS                                     AGE
istio-galley   10.32.0.17:15014,10.32.0.17:443,10.32.0.17:9901   14h
```

If the pods or endpoints aren't ready, check the pod logs and status for any indication
about why the webhook pod is failing to start and serve traffic:

```
$ kubectl logs -n istio-system istio-galley-755f8df6cb-zq4p8
```

See this book's GitHub repository for example output (*https://oreil.ly/rpU8s*) of an
`istio-galley` pod.

Debugging Envoy

Networking is difficult. Layers of abstraction and indirection make debugging network issues even more difficult.

Envoy's Administrative Console

Envoy's administrative interface runs on port 15000 (see Chapter 4 for an exhaustive
list of ports). You can access Envoy's administrative interface by using `kubectl` to
port-forward from your local machine to any given pod sidecarred with Envoy:

```
$ kubectl port-forward <pod> 15000:15000 &
```

To stop a port-forwarding job running in the background, run `kill %1` (assuming
you have no other background jobs running). For a list of active jobs, run `jobs`.

To see a YAML-formatted printout of that Envoy's configuration run the following:

```
$ curl http://localhost:15000/config_dump | yq r -
```

Or, bring up the full administrative console in your browser at http://localhost:15000.
Reference http://localhost:15000/help for a description of administrative actions

available. See Envoy's operations and admin docs (*https://oreil.ly/7DY65*) for a full description of all its administrative functions.

503 or 404 Requests

If you're seeing either of these two error codes when trying to access your service, know that although there are different causes, the most common culprits are:

- There's a disconnect between Envoy and Pilot. Here are the steps to remediate:

  1. Confirm Pilot is running. See "Troubleshooting Pilot" on page 112.

  2. Use `istioctl proxy-status` to confirm communication status between Pilot and Envoy. During normal operation, each xDS will show a status of SYNCED.

- There is a missing or incorrect network protocol in your Kubernetes service manifest. To remediate, configure your service manifest with the appropriate name for your service's exposed ports. For a list of protocol names, see "Workload Preparedness" on page 191.

- The Envoy configuration is capturing the route in the wrong upstream cluster. The `VirtualService` configuration is incorrect. Here are the steps to remediate:

  1. Identify an edge service (adjacent to an ingress gateway).

  2. Inspect its Envoy logs or use a tool such as Jaeger to confirm where failures are occurring.

Sidecar Injection

If you're having difficulty with sidecar injection, there may be a few different issues in your environment. Three factors could account for whether a sidecar is injected:

- The webhook `namespaceSelector`
- The default policy
- The per-pod override annotation

Verify that the following items are true:

Your pods don't run applications with UID 1337

Application containers should not run with UID 1337, as this is the UID used by the service proxy, Envoy. Currently the Envoy Sidecar Proxy *must* run as `istio-proxy` with UID 1337 and is not a centrally configurable deployment option.

Your admission controller is enabled

If you see an error like the following:

```
error: unable to recognize "istio.yaml": no matches for
    admissionregistration.k8s.io/, Kind=MutatingWebhookConfiguration
```

you are likely running Kubernetes version 1.9 or earlier, which might not have support for mutating admission webhooks or might not have it enabled and is the reason for the error.

The istio-injection label is present

As discussed in Chapter 5, for pods to benefit from automatic sidecar injection their namespace must bear an `istio-injection` label. So the injection Webhook will be invoked only for pods created in namespaces with the `istio-injection=enabled` label. Verify that the affected pods are within a namespace bearing this label:

```
$ kubectl get namespace -L istio-injection
NAME              STATUS   AGE   ISTIO-INJECTION
default           Active   39d   enabled
istio-system      Active   13h
kube-node-lease   Active   39d
kube-public       Active   39d
kube-system       Active   39d
```

The scope of the Webhook's namespaceSelect is correct

The Webhook's `namespaceSelector` determines whether the Webhook is scoped to opt-in or opt-out for the target namespace. The `namespaceSelector` for *opt-in* looks like this:

```
$ kubectl get mutatingwebhookconfiguration istio-sidecar-injector -o yaml
    | grep "namespaceSelector:" -A5

  namespaceSelector:
    matchLabels:
      istio-injection: enabled
  rules:
  - apiGroups:
    - ""
```

The `namespaceSelector` for *opt-out* looks like this:

```
  namespaceSelector:
    matchExpressions:
    - key: istio-injection
      operator: NotIn
      values:
      - disabled
  rules:
  - apiGroups:
```

```
    - ""
  Debugging Citadel
```

As is the case when troubleshooting other problems, consulting Citadel's logs and events can be insightful to diagnosing issues it might have.

```
$ kubectl logs -l istio=citadel -n istio-system
$ kubectl describe pod -l istio=citadel -n istio-system
```

It could be that the case that the istio-citadel pod isn't running, so verify its status:

```
$ kubectl get pod -l istio=citadel -n istio-system
NAME                               READY   STATUS    RESTARTS   AGE
istio-citadel-678b7c5cd4-ndn4n     1/1     Running   0          13h
```

Redeploy the istio-citadel pod if it isn't in a Running state.

Version Compatibility

You can't mix versions of Istio components, istioctl, and the Bookinfo sample application. For example, don't simultaneously run Istio v1.1, istioctl v.1.0, and Bookinfo v1.2. The same is generally true for patch versions as well, so for example, avoid running Istio v1.1.4 while using istioctl v1.1.3. To confirm the version of each Istio control-plane component you're running, run the following:

```
$ istioctl version --remote -o yaml
```

Alternatively, you can take a look at the image tag on one of the control-plane components. Using Pilot as an example, you can execute this:

```
$ kubectl get deployment istio-pilot -o yaml -n istio-system | grep image:
    | cut -d ':' -f3 | head –1
```

These debugging tools and their example use should serve you well; however, this is far from a complete list. Other failure and troubleshooting scenarios exist, and fortunately, so too, do other tools. With the proliferation of service meshes, the service mesh landscape has seen a number of helpful utilities and management tools (*https://oreil.ly/U6Vwa*) emerge. We anticipate the trend of growth of management-plane software to continue.

## CHAPTER 12

Real-World Considerations for Application Deployment

People adopt service meshes for many reasons, not least of which is to improve the reliability of services they deliver to their users. A key consideration of improving the reliability of a workload on Istio is understanding *Istio's* reliability characteristics. As you might expect, the reliability of the two are linked. Although use of Istio (or any service mesh) stands to dramatically lift the boats of all workloads (on and off the mesh), the introduction of additional components to the system, like a service proxy that creates a `services-network`, presents new modes of potential failure. Considerations for deploying Istio and workloads on Istio *reliably* is the focus of this chapter.

In earlier chapters, we talked about how Istio can improve your application's reliability (with outlier detection, circuit breakers, and retries, among others). We examined how Istio can allow you to control where traffic flows through your mesh very precisely, and how Istio helps you gain visibility into your deployment (by generating telemetry for your applications). We have addressed features of Istio that are helpful in protecting you against certain classes of failures, but we haven't addressed, in detail, how Istio helps when it comes to mitigating the most common sources of outages: deploying new versions of your applications. Fortunately, the ability to control traffic and see how that traffic is behaving is *exactly* what we need to minimize the risk of (re)deploying applications.

Let's dig into considerations for deploying Istio's control-plane components and walk through a case study of a canary deployment of an application. As we review how Istio can help us deploy our own applications more safely, we'll reflect on how Istio control-plane components interact at runtime and how their behavior affects that reliability.

Control-Plane Considerations

Each of Istio's components have a variety of failure modes, and their failures manifest in the mesh in different ways. To best understand these modes and their behavior, for each control-plane component, we review a common set of failure modes (components partitioned from a workload, partitioned from one another, etc.), any failure modes specific to that component, and how these issues manifest in the mesh at runtime. We cover the main failure modes, but it's impossible for us to be exhaustive. Our goal here is to arm you with the knowledge of behavior patterns and dependency implications and combine this with the information from the component-specific chapters in the hopes that you should be able to understand new failure modes when they appear.

In this section, we discuss most failures in terms of a *network* partition, which is really a stand-in for many failure modes. For example, the failure "Galley is partitioned from its config store," could be caused by many things; for example, an actual network partition, the config store serving 500 errors, the config store not accepting connections at all, or the config store serving at unacceptably high latencies. Irrespective of the root cause, for the purposes of understanding reliability characteristics of control-plane components, all of these failures are equivalent in that one component in the system cannot get the data it needs when it needs it.

It's also worth discussing Istio component upgrades at a high level. Historically, upgrading Istio has been a painful process, fraught with error (outage). As of Istio's 1.0 release, the project committed to ensuring smooth upgrade processes, but it's still an ongoing learning process for the project. For example, it was discovered after release that for the user configurations deployed by a small number of people, the upgrade from 1.0 to 1.1 would break applications traffic in the mesh. As a result of this incident and other learnings, the project has started several long-running initiatives around upgradability of the mesh-control plane and Istio's components generally (the control plane, but also node agents and data plane). These efforts primarily focus on the ability to canary control-plane components themselves. As of this writing, this work hasn't yet landed. For each component we look at in this chapter, we'll mention special upgrade considerations, but we will not cite specific known issues of upgrading from one version to another.

Galley

Galley is responsible for configuration distribution to other Istio control-plane components. When Galley is unavailable (partitioned from its own source of truth, the other Istio control-plane components; crash-looping; or otherwise) the primary symptom you'll see is the inability to push new configurations into your mesh. Even though the mesh should continue to function in its current steady state, you'll be unable to effect changes in the configuration of the mesh until Galley is restored.

A typical Istio mesh installation will have relatively few Galley instances. One or two (if you're running an HA pair) Galley instances per control-plane deployment is usual. Galley does not necessarily need to be "close" (in terms of network latency) to the rest of the control-plane components. Higher latency between Galley and the rest of the control plane means a longer time for user configurations to take effect; even a single global Galley instance controlling a control-plane instance on the other side of the world would have latency low enough for the mesh to function correctly.

Partitioned from the configuration store

When Galley cannot reach its configuration store no new configuration will flow from Galley into other Istio components. All of Istio's components cache their current state in memory—Galley is no exception; so as long as Galley itself doesn't die, it will continue to serve its current configuration to the rest of the control plane while attempting to reestablish a connection to the configuration store. If Galley itself dies and is restarted during this time, it will be unable to serve any configuration to the rest of the control plane until it reestablishes a connection to its own configuration store.

One way to mitigate this category of failure is to cache local configurations more persistently. Galley has the ability to ingest configurations from the local filesystem in addition to remote sources (like the Kubernetes API server). A base set of configurations can be provided on the local filesystem (persistent across restarts of Galley) that Galley can always serve while it attempts to establish a connection to remote configuration stores. Taken to the extreme, in systems with low rates of change, it's entirely possible to run Galley using *only* the filesystem-based configuration source.

When Galley is deployed on Kubernetes, it acts as a Validating Admission Controller, too; that is, Galley is responsible for validating configurations that's submitted to the Kubernetes API server. In this case, configurations pushed into Kubernetes will be rejected at push time (i.e., kubectl apply will fail).

Partitioned from other Istio components

When Galley is partitioned from other control-plane components, Galley itself won't fail, but those components will not receive configuration updates. See the section the previous section for details about their failure modes when they can't access Galley.

Partitioned from mesh workloads

Galley does not interact directly with workloads or nodes deployed in the mesh. It interacts only with other Istio control-plane components and Galley's own configuration store. Galley being unreachable for all of the workloads in the mesh is completely fine so long as the Istio control-plane components themselves can communicate with Galley.

Upgrades

Because of the nature of Galley's failure mode, an in-place or rolling upgrade of Galley is fairly easy (an in-place upgrade is effectively the same as a temporary partition in this context because the previous job is descheduled and a new one created to replace it). The other Istio components locate Galley by DNS and will attempt to reconnect to Galley as their connection is severed. Istio performs skew testing (in which we test different versions of control- and data-plane components together) to ensure that between any two adjacent versions (e.g., 1.0 to 1.1), upgrades are not breaking. There's no guarantee that skipping multiple versions is safe (e.g., 1.0 to 1.2).

Pilot

Pilot is responsible for configuring the service mesh's data plane at runtime. When it's unavailable, you'll be unable to change the mesh's current networking configuration; new workloads will not be able to start, but existing workloads will continue to serve under the configuration they had just prior to loss of communication with Pilot. Service proxies will retain this same configuration until either they reestablish a connection to Pilot or until they restart. Other data-plane configurations that require runtime (not bootstrap) configurations—for example, updates to policy or telemetry settings across the mesh—will also not take effect until Pilot recovers.

A typical service mesh deployment will have several Pilot instances. Pilot, like the other Istio control-plane components, is a stateless service that can be horizontally scale as needed. In fact, this is the recommended best practice for production deployments. Underlying platforms like Kubernetes make such production configurations relatively simple with support for horizontal autoscaling of pods out of the box. Latency between the service registry, Pilot, and the service proxies under Pilot management is the critical path in updating endpoints in the mesh as workloads are scheduled or move around. Keeping this latency low results in better overall mesh performance. Generally, Pilot should be "near" (lower latency to reach) the service proxies for which it is providing configuration. Pilot's performance is less sensitive to its distance from *its* configuration sources.

There is one pain point related to scaling Pilot that's worth discussing. Because Envoy uses a gRPC stream to communicate configuration, there is no per-request load balancing across Pilot instances. Instead, each Envoy in an Istio deployment is sticky to its associated Pilot. A given Envoy will not communicate to another Pilot unless its associated Pilot severs the connection (or dies, severing its connections). For this reason, scaling up Pilots can be tricky. Often, you'll need to scale out several instances and then kill an overloaded Pilot instance to force Envoys to rebalance across the newly deployed Pilot instances. This maintenance issue is being addressed in upcoming Istio releases in which Pilot will shed load by closing some connections itself when overloaded, forcing Envoys to reconnect or find a new instance.

Partitioned from the configuration store

As with the other Istio components, Pilot caches its current state in memory. The configuration in Pilot is divided into two categories: Istio networking configuration and environmental state from service registries.

When Pilot is unable to communicate with its configuration store for Istio networking configuration (Galley or the Kubernetes API server in older versions of Istio), it will continue to serve out of its currently cached state. New workloads will be able to be scheduled and their service proxies will receive configurations based on Pilot's currently cached configuration. If Pilot itself restarts while it's unable to communicate with the configuration store (or a new instance of Pilot is started), it will be unable to serve configurations for any service proxies that communicate with it.

When Pilot is unable to communicate with its service registries, it will again serve its current state out of memory while attempting to reconnect to the source. During this time, new services introduced into the mesh (e.g., the creation of a new Service resource in Kubernetes) will not be routable by workloads in the mesh. Similarly, new endpoints won't be pushed to Envoy service proxies—this means that while Pilot is disconnected from its service discovery source, workloads being descheduled or otherwise moved will not have their network endpoints removed from the load-balancing set of the other service proxies in the mesh, and can still attempt to send traffic to those now-dead endpoints. Setting automatic retries with outlier detection across your deployment will help keep application traffic healthy during transient failures like this. And as before, if Pilot itself restarts in this window when the service registry is unavailable, *no* services from that registry will be routable in the mesh.

Partitioned from other Istio components

Pilot receives its network identity from Citadel, just like the other Istio components; being unable to reach Citadel when Pilot needs a new identity document (e.g., when a new instance is scheduled or the current credential expires) will result in workloads being unable to communicate with Pilot. (See "Citadel" on page 211 for more information.) Troubleshooting the inability to communicate with Galley was described in the previous section and in the section on Galley. Pilot does not communicate directly with Mixer, so being able to contact either the Mixer policy or telemetry services does not affect Pilot at runtime.

Partitioned from mesh workloads

When workloads in the mesh cannot communicate with Pilot, service proxies for those workloads cannot receive new runtime configurations. Specifically missing will be updates to networking configuration, service-to-service authorization policy, and addition of new services, and endpoint changes will not be pushed to service proxies. As with every other Istio component, service proxies cache their current configuration and will continue to serve that configuration until they reestablish a connection to some Pilot instance. While Pilot is unavailable, newly scheduled workloads will not receive any configuration and therefore will not be able to communicate over the network at all (Istio configures the sidecar to fail closed). Newly scheduled workloads will also not be able to receive an identity from Citadel, because their identity is first populated by Pilot. Existing workloads will continue to serve using their current identity (as of the time they lost contact with Pilot) and will continue to be able to receive fresh credentials for that identity from Citadel even while Pilot is unavailable.

As we discussed earlier, configuring default retry, circuit breaking, and outlier detection policies across your mesh can help mitigate the impact of the transient Pilot outages that cause stale runtime configurations. One key benefit of client-side load balancing is the ability for individual clients to choose the servers they communicate with based on how available the server seems to the client. The mesh continues to function well with a degraded Pilot as long as the rate of change of the rest of the deployment is low and good network resiliency policies are in place across the mesh.

Upgrades

Like Galley, upgrading Pilot in a live deployment is similar to a network partition. In particular, even though the data plane will continue to serve, updates (like newly scheduled or descheduled workloads) will not propagate to Envoy instances. As we noted at the beginning of the Pilot section, Envoys do not load-balance requests across Pilot instances, therefore deploying a new Pilot side by side with an old one is not sufficient: you really need to perform a rolling upgrade (in which the new version replaces the old, shifting Envoy traffic as the old instances die) or manually deschedule old Pilot instances as new ones are brought up.

These restrictions are in part due to limitations in Envoy. Envoy takes a bootstrap configuration, which is immutable; part of this configuration is Pilot's address. To update the bootstrap configuration, Envoy must be restarted, and the full suite of Envoy's configuration is not available for configuring how Envoy talks to Pilot. For example, it is not possible to use Envoy's (or Istio's) own configuration to perform a percentage-based rollout of a new Pilot for Envoy to consume. (This is an intentional design decision on Envoy's part to limit a large class of failures; the control plane misconfigures Envoy such that it is not able to communicate with the control plane again to receive correcting configuration.) Therefore, we're limited in the techniques available for rolling out new Pilot versions incrementally.

Mixer

Mixer has two modes of operation with very different failure modes. In *Policy* mode, Mixer is part of the request path, and failures directly affect user traffic. This is because policy is necessarily blocking for requests. In *Telemetry* mode, Mixer is out of the request path and failures affect only the ability of the mesh to produce telemetry (this, of course, can result in all sorts of alarms going off as telemetry fails to come in for part of the mesh). The sections that follow address failure modes common to both and call out the special considerations for each mode separately.

Mixer is written almost as a router: its configuration really just describes how to create values from a set of data and where to forward those values. As a result, in both modes of operation Mixer usually communicates with a set of remote backends for every request it receives. This means Mixer is particularly sensitive to network partitions and increased network latency, much more so than the other control-plane components. It's also important to note that in today's model of a Mixer deployment, Istio assumes that the backends that Mixer communicates with are not in the mesh themselves. Istio makes this assumption for a number of reasons; for example, to avoid recursive calls. (Mixer sends traces to the collector, which triggers the collector's sidecar to send a trace to Mixer; Mixer sends that trace to the collector, which triggers the collector's sidecar.) The saving grace is that Mixer, unlike Pilot, sits behind a sidecar itself. This makes it possible to use Istio configuration to control how Mixer communicates with backends (including resiliency configuration like circuit breaking and automatic retries).

Partitioned from the configuration store

Like the other Istio components, Mixer holds its current serving configuration in memory. A partition from Galley means that it won't receive new configurations, but it won't hinder Mixer's ability to keep executing its current configuration. If Mixer dies and is restarted while Galley is unavailable, Mixer will serve only its default configuration. We discuss the behavior of Mixer serving its default configuration in each mode separately in a moment. In both modes, it is possible to provide Mixer with a different default configuration by giving it configurations from the local filesystem.

Mixer policies. Mixer policy can be set at installation to default to open or closed connections when unconfigured. Istio's default installation ships with a default-open configuration that applies no policy. With that configuration, a service proxy calling *check* against an unconfigured Mixer will always allow traffic. It does this so that installing Istio into an existing cluster does not break all traffic. If you are using Mixer to apply policy that is nonoptional, you should configure Mixer to default-closed when unconfigured during Istio installation. Authorization policy is a good example of policy that some service teams deem nonoptional. Other service teams choose to tolerate rate limiting or even abuse detection failing part of the time in favor of serving user traffic, so in this context, these policies could be considered "optional."

Mixer telemetry. These are not in the request path, so their failing will never affect traffic in the mesh. An unconfigured Mixer telemetry will accept *report* data from service proxies in the mesh; however, it will not generate telemetry with it (an unconfigured Mixer's *report* is a no-op). This situation can cause a pager storm as alerts for every affected service might trigger at the same time due to missing metrics.

Unfortunately, Mixer does not support a mode in which it reads configurations both from a local filesystem and from a remote configuration server. So, when using a remote configuration server (i.e., Pilot), today, you cannot set a default configuration for Mixer other than high-level flags (e.g., *policy* defaulting to open or closed). This is a known area for improvement, and subsequent versions of Istio should begin to address this.

Partitioned from other Istio components

For the most part, other Istio components do not communicate with Mixer, nor do they have a runtime dependency on Mixer. For Istio components (e.g., Pilot) that run behind service proxies that enforce policy, their failure mode when they're unable to communicate with Mixer is identical to any other workload in the mesh. Otherwise, there are no special runtime dependencies between the other components and Mixer.

Partitioned from mesh workloads

When workloads cannot communicate with Mixer, they fail, as you might expect. For policy, the service proxy will enforce the default behavior set at install time (either fail open or closed). For telemetry, the service proxies will buffer as much data as they can until they're able to forward it on to Mixer again. Service proxies use a fixed-size circular buffer to temporarily store *report* metadata that they are attempting to forward to Mixer, so eventually data will be lost. The size of the buffer is configurable in the flags passed to the service proxy at startup. This configuration item is not exposed in the Helm chart today.

Upgrades

Proxies use the protocol service *unary* to communicate with Mixer, unlike how the service proxies communicate with Pilot (Envoy using gRPC streams to Pilot's xDS interface). That is to say, messages are sent individually and not streamed. Therefore, each request can be load balanced. This makes it a lot easier to roll out new versions of Mixer, where we can use Envoy and Istio's regular primitives to canary a new version automatically.

When you're upgrading Mixer policies, beware of the latency spike that you'll see when transitioning to a new instance. Mixer policies cache policy decisions very aggressively, and when you transition traffic to a new instance, you'll see latencies spike as checks miss cache and call policy backends for a decision. This means that your policy backends will also see an increase in traffic during the new instance's cache-warming period. This is unlikely to affect your 50th percentile latency, but it can affect your 99th percentile.

There aren't any special considerations for a Mixer telemetry, though the way that Mixer lazily loads its runtime configuration means that you're likely to see very high latency for the first few *report* requests. Because *reports* are asynchronous and out-of-band of your traffic, this shouldn't manifest as slowdowns in user traffic.

Citadel

Citadel is responsible for identity issuance and rotation in the service mesh. When Citadel is unavailable, nothing will happen until certificates begin to expire. Then, you'll see failures to establish communication across the mesh. Existing traffic will continue to function while Citadel is down, but new workloads will not be able to communicate and new connections cannot be established (by either new or existing workloads) if the workload's certificates expire while it's unable to communicate with Citadel. When you're using mTLS across Istio control-plane components, which is the default installation setting, the startup of all other control-plane components depends on Citadel starting up. This is because Citadel needs to mint an identity for each control-plane component before communication is allowed.

Partitioned from the configuration store

Like the other components, Citadel will continue to serve with its current state when it's unable to reach its configuration store. Unlike most of the other control-plane components, Citadel receives little configuration from Galley, instead being more tightly coupled to its environmental configuration sources (in particular, the Kubernetes API server), which it uses to discover the set of identities for which it will mint certificates. When these identity sources are unavailable, Citadel is unable to mint certificates for new workloads and might be unable to rotate certificates for existing ones.

Partitioned from other Istio components

The other Istio components are just like normal mesh workloads from Citadel's perspective: none of the control-plane components are special. The next section discusses this further.

Partitioned from mesh workloads

When workloads in the mesh can't communicate with Citadel, they cannot receive new identity certificates. This means that new workloads starting up will be unable to communicate with anything in the mesh that requires mTLS because Citadel cannot mint an identity for those workloads. Existing workloads whose certificates are expiring will be unable to establish new connections, but their existing connections will remain open and valid until they receive a new certificate or close them. This failure to communicate will manifest as TCP handshakes failing, producing the dreaded "connection reset by peer" error. If you set shorter-lived certificates—for instance, a few hours—some edge cases around certificate rotation can manifest as 503s (due to a connection reset error) in the deployment. It is an ongoing effort in Istio to eliminate all 503s like these from the deployment, and some edge cases in certificate rotation are the last remaining source of these errors.

You should also note that to avoid "thundering-herd" problems, individual workloads will request refreshed certificates at random intervals before their certificate expires (to prevent every workload from asking for a new certificate every hour on the hour, for example). This means that, when partitioned from Citadel, various workloads for the same service might be unable to communicate, whereas others are still able to communicate.

Upgrades

Because of the random nature of certificate refresh requests, there's no easy way to "schedule downtime" for Citadel, even though it's called only very intermittently by workloads in the mesh. However, a new Citadel can be deployed along with an existing instance, and the existing instance can be drained (or killed entirely; e.g., in Kubernetes) to force traffic in the mesh to the new instance without interruption. Given that Citadel eagerly attempts to create certificates for all identities in the mesh at startup and that it cannot issue certificates until it finishes this process, you'll likely want to deploy a new version of Citadel and wait for it to warm up before sending traffic to it.

Case Study: Canary Deployment

The information in the previous sections about how Istio's control-plane components interact should help you to build a mental model for how the mesh as a whole interacts and how the failure of each component will manifest within or affect your applications. With this knowledge in-hand, you should be able to begin developing plans for safely and reliably running and managing Istio in production. Now, the question becomes, how do you use Istio's functionality to improve the reliability of the applications in your deployment?

Nearly every outage is the result of some change(s). Controlling how changes are deployed into production and how they take effect are critical for controlling outages. For a service, deploying a new binary is the most common change, accompanied by a close second of deploying updated configuration for that service. We recommend that you treat management of changes—configuration and binary changes—identically. You'll find that although binary deployments might cause more outages today, as your production deployment matures, it's likely that the root cause of most outages will shift to configuration. By handling both in a single, consistent manner you can build a single set of practices and processes for mitigating service outages regardless of the root cause. Hopefully, it's atypical to have an outage be just like previous outages you've experienced (because the issue that has caused that outage has been addressed). Assuming so, it follows that, generally speaking, there is no one-size-fits-all approach to problem resolution, but that in emergency situations having a known set of patterns to act against saves time, money, and error budget. Make sense? So, then, how can you safely use Istio to deploy a new binary?

Canarying is the process of gradually deploying a change, carefully controlling how it takes effect and who it affects. For example, it's common for a company to have its employees test the next version of a product during development before it rolls out to customers; this is a canary. With Istio, we have a wide range of options to use in deciding how to route traffic to any groups of instances of a service—many of which are covered in Chapter 8. Here, we walk through a case study using a percentage-based traffic split to canary a new deployment of a service. To prepare a test environment in which we can see our canary in real time, in Example 12-1 we first create a simple deployment in Kubernetes with a service (see httpbin-svc-depl.yaml (*https:// oreil.ly/lmmyS*) in this book's GitHub repository).

> Notice the `apiVersion: v1` label. It's common in the Kubernetes community to use the `version` label to denote versions of deployments, and to use the `app` label to select a set of deployments for a service. A lot of tooling, including Istio's own default dashboards, assumes the `version` label when drawing service graphs. We use this same label in our case study to control traffic routing.

Example 12-1. A Kubernetes service and deployment definition for the httpbin app

```
apiVersion: v1
kind: Service
metadata:
  name: httpbin
  labels:
    app: httpbin
spec:
  ports:
  - name: http
    port: 8000
    targetPort: 80
  selector:
    app: httpbin
---
apiVersion: extensions/v1beta1
kind: Deployment
metadata:
  name: httpbin-v1
spec:
  replicas: 1
  template:
```

```
metadata:
  labels:
    app: httpbin
    version: v1
spec:
  containers:
  - image: docker.io/kennethreitz/httpbin
    imagePullPolicy: IfNotPresent
    name: httpbin
    ports:
    - containerPort: 80
```

We can send traffic to the httpbin service within our cluster and we should see metrics appear. To make this easier, we can expose httpbin on our Gateway, as shown in Example 12-2, so that it's accessible outside of our cluster (i.e., from our local machine). See httpbin-gw-vs.yaml (*https://oreil.ly/PwWAI*) on this book's GitHub repository for the following example:

Example 12-2. An Istio Gateway and VirtualService exposing the httpbin service on the istio-ingressgateway deployment

```
apiVersion: networking.istio.io/v1alpha3
kind: Gateway
metadata:
  name: httpbin-gateway
spec:
  selector:
    istio: ingressgateway
  servers:
  - port:
      number: 80
      name: http
      protocol: HTTP
    hosts:
    - "*"
...
apiVersion: networking.istio.io/v1alpha3
kind: VirtualService
metadata:
  name: httpbin
spec:
  hosts:
  - "httpbin.svc.default.cluster.local"
  gateways:
  - httpbin-gateway
  http:
  - route:
    - destination:
        host: httpbin
```

```
  port:
    number: 8000
```

 We use `hosts: "*"` here to make it easier to `curl` the Gateway's IP address. If you have a DNS name for your `istio-ingessgateway` service, or already know the IP address, you can use that in the value for the `hosts` field in the `Gateway` and `VirtualService` (rather than using "*").

We can issue a `curl` from our local machine to verify, as demonstrated in Example 12-3.

Example 12-3. A curl command issuing a request to the httpbin service

```
$ curl ${ISTIO_INGRESS_IP}/status/200
```

Now, to canary a new version of the `httpbin` application, we could just create a new deployment. This would result in a round-robin distribution of load across all of the `httpbin` instances in our cluster. If there are many instances of `httpbin` running with lots of traffic, this might be acceptable; but that's not often the case. Instead, we'll use Istio to ensure that traffic stays pinned to the known good version while we roll out a new deployment and then gradually shift traffic over.

To do this, we need to create a few resources. First, we need to create a `Destination Rule` for our `httpbin` service that lets us describe subsets of the deployment. Then, we use those subsets in our `VirtualService` to make sure traffic stays directed at v1 even as we roll out v2, as shown in Example 12-4 (see httpbin-destination-v2.yaml (*https://oreil.ly/vzcPD*) on this book's GitHub repository).

Example 12-4. An Istio DestinationRule for the httpbin service that declares two subsets

```
apiVersion: networking.istio.io/v1alpha3
kind: DestinationRule
metadata:
  name: httpbin
spec:
  host: httpbin
  subsets:
  - name: v1
    labels:
      version: v1
  - name: v2
    labels:
      version: v2
```

We declare two subsets: the v1 subset for the workloads we've already deployed, and the v2 subset for the workloads we're about to deploy.

Notice that we make sure we use the `version: v1` label, with which we originally deployed our application. Also, note that we can define a new subset, v2, which targets labels that we *haven't* deployed yet. This is totally fine. When we do deploy workloads with the `version: v2` label, the `DestinationRule` will target them. Until then, traffic pointed to the `httpbin` v2 subset will result in a 500 error (because there's no healthy server in the v2 set).

Now, let's update our `VirtualService` to use the subset shown in Example 12-5 (see httpbin-vs-v1.yaml (*https://oreil.ly/a80aT*) on this book's GitHub repository).

Example 12-5. The VirtualService from Example 12-2, updated to include a subset in its destination clause

```
apiVersion: networking.istio.io/v1alpha3
kind: VirtualService
metadata:
  name: httpbin
spec:
  hosts:
  - "*"
  gateways:
  - httpbin-gateway
  - mesh # Also direct traffic in the mesh with the same VirtualService
  http:
  - route:
    - destination:
        host: httpbin
        subset: v1
        port:
          number: 8000
```

This ensures that all traffic, both within the mesh (due to `gateways: mesh`) and at ingress (`gateways: httpbin-gateway`), is pinned to the subset of `httpbin` that is v1. Now, it's safe for us to deploy a new version of `httpbin` that we're confident will not receive user traffic, as illustrated in Example 12-6 (see httpbin-depl-v2.yaml (*https://oreil.ly/uXK71*) on this book's GitHub repository).

Example 12-6. A second deployment of httpbin with a version: v2 label

```
apiVersion: extensions/v1beta1
kind: Deployment
metadata:
  name: httpbin-v2
spec:
  replicas: 1
```

```
template:
  metadata:
    labels:
      app: httpbin
      version: v2
  spec:
    containers:
    - image: docker.io/kennethreitz/httpbin
      imagePullPolicy: IfNotPresent
      name: httpbin
      ports:
      - containerPort: 80
```

We can continue to send traffic to the httpbin service, outside the cluster or within it, and now we should see traffic arrive at this new deployment. You can use Istio's metrics to verify this.

Now, we can finally canary this new deployment. We do this in Example 12-7 by directing 5% of our traffic to the new deployment, observing our service's response codes and latency via Istio's metrics to ensure the rollout looks good, and then ramping up the percentage gradually over time (see httpbin-vs-v2-5.yaml (*https://oreil.ly/ rB9cH*) on this book's GitHub repository).

Example 12-7. The VirtualService from Example 12-6 updated to send 5% of traffic to httpbin's v2 subset

```
apiVersion: networking.istio.io/v1alpha3
kind: VirtualService
metadata:
  name: httpbin
spec:
  hosts:
  - "*"
  gateways:
  - httpbin-gateway
  - mesh # Also direct traffic in the mesh with the same VirtualService
  http:
  - route:
    - destination:
        host: httpbin
        subset: v1
        port:
          number: 8000
      weight: 95
    - destination:
        host: httpbin
        subset: v2
        port:
          number: 8000
      weight: 5
```

We can continue this process by incrementally increasing the weight for `subset: v2` and decreasing the weight for `subset: v1` in step. Keep in mind that all weights must add up to 100(%) and that you can have as many subsets receiving traffic at a time as you'd like (not just the two we use in this example).

After we have rolled out the new deployment, we then have to make a choice. Eiher we can clean up the `DestinationRule`, removing our (now-unused) subsets, or we can leave the old ones in place. We'd recommend a middle ground: keep your `DestinationRules` and `VirtualServices` fixed for dealing with two subsets, the current and next. In our example, we can keep subsets v1 and v2 around until it's time to roll out v3. Then, we can replace v1 with v3 and do our entire rollout procedure again, migrating incrementally from v2 to v3. Then, we'll have configurations (a `DestinationRule` and `VirtualService`) for subsets v2 and v3 in hand, and when it's time for v4, we replace v2 and canary from v3 to v4 as before, and so on. This has the side effect of greatly lowering the amount of configurations that need to be changed in an emergency situation when you need to roll back to the previously known good deployment: we already have the configuration for the previous known good deployment and all we need to do is redeploy the binary and change the weights in our `VirtualService`.

Cross-Cluster Deployments

As we discussed in Chapter 8, techniques for routing traffic aren't restricted for use only with services within the same cluster. Every company making a serious investment in Kubernetes must deal with the realities of managing and deploying into multiple clusters. Multiple clusters are commonly used to create multiple, isolated failure domains. If you're using clusters to create failure domains, it's important to be able to shift traffic across your clusters so that you can route around failures at runtime. Using the same traffic-splitting techniques we use for canarying, we can also incrementally (or all at once) force traffic from one cluster to another. Istio supports this as a first-class use case. (See Chapter 13 for more details.) To quickly highlight how this works, suppose that we have a remote cluster with an ingress IP address of 1.2.3.4 that also hosts the `httpbin` service. In our first cluster with the `httpbin` service, shown in Example 12-8, we can create a new Istio `ServiceEntry` pointing at the ingress of that new cluster (see httpbin-cross-cluster-svcentry.yaml (*https://oreil.ly/ PGfU5*) on this book's GitHub repository).

Example 12-8. A ServiceEntry for httpbin.remote.global

```
apiVersion: networking.istio.io/v1alpha3
kind: ServiceEntry
metadata:
  name: httpbin-remote
spec:
```

```
hosts:
- httpbin.remote.global # remote postfix is used for Istioa's DNS plugin
location: MESH_INTERNAL # make sure we use mTLS
ports:
- name: http
  number: 8000
  protocol: http
resolution: DNS
addresses:
# Does not need to be routable, but needs to be unique for each service you're
# routing across clusters; used by Istio's DNS plug-in
- 127.255.0.2
endpoints:
- address: 1.2.3.4 # address of our remote cluster's ingress
  ports:
    # Do not change this port value if you're using the Istio multi cluster
      installation
    http: 15443
```

In our local cluster, we can update our `VirtualService` to force traffic directed to `httpbin` over to the remote cluster, as demonstrated in Example 12-9 (see httpbin-cross-cluster-vs.yaml (*https://oreil.ly/j7X6l*) on this book's GitHub repository).

Example 12-9. Updated version of Example 12-5

```
apiVersion: networking.istio.io/v1alpha3
kind: VirtualService
metadata:
  name: httpbin
spec:
  hosts:
  - "*"
  gateways:
  - httpbin-gateway
  - mesh # Also direct traffic in the mesh with the same VirtualService
  http:
  - route:
    - destination:
        host: httpbin.remote.global
        port:
          number: 8000
```

This will route traffic both at ingress into our local cluster and for traffic inside the mesh in the local cluster to call out to the remote cluster when trying to contact `httpbin`. Because in our `ServiceEntry` we declare that the endpoint is `MESH_INTER NAL`, we're guaranteed that mTLS will be used end to end in the communication across clusters, so there's no need to even set up VPN connectivity across the cluster. We can route over the internet, if needed.

In this chapter, we took a whirlwind tour of control-plane component failure modes as well as the effects of those failures on the service mesh from sibling control-plane components to data-plane service proxies and the workloads to which they are side-carred. We walked through a case study for safely deploying a new version of an existing service so that we had a high level of control over how users accessed the new version, inclusive of retaining the ability to rollback user traffic to the old version, if needed. Finally, we looked at a very brief example of using the same traffic routing primitives we used for canaries to control failover across clusters. Istio shines in this area, enabling fairly low effort active/passive and active/active deployments.

## CHAPTER 13

Advanced Scenarios

Single-cluster service mesh deployments might be all that is required in some environments. But other environments might call on the need for multiple clusters and single, global service mesh deployment or federation of independent service mesh deployments. Such environments can include consideration for existing monoliths or other external services. And although we're all excited to see the day when microservices rule the world and monolithic applications are relegated to the dusty pages of history, we're not there yet. The Istio project understands this and supports a variety of deployment and configuration models.

This chapter reviews a handful of the more common advanced topologies. Advanced topologies are useful in environments in which the focus strictly comprises geographically proximate microservices or environments that distribute service meshes across regions or providers.

Types of Advanced Topologies

Although numerous topology configurations are possible, here we discuss a core few that you can morph into other configurations. Let's categorize these few into two foundational topologies deployed across a single cluster or multiple clusters.

Single-Cluster Meshes

An advanced single-cluster topology is that of *mesh expansion*. Mesh expansion is a topology that includes running traditional, nonmicroservice workloads (so, monolithic apps) on bare metal or VMs (or both) on your Istio service mesh. Though these apps don't receive all of the benefits offered by the service mesh, incorporating them into the service mesh does allow you to begin to gain insight into and control over how these services are communicating with one another. It lays the groundwork for a migration into a cloud native architecture or for divvying workload across Kubernetes and non-Kubernetes nodes.

We dig into that a bit more, later in this chapter. The point here is to associate *mesh expansion* with onboarding brownfield applications onto a mesh where you can observe the traffic, begin breaking up a monolith by "strangling" it by siphoning off traffic through route rules, or test these services when they're *not* running on the VM or host machine anymore.

Multiple-Cluster Meshes

Two other types of advanced topologies are that of Istio *multicluster* and *cross-cluster* models. We put these two topologies into the same multiple-cluster-mesh (federation) category because, in essence, they intend to solve the same problem of intercluster communication. They provide for communication between disparate Kubernetes clusters running individual service meshes, unifying them either under one control plane or across two control planes. But this is where language becomes a bit tricky and confusion can creep in.

To keep it simple, we'll summarize these two approaches now and examine them further later in the chapter.

Istio multicluster (single mesh)

Istio multicluster (single mesh) is a centralized approach for connecting multiple service meshes into a single service mesh. You do this by selecting a cluster that serves as the master cluster, with the others being remote clusters. We use *local* and *remote* as the terms to label which cluster's data plane is local to the centralized control plane and which cluster's data plane is remote from the centralized control plane.

A single-control-plane Istio deployment can span across multiple clusters as long as there is network connectivity between them and no IP address range overlap. Figure 13-1 illustrates how Istio v1.0 supports this flat-network model across clusters. You can extend Istio v1.0 to nonflat networks, where there is IP address conflict between clusters.

Using Network Address Translation (NAT) and a combination of VPNs, Istio Gateways, or other network services, you can conjoin clusters into the same administrative domain (under the same single control plane). It's possible to federate multiple control planes in v1.0, but this requires a lot of manual tweaking and configuration within Istio. Irrespective of the approach to networking clusters together, to enable service name resolution and verifiable identities, all namespaces, services, and service accounts need to be identically defined in each cluster.

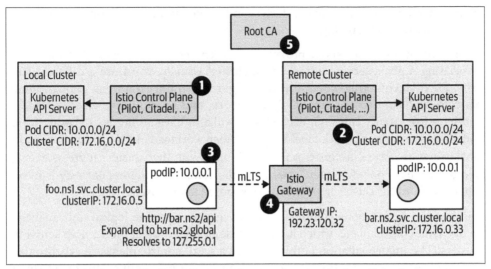

Figure 13-1. The Istio multicluster approach: a single-control-plane Istio deployment with direct connection (flat networking) across clusters

In Istio v1.1, flat networking is no longer required. Two additional features have emerged that enable different multicluster scenarios:

Split horizon (EDS)
Pilot implements Envoy's EDS API and uses it to configure service proxies in the data plane with information about services and endpoints local to a given service proxy's cluster only. With split-horizon EDS, Pilot presents endpoints relevant to the cluster where the connected service proxy is, enabling Istio to route requests to different endpoints, depending on the location of the requested source. Istio Gateways intercept and parse TLS handshakes and use SNI data to decide destination service endpoints.

SNI-based routing
This uses the SNI TLS extension to make routing decisions for intercluster connectivity and communications.

As you saw in Chapter 5, EDS is part of Envoy's API. Split horizon is a networking concept in which routing loops are avoided by prohibiting a router from advertising a route back onto the interface from which it was learned. So, in Istio's case, as Pilot configures the service proxies in the data plane with service and endpoint information, it does so with information about endpoints relevant to the cluster where the connected service proxies run.

While naming of services, ServiceAccounts, and so on needs to be consistent across clusters, v1.1 improves Istio's awareness of clusters and locality. Kubernetes labels and annotations are used to facilitate cluster awareness both on a per-network basis (associating each network with a given cluster) and a geographic basis for more intelligent, locality-based load balancing.

Upon initialization, the service proxy assigns each network a cluster label, inherently associating a given service instance to a cluster. Usually, you'd use a different label value for each cluster; however, this is configurable to the extent that perhaps multiple clusters belong to the same logical network, and so should be directly routable and have low latency (ideally). Each cluster will also have an ingress `Gateway`, which will share the same network label value as other workloads in the cluster. Matching label values associates in-cluster service endpoints with that cluster's ingress `Gateway`. Because it's used only for intercluster communication, the ingress `Gateway` is ideally separated from the cluster ingress and not exposed to end users.

Multicluster deployments combine multiple clusters into one logical unit, managed by one Istio control plane, which has a single logical view of all the services across the clusters. The implementation of this could be a set of control planes all synchronized with replicated configuration (typically using additional tooling, driven by shared CI/CD pipelines and/or GitOps practices) or one "physical" control plane that operates multiple data planes as one single service mesh. Either way, you have a set of clusters that are part of the same mesh.

Istio needs to know which cluster these workloads belong to. Akin to the use of Kubernetes labels for locality-based load balancing, Istio assigns each cluster a "network" label. These are again used to make Istio cluster-aware in terms of which cluster a given network is associated with. Typically, we would use a different label value for each cluster, but this can be tweaked if you know that multiple clusters are part of the same logical network (e.g., directly routable, low latency).

Istio cross-cluster (mesh federation)

Istio cross-cluster (mesh federation) is a decentralized approach to unifying service meshes. Each cluster runs its own control plane and data plane. You can have two or more clusters participating in the service mesh regardless of their region or cloud provider. Cross-cluster deployments facilitate for relatively different configurations per service mesh under different administrative domains running in different regions. With those individual administrative domains in mind, an advantage to the mesh federation pattern is that you can selectively make connections between clusters and, in turn, so can the exposure of one cluster's services to other clusters.

Improving Cross-Cluster Load Balancing

When running a service in a single cluster, you'll typically run multiple replicas of its pods to load balance inbound requests of that service. Doing so helps foremost with scalability (and with availability in the context of handling scale, but not in the context of failure domains). When running a service across multiple clusters, you might load balance inbound requests across pods in both clusters. Doing so helps not only with scalability, but with availability (resiliency); however, while load balancing requests across clusters, you generally want locality-aware load balancing, meaning that you don't want requests for a given service load balanced to a remote cluster, *if* those requests can be locally satisfied (sent to pods in the local cluster).

In general, you'll want to keep traffic local. Locality-based load balancing supports this behavior such that when all endpoints are healthy, awareness of locality is used to keep load-balanced traffic in the closest possible proximity. With the release of Istio v1.1, locality-based load balancing has been introduced (following the path new features do, it is experimentally supported in 1.1 and off by default). Istio defines locality as a geographic location using a combination of region, zone, and subzone concepts to prioritize load-balancing pools to control the geographic location where requests are sent.

As a property of the specific deployment environment, Istio will source locality information from the underlying platform. Using Kubernetes as the example platform, note that Kubernetes has a set of reserved labels and annotations within the kubernetes.io namespace. When deployed in a public cloud, `kubelets` on each node in a cluster will populate reserved labels like `failure-domain.beta.kubernetes.io/region`, from which Istio can glean region, zone, and subzone locality information.

This new feature enables two modes of load balancing: *distribute* and *failover*. Distribute mode facilitates locality-prioritized load balancing. When some endpoints in a locality are unhealthy, Istio's service proxy, Envoy, adjusts the locality weight to reflect this using a weighted round-robin schedule. Failover mode ensures that when endpoints in the local region become unhealthy, traffic is rerouted to remote region(s). Configure the mapping of which region another region should failover to.

Even with v1.1's enhancements for multicluster support, not all possible load-balancing algorithms have emerged in Istio. It currently supports round robin, random, weighted, and least-requests load-balancing modes. Single-cluster load balancing is still improving, and Envoy supports several other sophisticated load-balancing algorithms.

Use Cases

As you can see by the advanced configurations we've touched on, there are a slew of use cases. While keeping in mind our mantra that you should be able to secure, observe, control, and connect your services regardless of where they are running or what they are running on (public, private, or hybrid cloud), let's outline what use cases these advanced models of deployment enable.

HA (cross-region)
> With both multicluster and cross-cluster, you can enable a cross-region story. This means that you can have a Kubernetes cluster deployed in two separate regions with service traffic being routed, securely, across those two regions. It is also possible to do failover between these regions with cross-cluster setups so that when one region drops, your application doesn't necessarily drop.

Cross-provider
> Expanding on cross-region, both topologies can support multicloud setups between providers; however, the requirements to do this, and also cross-region, differ significantly. We dig into that further in a later section. But, simply put, Istio allows you to achieve multicloud service mesh deployments.

Deployment strategies
> With a multicluster setup, you can put a canary online on lower-cost instances at a lower-cost provider. Imagine spinning up a canary at DigitalOcean to which you can pass 1% of traffic from your production environment running on IBM Cloud. This is possible with both topologies. Similar logic follows for strategies like A/B testing and blue/green deployments.

Distributed tracing for the monolith
> Using service mesh expansion, your monolithic app becomes less opaque. After you've expanded your mesh to include traditional applications running on VMs or metal, you can gather tracing data and more.

Migration

Using cross-cluster, you can move your service across regions or across providers using Istio to control the routing of your service traffic. One of the more interesting migration scenarios is the ability to take brownfield applications and transition them piecemeal into Kubernetes. This helps to give your brownfield application a bit of cloud native varnish to it. Now, your brownfield can communicate, if you wanted it to, with new services that you're deploying within the cluster.

All of these scenarios will begin to make sense as we dig deeper into each one later in the chapter. After you have finished the exercises, you should have a basic understanding of how to set up each and how each works. We will be using the Bookinfo sample application throughout to illustrate the differences.

Choosing a Topology

Each deployment topology design comes with implementation concessions. It's highly likely that the approach you select will be and probably should be dictated by where your data (or compute) lives. If you're using only clusters in the public cloud, cross-cluster might make better sense. If you're running some on-premises clusters with a cluster or two in the public clouds, multicluster might make sense. This is not to say that you can't use cross-cluster between on-premises and the public cloud providers, especially as on-premises begins to model itself on how public cloud is delivered—for example, solutions like NetApp HCI, Azure Stack, GKE On-Prem, and more.

Cross-Cluster or Multicluster?

Let's dive into the deep end of the pool. As we explained previously, the best way to think about Istio multicluster versus cross-cluster is to think *centralized* versus *decentralized* control planes, respectively. Over time, these have become the two dominant approaches to connecting multiple Kubernetes clusters running a service mesh together. Both have their advantages and disadvantages. Let's walk through those pros and cons, beginning with multicluster.

Each data plane, whether local to or remote from the central control plane, must have connectivity with management components like Pilot and Mixer. Local and remote data planes also need to be able to push telemetry to the central control plane. All clusters participating in the service mesh must have unique network ranges and be routable among themselves. A common approach to facilitating connectivity across providers or across regions is to use private tunnels between clusters. Depending on your environment, this could be a VPN between on-premises cluster(s) and provider or across provider regions. Rancher's Submariner (*https://submariner.io*) or Amazon VPC peering are two example technologies that you might use. More and more people are using capabilities inherent to Istio itself by taking advantage of secure, gateway-to-gateway communication.

An Istio v1.1 multicluster environment necessitates that only one cluster run the majority of control-plane components with communication being routed to those components from the remote installations. The remote clusters would be set up with automatic sidecar injection and Citadel (must share a root CA). You can extend networking to support nonflat networks using NAT or VPN.

One use case for this type of deployment would be to bridge an on-premises Istio service mesh into the public cloud via a VPN. This allows developers to verify, through things like canaries or A/B testing, or something custom, their service on a cloud provider, reducing the need to have that traffic reach the on-premises production environment. It would allow for an easier migration—step by step—into the public cloud or a more hybrid approach if regulatory requirements bind you to locality. This is one of many stories that open up when you have hybrid connectivity into the public cloud from a private environment.

It also isn't a requirement that you colocate the workload where your control plane runs. For some use cases, a centralized control plane dedicated to those components and remote data planes where workload runs might make sense, although this style topology does increase the risk of partition between control and data planes to the extent that the network between them isn't highly resilient.

Our second deployment option is Istio cross-cluster, as illustrated in Figure 13-2.

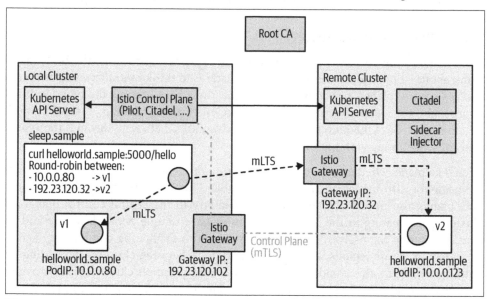

Figure 13-2. Istio v1.1 cross-cluster topology with cluster-aware service routing: a single control plane spanning multiple Kubernetes clusters

Cross-cluster deployments allow for a decentralized group of Istio service meshes to be federated using Istio route rules deployed within each service mesh. In this scenario, each Kubernetes cluster is running its own instance of the control plane. Both are being used to run workloads.

Let's walk through the flow for a cross-cluster call to be made. Understanding what systems are invoked and what steps support this flow aids in understanding cross-cluster behavior:

1. Client workload resolves remote services' name to a network endpoint (i.e., using Kubernetes DNS or other service registry such as Consul). Inherently, this means that as a prerequisite, the remote service must be registered in the client's local name server (DNS) or service registry in order for the client workload to successfully resolve its name to an endpoint.

2. With the network endpoint resolved, the client calls the remote service. These requests are intercepted by the local service proxy. The request is then mapped to an upstream and specific endpoint and then routed. Depending on the topology and security configuration, the client service proxy might connect directly to the remote endpoint. Or it might connect via an engress and/or ingress gateway.

3. The remote service proxy accepts the connection and validates the identities using mTLS exchange (herein lies the implicit requirement for each clusters' service certificates to share a common root of trust—whether signed by the same or different Citadels).

4. If an authorization policy is to be consulted, a check might need to be sent. Both the client and remote service identities (from each of the different clusters) are sent to Mixer for evaluation.

From an operator point of view, the requirements are simpler for cross-cluster than they are for multicluster—considering that you don't need to set up a direct connect, VPN, VPC peering, or something similar, that is. That said, you do have the requirement of some type of ingress endpoint with which the cluster can communicate and the port open to communicate across that tunnel.

Each cluster must be able to communicate with each destination cluster on the port you've chosen; for example, 80 or 443. On a public cloud provider this would translate to a public ingress on each side. For example, you would need to ensure your source cluster can communicate via elastic load balancing to the target cluster, and vice versa. The ingress is used as a `ServiceEntry` within Istio.

Let's pause here and recap the definition of a `ServiceEntry` from Chapter 8. A `ServiceEntry` contains a variety of properties that define it—host, address, port, protocol, and endpoint. A `ServiceEntry` is used to inform Istio about a service that hasn't been autodiscovered by Istio already. `ServiceEntrys` can identify services either outside of the mesh or services internal to the mesh.

A cross-cluster topology can benefit you by removing the need for a VPN to connect each cluster together as you must do with multicluster (unless you're using v1.1's cluster-aware routing using Istio `Gateways`). It also protects you from having a single point of failure. The downside will be policies, which, for now, remain unique to each environment. If you want to apply the same policy globally, you'll need to do so individually in each cluster. Solutions such as Galley will hopefully provide configuration management services for Istio.

Additionally, since these are disparate Kubernetes clusters you still need to find a solution for replicating objects that you need to be in both environments. In Kubernetes, you can solve this through Kubernetes Federation, which would allow you to ensure that most objects are federated and created on each cluster participating as members in the federation.

 Given the early state of Kubernetes Federation v2, it might be prudent to utilize alternative GitOps-based approaches as v2 matures.

Another consideration to address is that of cloud load balancing if you've chosen to go down the path of running your services across multiple cloud providers and want true redundancy.

Configuring Cross-Cluster

Let's walk through an example of deploying two or more clusters using a cross-cluster topology. In this exercise, we do not need to ensure unique networks exist across all clusters that will participate in each mesh. Their Gateways must be able to route to one another without issue. With a cross-cluster topology, service proxies will communicate with their local control plane for management, authz, telemetry, and so on. We assume that you are familiar with how to install and build a Kubernetes cluster. If you don't want to go through the hassle, you can opt to deploy two or more clusters on a managed Kubernetes cluster for speediness of walking through this exercise (not necessarily for how to run Kubernetes at large).

A few prerequisites are needed for this exercise:

1. You'll need ClusterAdmin access on each Kubernetes cluster, and ensure you have kubectl access to both clusters. You won't need shell access.

2. Gateways in each cluster provide cluster-to-cluster connectivity needed for cross-cluster service communication, via TLS. The istio-ingressgateway service's IP address in each cluster must be accessible from all other clusters.

3. The aforementioned cross-cluster communication requires use of mTLS between services, which unto its own requires a shared root CA. To satisfy this requirement, each cluster's Citadel needs to be configured with intermediate CA credentials generated by a shared root CA.

4. Each Kubernetes cluster running Istio should be running at the same version (1.12 or higher) with Istio installed running 1.0 or higher. You can use a managed Kubernetes service like NetApp Kubernetes Services (NKS), Google Kubernetes Engine (GKE), or Azure Kubernetes Service (AKS)—it might shave some time off the exercise. Of course, you don't need to use those services; however, any CNCF–conformant Kubernetes distribution will suffice.

Handily, Helm charts exist that automate much of this setup. Let's walk through what each step does to see what's happening under the hood:

1. Deploy two or more Kubernetes clusters. Following the installation process outlined in Chapter 4 will work.

2. As shown in the Istio documentation (*https://istio.io/docs/*), generate a multicluster-gateways Istio configuration file using Helm, using Helm's templat-

ing feature. Ensure that `helm` is installed locally and from the stio package directory by running the following command:

```
$ helm template install/kubernetes/helm/istio --name istio
    --namespace istio-system -f \ install/kubernetes/helm/istio
    /example-values/values-istio-multicluster-gateways.yaml >
    $HOME/istio.yaml
```

Implicit in this setup is the need for certificates to share a common root of trust,
even when signed by different Citadels. To have mTLS working correctly across
clusters, we must use a shared root CA. So long as these same certificates exist in
each cluster and Citadel can issue and provide identities to those service proxies,
cross-cluster communication can be secured with mTLS. We describe Citadel in-
depth in Chapter 6.

3. Install Istio's CRDs on each cluster:

```
$ kubectl apply -f install/kubernetes/helm/istio-init/files/crd/
```

4. You will need to create a control plane in each cluster. Each cluster's control plane
needs to be identically configured. Begin by creating the `istio-system` namespace manually on your Kubernetes cluster:

```
$ kubectl create ns istio-system
```

5. On each cluster, instantiate the secrets by running the following:

```
$ kubectl create namespace istio-system
$ kubectl create secret generic cacerts -n istio-system \
    --from-file=samples/certs/ca-cert.pem \
    --from-file=samples/certs/ca-key.pem \
    --from-file=samples/certs/root-cert.pem \
    --from-file=samples/certs/cert-chain.pem
```

6. Next, apply the Helm template output you generated earlier:

```
$ kubectl apply -f $HOME/istio.yaml
```

7. You'll want to ensure that the clusters all have automatic sidecar injection enabled
(which should already be the case):

```
$ kubectl label namespace default istio-injection=enabled
```

Configure DNS and Deploy Bookinfo

In our example, we'll be deploying Bookinfo, the default Istio demo app, to both clusters. Ensure that CoreDNS is configured for cross-cluster name resolution and apply
the `ConfigMap` update shown in Example 13-1 on each cluster (see *istiocoredns.yaml*
(*https://oreil.ly/Dmy1v*) in this book's GitHub repository).

Example 13-1. Cross-cluster CoreDNS ConfigMap

```
apiVersion: v1
kind: ConfigMap
metadata:
  name: coredns
  namespace: kube-system
data:
  Corefile: |
    .:53 {
        errors
        health
        kubernetes cluster.local in-addr.arpa ip6.arpa {
           pods insecure
           upstream
           fallthrough in-addr.arpa ip6.arpa
        }
        prometheus :9153
        proxy . /etc/resolv.conf
        cache 30
        loadbalance
        loop
        reload

    }
    global:53 {
        errors
        cache 30
        proxy . $(kubectl -n istio-system get svc istiocoredns
             -o jsonpath={.spec.clusterIP})
    }
```

Let's set up and configure Istio rules for `Gateways`, `ServiceEntries`, and `VirtualSer` `vices`. Refer to Chapter 8 for a detailed explanation of these core networking constructs in Istio. First, you need to create your `Gateway` on each cluster, *Cluster A* and *Cluster B*, as shown in Example 13-2. Use gateway configuration against both clusters (see *ingress-gw.yaml* (*https://oreil.ly/MCnpt*) in this book's GitHub repository).

Example 13-2. Creating a Gateway per cluster

```
apiVersion: networking.istio.io/v1alpha3
kind: Gateway
metadata:
  generation: 1
  name: ingress-gateway
  namespace: "default"
  resourceVersion: ""
  selfLink: /apis/networking.istio.io/v1alpha3/namespaces/default/gateways
          /ingress-gateway
  uid: ""
```

```
spec:
  selector:
    istio: ingressgateway
  servers:
  - hosts:
    - '*'
    port:
      name: http
      number: 80
      protocol: HTTP
  - hosts:
    - '*'
    port:
      name: https
      number: 443
      protocol: HTTPS
    tls:
      caCertificates: /etc/istio/ingressgateway-ca-certs/ca-chain.cert.pem
      mode: MUTUAL
      privateKey: /etc/istio/ingressgateway-certs/tls.key
      serverCertificate: /etc/istio/ingressgateway-certs/tls.crt
```

Use of a public cloud provider as infrastructure for this example might (or might not) facilitate exposing a public ingress gateway for both clusters more quickly than on-premises deployment. Cross-cluster requires an external IP to allow service traffic to transit the public internet. It also illustrates how Istio can help you elegantly solve multicloud, cluster communication.

With the external IP address in hand, set your context to *Cluster A* and apply the following again with kubectl. You will need to populate the endpoints entry with *Cluster B*'s ingress and the hosts entry with the remote cluster service name, as shown in Example 13-3 (see *egress-serviceentry-a.yaml* (*https://oreil.ly/ongFN*) in this book's GitHub repository).

Example 13-3. Egress ServiceEntry pointing to Cluster B

```
apiVersion: networking.istio.io/v1alpha3
kind: ServiceEntry
metadata:
  generation: 1
  name: egress-service-entry
  namespace: "default"
  resourceVersion: ""
  selfLink: /apis/networking.istio.io/v1alpha3/namespaces/default
          /serviceentries/egress-service-entry
  uid: ""
spec:
  endpoints:
  - address: # <external IP address here>
  hosts:
```

```
  - svc.cluster-b.remote
  location: MESH_EXTERNAL
  ports:
  - name: https
    number: 443
    protocol: HTTPS
  resolution: DNS
```

Now, switch your context to *Cluster B* and create the `ServiceEntry` in Example 13-4 on the other cluster. Before you do this, ensure you've changed the `endpoints` and `hosts` entry to point to *Cluster A*. Remember, you must be able to reach the endpoints from within the cluster (see *egress-serviceentry-b.yaml* (*https://oreil.ly/5Rq1o*) in this book's GitHub repository).

Example 13-4. Egress ServiceEntry pointing to Cluster A

```
apiVersion: networking.istio.io/v1alpha3
kind: ServiceEntry
metadata:
  generation: 1
  name: egress-service-entry
  namespace: "default"
  resourceVersion: ""
  selfLink: /apis/networking.istio.io/v1alpha3/namespaces/default/serviceentries
           /egress-service-entry
  uid: ""
spec:
  endpoints:
  - address: # <external IP address here>
  hosts:
  - svc.cluster-a.remote
  location: MESH_EXTERNAL
  ports:
  - name: https
    number: 443
    protocol: HTTPS
  resolution: DNS
```

At this point, you're ready to split traffic up across both clusters. In this example, we're going to split traffic from *Cluster A* to *Cluster B*. You do this by using a `Destina tionRule`. We are using Bookinfo's *Reviews* service as our example. In this setup, both services are running on both clusters (but not necessary considering that we updated the CoreDNS configuration earlier).

A `DestinationRule` tells Istio where to send the traffic. These rules can specify various configuration options. In the following example we're creating a `Destination Rule` that allows for mTLS origination for egress traffic on port 443.

You will want to switch to the context of *Cluster A* and then apply the rule shown in Example 13-5. Our `host` attribute defines our remote *Cluster B*. Our traffic will route across 443 to the external cluster, too (see *reviews-destinationrule.yaml* (*https://oreil.ly/MQYBN*) in this book's GitHub repository).

Example 13-5. DestinationRule routing Reviews traffic to Cluster B

```
apiVersion: networking.istio.io/v1alpha3
kind: DestinationRule
metadata:
  generation: 1
  name: reviews-tls-origination
  namespace: "default"
  resourceVersion: ""
  selfLink: /apis/networking.istio.io/v1alpha3/namespaces/default/destinationrules
          /reviews-tls-origination
  uid: ""
spec:
  host: svc.cluster-b.remote
  trafficPolicy:
    portLevelSettings:
    - port:
        number: 443
      tls:
        caCertificates: /etc/certs/cert-chain.pem
        clientCertificate: /etc/certs/cert-chain.pem
        mode: MUTUAL
        privateKey: /etc/certs/key.pem
```

We then create a *VirtualService* on *Cluster A*, too. Remember, we're looking to split traffic from *A* to *B*. In Example 13-6, we route 50% of our traffic destined to our `Reviews` service to *Cluster B* while leaving the remaining 50% going to the service running locally in *Cluster A* (see *reviews-virtualservice.yaml* (*https://oreil.ly/hYYtb*) in this book's GitHub repository).

Example 13-6. VirtualService for Reviews traffic splitting between clusters

```
apiVersion: networking.istio.io/v1alpha3
kind: VirtualService
metadata:
  generation: 1
  name: reviews-egress-splitter-virtual-service
  namespace: "default"
  resourceVersion: ""
  selfLink: /apis/networking.istio.io/v1alpha3/namespaces/default/virtualservices
          /reviews-egress-splitter-virtual-service
  uid: ""
spec:
  hosts:
```

```
    - reviews.default.svc.cluster.local
  http:
  - rewrite:
      authority: reviews.default.svc.cluster-b.remote
    route:
    - destination:
        host: svc.cluster-b.remote
        port:
          number: 443
      weight: 50
    - destination:
        host: reviews
      weight: 50
```

We then need to add some additional VirtualServices to allow ingress traffic to
actually reach the Reviews service; in other words, users browsing the app from the
public internet. Example 13-7 creates this and should be done on *Cluster A*. We
define the previous gateway we created earlier on in the chapter as well as the URI for
the service (see *bookinfo-vs.yaml (https://oreil.ly/NkXU9)* in this book's GitHub repository).

Example 13-7. A VirtualService on Cluster A to map inbound traffic to ProductPage

```
apiVersion: networking.istio.io/v1alpha3
kind: VirtualService
metadata:
  generation: 1
  name: bookinfo-vs
  namespace: "default"
  resourceVersion: ""
  selfLink: /apis/networking.istio.io/v1alpha3/namespaces/default
          /virtualservices/bookinfo-vs
  uid: ""
spec:
  gateways:
  - ingress-gateway
  hosts:
  - '*'
  http:
  - match:
    - uri:
        prefix: /productpage
    route:
    - destination:
        host: productpage
```

Finally, on *Cluster B*, we create another VirtualService to allow traffic to hit the service directly. In Example 13-8, we're defining the remote service in our hosts

attribute and the route destination (see *reviews-ingress-virtual-service.yaml* (*https://oreil.ly/QZTLq*) in this book's GitHub repository).

Example 13-8. A VirtualService on Cluster B to map traffic to `Reviews`

```
apiVersion: networking.istio.io/v1alpha3
kind: VirtualService
metadata:
  generation: 1
  name: reviews-ingress-virtual-service
  namespace: "default"
  resourceVersion: ""
  selfLink: /apis/networking.istio.io/v1alpha3/namespaces/default/virtualservices
           /reviews-ingress-virtual-service
  uid: ""
spec:
  gateways:
  - ingress-gateway
  hosts:
  - reviews.default.svc.cluster-b.remote
  http:
  - route:
    - destination:
        host: reviews
```

By this point, you should be able to see 50% of your traffic hitting the service on *A* and 50% hitting the service on *B*. And we've unified the service mesh across two different clusters.

Using this chapter's example, you can play around with various scenarios beyond splitting traffic equally. Cross-cluster enables other use cases—most prominent that of failover—potentially including circuit breaking across providers or regions, performing canaries on lower-cost clusters elsewhere, and more.

Networking comes to the forefront of concerns when planning advanced topologies. It's worth noting that Istio multicluster does not equal multicloud out of the box. Remember, the requirement is that all Kubernetes clusters must be able to route traffic to one another with no network overlap. If not planned properly, operation teams could run into headaches when they do choose to move toward unifying their infrastructure under a single service mesh like Istio. So, before you begin to look at adopting Istio multicluster, first inspect your current network setup and topology. Were you using the same network address space each time you built a new cluster? If so, you might need to re-IP your clusters. Can your service traffic reach all services in both clusters? If not, you need to ensure that you can route traffic.

Index

round-robin load balancing strategy, 151
splitting service into subsets, 130, 147
TLS settings, 129
development, 21
cloud native, 24
DevOps, 21
Discovery Service (xDS) responses generated
by Pilot, 109
Discovery Service APIs (xDS APIs), 109
discovery services for Envoy's APIs (or xDS),
84, 108
distributed systems
key importance of observability, 30
network challenges addressed by Istio, 41
distributed tracing, 29
(see also traces)
costs of, 28
for the monolith, 226
DNS, 17, 124
configuring CoreDNS for cross-cluster
name resolution, 231
egress Gateway using, 157
entries not populated based on Istio Service-
Entrys, 127
ServiceEntry with, 126
Docker
release schedule, time-based, 13
running envoy in a Docker container, 87
Docker Desktop
deploying Kubernetes on, 52
installing Kubernetes Dashboard, 52
preparing as installation environment for
Istio, 49
configuring Docker Desktop, 50
support for running Kubernetes standalone
server and client, 50
downstream and upstream, 83

E

EDS (endpoint discovery service), split horizon, 223
egress, 36
egress gateways, 43
in demo deployment of Istio, 62
routing outbound traffic through, 43
egress traffic, managing, 156
endpoints
clusters and, 109
Envoy configuration, 84

examining state of service proxies connected to Pilot, 112
information about, pushed to service proxy
from Pilot, 124
lame-ducking, 151
no endpoints available for Galley service,
198
processing in ServiceEntry, 109
service, 18
split horizon endpoint discovery service,
223
environments, 17
in zones, 19
multienvironment (or hybrid), 17
Envoy (data-plane component), 11
Envoy proxy, 40, 93
APIs, push based, 85
debugging, 198-201
503 or 404 requests, 199
sidecar injection, 199
Discovery Service (xDS) APIs, 109, 110
functionality, 83-88
administration console, 86
certificates and protecting traffic, 85
core constructs, 84
generating initial trace headers, 179
in Istio, 76
intercepting all incoming/outgoing requests
at runtime, 123
istioctl tools for inspecting configuration,
111
minimizing performance overhead, 47
overview, 74-76
reasons for using Envoy, 75
ProxyConfig object, 107
redirection of traffic to, using iptables, 74
role in identity certificates (SVIDs) management, 97
telemetry reports sent by, 163
error budget, 148
errors, 31
Eureka, 69
extensibility of Istio, 44
adapters, 46
customizable sidecars, 45
extensibility of Mixer, 160

F

facade services, 10

O

observability
  brought by service meshes, 5
  cloud native applications, 22
  defined, 25
  key importance in distributed systems, reasons for, 30
  monitoring versus, 25, 31
  pillars of, 27
    combining, 29
    cost/value comparison, 29
    logs, 27
    metrics, 27
    traces, 28
  provided by service meshes, 9
  uniform, 25
  uniform, with service meshes, 32
    interfacing with monitoring systems, 33
Open Policy Agent (OPA) adapter, 169
OpenTelemetry, 179
operations, 21
  cloud native, 24
orchestration frameworks, 17
out-of-proccss adaptcrs, 167
outlier detection, 151

P

packaging
  cloud native, 24
percentage-based traffic split in canary deployment, 149
performance
  costs of using Istio features, 47
  traces and, 180
physical listeners, 109
Pilot, 19, 37, 45, 105-122
  configuration serving, 109-110
  configuring, 105-109
    mesh configuration, 106-107
    networking configuration, 108
    service discovery, 108
  ControlZ introspection of, 188
  debugging, 111-122
    tools for, 111
    tracing configuration, 114-122
    troubleshooting Pilot, 112-114
  disallowing egress traffic to undefined endpoints, 85

disconnect between Envoy and, remediating, 199
failure modes, 206-208
  partitioned from configuration store, 207
  partitioned from other components, 207
  partitioned from workloads, 207
  upgrades, 208
memory requirements, 50
pilot-agent running with Envoy in istio-proxy container, 86
policies affecting traffic, 170
role in identity certificates (SVIDs) management, 97
traffic policy configured by, 74
troubleshooting, 196
use of Envoy ADS, 85
validation of configurations consumed by, 197
planes, 36
  (see also control plane; data plane)
pods
  associating with services, 192
  configuration allowing NET_ADMIN capability, 193
  service account as pod identity, 91
  verifying Citadel pod is running, 201
  verifying status of Galley pod, 198
policies in the mesh, Mixer and, 159-173
  adapters, 166
  attributes, 165-166
  creating Mixer policy and using adapters, 167-173
    Open Policy Agent (OPA) adapter, 169
    Prometheus adapter, 170-172
  failures of Mixer in policy mode, 208
  how Mixer policies work, 163-164
    enabling policy enforcement, 163
    reporting telemetry, 163
  Mixer architecture, 160-163
    enforcing policy, 161
  policies coming from Pilot vs. Mixer, 170
ports
  identifying port for Bookinfo Istio app exposed on ingress gateway, 66
  naming of service ports, 192
  network ports used by Istio, 66
precondition check adapters, 167, 169
probabilistic sampling, 28

W
webhooks
mutating admission, 80, 200
namespaceSelector, verifying scope of, 200
validating webhooks in Galley, 197
Webhook Admission controller, reliance on labels, 82
Workload API, 92, 92
workload principals, 17
defined, 19
workloads, 18
belonging to a Gateway, 141
Citadel partitioned from mesh workloads, 211
defined, 18
Galley partitioned from mesh workloads, 205
improving reliability on Istio, 203
Individual Workloads View on Grafana dashboard, 184
Mixer partitioned from mesh workloads, 210
Pilot partitioned from mesh workloads, 207
workload name, 18
workload preparedness, 191-194
application configuration, 191
network traffic and ports, 191
pods, 193
services and deployments, 192

X
x-request-id trace header, 179
xDS APIs, 110
(see also Discovery Service (xDS) APIs; Envoy proxy)

Z
Zipkin, using for tracing
removing references of Zipkin URL from Mixer deployment, 181
zones (Istio control plane), 19

About the Authors

Lee Calcote is an innovative product and technology leader, passionate about empowering engineers with efficient and effective solutions. As the founder of Layer5, he's at the forefront of the cloud native movement. Open source, advanced, and emerging technologies have been a consistent focus through Lee's tenure at Solar-Winds, Seagate, Cisco, and Schneider Electric. An advisor, author, and speaker, Lee is active in the community as a Docker Captain, Cloud Native Ambassador, and Google Summer of Code Mentor.

Zack Butcher is a founding engineer at Tetrate and a core contributor to the Istio project. He's always been drawn to hard problems, from developing web applications for IE6 to working on service management, access control, and the central resource hierarchy for Google Cloud Platform. Tetrate is a small company, and he wears many hats there, including system architecture, sales, writing, and speaking.

Colophon

The animal on the cover of *Istio: Up and Running* is Sabine's gull (*Xema sabini*). After this small gull completes its breeding season in the arctic tundra environments of northern Alaska, Nunavat, and Greenland, populations then disperse to rich coastal feeding grounds off of northern South America and southwestern Africa.

Breeding adults have a dark gray head with a black ring at the base of the neck; extended wings are pale gray above with a black leading edge and a triangle of white in the interior. Adults also have red eyes, dark gray legs and feet, and a black bill with a yellow tip. First-year juvenile birds have duller plumage that features browns instead of the adult's darker colors. These birds average just over 12 inches long (small in comparison to the more familiar herring gull, which averages two feet in length).

During nesting season, this small gull eats insects, but during the rest of its year, spent in coastal waters, its diet consists mostly of small fish, crustaceans, and plankton. These birds are drawn to sites where upwellings of cold currents—such as the Peru Current, off Peru's northwest coast; and the Benguela, rising southwest of Africa—bring deep-water nutrients to the surface, creating a feeding bonanza for many types of sea life.

English scientist William Elford Leach named this bird for western science; its species name honors Edward Sabine, who first described it. Leach found this bird unique enough to require a new genus (it remains Xema's only member), a judgment still disputed by some. An important figure in early nineteenth-century British zoology and taxonomy, Leach was known for a whimsical and personal approach to naming, at times using anagrams of the names of colleagues and acquaintances—though he also used names from classical mythology, choices more in line with his particular cultural as well as scientific traditions.

Many of the animals on O'Reilly covers are endangered; all of them are important to the world.

Color illustration by Karen Montgomery, based on a black and white engraving from *British Birds*. The cover fonts are Gilroy Semibold and Guardian Sans. The text font is Adobe Minion Pro; the heading font is Adobe Myriad Condensed; and the code font is Dalton Maag's Ubuntu Mono.

O'REILLY®

There's much more where this came from.

Experience books, videos, live online training courses, and more from O'Reilly and our 200+ partners—all in one place.

Learn more at oreilly.com/online-learning

Milton Keynes UK
Ingram Content Group UK Ltd.
UKHW010809150824
446957UK00006B/129